T0320159

Economics in the Shadows of Darwin and Marx

To Sarah and James

Economics in the Shadows of Darwin and Marx

Essays on Institutional and Evolutionary Themes

Geoffrey M. Hodgson

Research Professor in Business Studies, University of Hertfordshire, UK

Edward Elgar

Cheltenham, UK • Northampton, MA, USA

Published by
Edward Elgar Publishing Limited
Glensanda House
Montpellier Parade
Cheltenham
Glos GL50 1UA
UK

Edward Elgar Publishing, Inc.
136 West Street
Suite 202
Northampton
Massachusetts 01060
USA

A catalogue record for this book
is available from the British Library

Library of Congress Cataloguing in Publication Data
Hodgson, Geoffrey Martin, 1946-
Economics in the shadows of Darwin and Marx : essays on institutional and evolutionary themes / Geoffrey M. Hodgson.
p. cm.
Includes bibliographical references and index.
1. Evolutionary economics. 2. Institutional economics. 3. Evolutionary economics. 4. Social Darwinism. 5. Marxian economics. I. Title.

HB99.5.H633 2006
330.1--dc22

2006011741

ISBN-13: 978 1 84542 497 8 (cased)
ISBN-10: 1 84542 497 2 (cased)

Printed and bound in Great Britain by MPG Books Ltd, Bodmin, Cornwall

Contents

Figures

Preface and Acknowledgements

When in the early 1980s I began writing on evolutionary and institutional themes in economics, I felt almost a lone voice. Gradually, however, due to the efforts of many scholars, the situation changed. Today evolutionary and institutional ideas are commonplace, and have made their way into the mainstream. As economics has entered the twenty-first century it has reached an exciting stage of its development, while retaining some of its less productive preoccupations. This book is an attempt to contribute to this rapidly changing programme of research, by further developing some institutional and evolutionary ideas.

The title and themes of this volume reflect the ongoing influence of two great Victorian thinkers. Despite the enduring importance of the contribution of Karl Marx to the social sciences, I argue that aspects of his legacy remain problematic. Institutional and evolutionary approaches in economics can learn a great deal from the fundamental ideas of Charles Darwin, whose excursions into the social sciences were tiny by comparison. Darwinism embraces notions of algorithmic change that contrast with the grand scenarios of sequential historic transition within Marxism. Overall, Darwinism is more appropriate than Marxism for the modern behavioural sciences. All this is explored below. For reasons attributable to the present and the past, all social scientists in the twenty-first century somehow have to settle their accounts with both Darwin and Marx.

The papers included here were all written since 1999. At the start of that year I moved from the University of Cambridge to the University of Hertfordshire. Since then I have also published on other themes, including two volumes on the history of institutional economics (Hodgson, 2001b, 2004a), some essays on the nature of the firm, and several more on the application of Darwinian principles to socio-economic evolution. I plan to publish in the future a separate book on the theory of the firm, and Thorbjørn Knudsen and I are preparing a book explaining in detail the Darwinian mechanisms of evolution in economies and societies.

I am very grateful to Howard Aldrich, Masahiko Aoki, Margaret Archer, Brian Arthur, Robert Aunger, Robert Bannister, Markus Becker, Kenneth Binmore, Mark Blaug, Marion Blute, Max Boisot, Alex Callinicos, Richard Carter, Ana Celia Castro, Carolina Cavalcante, Victoria Chick, Gregory Claeys, John B. Davis, Wilfred Dolfsma, Denise Dollimore, Sheila Dow, Stephen Dunn, Raul Espejo, Ronaldo Fiani, Steve Fleetwood, Ben Fletcher, Edward Fullbrook, Chris Fuller, Gerald Gaus, Ian Gough, Avner Greif, Jane Hardy, David Hull, Anthony Kasozi, Matthias Klaes, Thorbjørn Knudsen,

John Laurent, Clive Lawson, Tony Lawson, Nathalie Lazaric, Fred Lee, Axel Leijonhufvud, Uskali Mäki, Paul Milgrom, Stephen Nash, Richard Nelson, Douglass North, Paul Ormerod, Pavel Pelikan, Stephen Pratten, Erik Reinert, Peter Richerson, J. Barkley Rosser, Jochen Runde, John Searle, Colin Shaper, Giles Slinger, Koye Somefun, Irene van Staveren, Ian Steedman, Robert Sugden, Margherita Turvani, Viktor Vanberg, Kumaraswamy Velupillai, Jack Vromen, Sidney Winter, Ulrich Witt, John van Wyhe, several anonymous referees and many others for critical and helpful comments.

Warm thanks are also due to Thorbjørn Knudsen for agreeing to the publication of a chapter based on a jointly-authored essay, to Alex Callinicos for giving me permission to print his contribution to a debate that we held in 2001 and to Douglass North for allowing me to reproduce extracts from our correspondence. The following publishers are thanked for permission to use material from previously published articles: the Association for Evolutionary Economics, Blackwell Publishing, Elsevier Publishing, Oxford University Press and Routledge.

Above all I wish to express my gratitude to my friends and family, whose support has made this work possible.

1. Introduction

> From the viewpoint of pure economic theory, Karl Marx can be regarded as a minor post-Ricardian.
>
> Paul A. Samuelson, 'Economists and the History of Ideas' (1962)

> All this prattle about biological methods in economics ... of birds and bees, giant trees in the forest, and declining entrepreneurial dynasties ...
>
> Paul A. Samuelson, 'The Monopolistic Revolution' (1967)

Many economists would still follow Paul Samuelson and regard Charles Darwin and even Karl Marx as having little relevance for their subject.[1] Marxian economics is absent from most undergraduate and postgraduate curricula. Many economists would not describe Marx as an economist anyway, because his analysis does not fit into the narrow mould of economics as the 'science of choice'. And who would be so daft as to suggest that Darwin, the biologist, has anything to do with economics? We might play with biological metaphors and analogies, but many would agree with Joseph Schumpeter (1954, p. 789) when he argued that economic phenomena 'would have to be analyzed with reference to economic facts alone and no appeal to biology would be of the slightest use'.

However, the exclusion of Marx from economics is unwarranted, even if one is critical of his doctrines. Sciences should not be defined by their methods or assumptions, but by their objects of analysis. Economics should thus be the science of the economy. Marx's *Capital* is about the workings of the capitalist economy, and should thus qualify as economics.

Figure 1.1 below shows that citations to Marx remain high in core mainstream journals of economics, despite the unfashionable status of his ideas. There are good reasons why the spectre of Marx has haunted economics. While several of his other forecasts were wrong, Marx correctly predicted the globalization of markets and the growth of giant firms. Nobel prize winner Lawrence Klein (1947) saw Marxian economics as 'probably the origin of macro-economics'. Overall, Marx made a major contribution to our understanding of the nature and dynamics of the capitalist system.[2]

---

[1] This chapter was first drafted for this volume.

[2] While rejecting his labour theory of value and his theory of the tendency of the rate of profit to fall, Hodgson (1991) argued that Marx had still made a major contribution to economic science. I take the same view today.

The great twentieth-century debate between capitalist markets and socialist planning also put Marx at centre stage. During the Cold War, economists in the West attempted with neoclassical theory to demonstrate the superior efficiency of the market system. Ranged against them were Soviet economists, officially of Marxist hue. Ironically, the theoretical weapons adopted on each side were ill suited to explain the system to which they were affiliated. Neoclassical theory fails to capture the evolutionary and dynamic features of capitalism, and Marx's writings have very little to say about the workings of socialism. Ironically, both Marxism and neoclassical theory share a common ancestor in the economics of David Ricardo. This Cold War debate was largely between two branches of Ricardian economics!

In his 1933 essay on Thomas Robert Malthus, John Maynard Keynes (1972, pp. 100–101) alluded to an alternative tradition and lamented: 'If only Malthus, instead of Ricardo, had been the parent stem from which nineteenth-century economics proceeded, what a much wiser and richer place the world would be today!' Malthus's mode of thinking was less *a prioristic* and more historically oriented than the formal economics of today. His emphasis on dynamism and variety was a crucial inspiration for Darwin. The Malthusian tradition contrasts with Ricardianism and its descendants.

However, even after the collapse of the Soviet Empire in 1989–1991, in some quarters Marxian ideas remain influential. Marxism seems to offer a theoretically systematic and politically radical alternative to orthodoxy. While I am critical of its theory and outlook, Marxism has to be brought into the discussion, so that it may be gainfully understood and surpassed.

Economics has often borrowed ideas from biology. However, biological metaphors and analogies are not merely literary frills. Philosophers such as Mary Hesse (1966) and Max Black (1962) have established that metaphors are constitutive of science. Because biology and economics both address complex evolving systems, there are good reasons to consider Darwinian and other biological metaphors within economics (Hodgson, 1993, 1999b).

There are even stronger arguments for bringing Darwinian ideas into the social sciences. First, as shown in Chapter 2, the philosophical underpinnings of Darwinism are highly relevant for the social sciences.

Second, while the detailed mechanisms of social and biological evolution are very different, they share some general features at a highly abstract level, concerning variation, inheritance and selection. It is not simply that economic evolution is *analogous* to biological evolution in some way. At an abstract level economic evolution *is* Darwinian, in the sense that it involves the key mechanisms of variation, inheritance and selection (Hodgson, 2002b, 2004a).

I also wish to claim – which at first sight may seem extraordinary – that Darwinism offers a more fruitful philosophical worldview for the social sciences than Marxism. This is despite the fact that Marx made an immense contribution to our understanding of how the capitalist system works, and Darwin had much less to say about social structures or human history.

I am not suggesting that Darwinism itself offers adequate policy guidance. Values and normative statements are much more prominent in Marxism. It has been an infamous error to attempt to use Darwinism to support particular political policies. The strength of Darwinism lies not in any direct guidance for policy but in its explanatory rubric and its basic philosophical outlook.

Furthermore, I am not proposing that explanations of socio-economic phenomena can or should be reduced largely to biological terms. For reasons elaborated elsewhere (Hodgson, 1993, 2004a), biological reductionism is not a viable strategy for the social sciences.

Instead, this call for a Darwinian turn in the social sciences relies on arguments similar to those made by David Ritchie (1896), Thorstein Veblen (1899, 1919) and Albert Keller (1915) long ago. Their works emerged during a spell of interest in Darwinian themes in social science in the early years of the twentieth century. Their ideas lay underdeveloped in the subsequent years, when any intellectual intercourse between the social and the biological sciences was highly unpopular. Only recently has the situation changed, when Darwinian themes have again re-emerged in the social sciences.

When Marx lambasted Malthus he dismissed the problem of overpopulation with finite resources, which we face with some urgency today. Darwinism spans the natural and the human world, and reminds us of the ecological context of human activity. Marxism emphasizes class, but has relatively little to say about the enduring issues of gender or ethnicity. When freed of racist or sexist pseudo-science, Darwinian theory can add to our understanding of some of these phenomena (Lopreato and Crippen, 1999).

Citation analysis illustrates the ups and downs in interest in Marxism and Darwinism by economists. Figure 1.1 charts the number of items (including articles and reviews) in the *American Economic Review* (founded 1911), *Economic Journal* (founded 1891), *Journal of Political Economy* (founded 1892) and *Quarterly Journal of Economics* (founded 1886), that cited Marx (plus derivative words such as Marxism), Darwin (plus derivative words such as Darwinism), Veblen (plus derivative words such as Veblenian), and Walras (plus derivative words such as Walrasian). Walras serves as a benchmark figure to indicate the rise of the pre-eminent post-war version of neoclassical economics. Indeed, this citation analysis identifies the rise and prominence of Walrasian economics from the 1950s to the 1980s.

The tiny and short-lived flurry of interest in Darwinism in these leading journals in economics did not survive the First World War. By contrast, interest in Marxism in the same publications grew to a zenith in the 1950s, during the Cold War. In the 1990s, after the collapse of the Eastern Bloc, citations to Marx and Marxism declined.

Figure 1.1 Appearances of Darwin, Marx, Veblen and Walras in Four Leading Journals in Economics

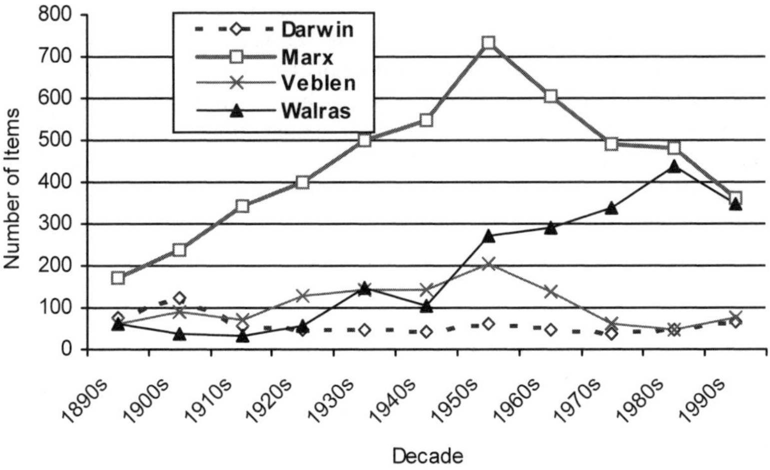

In Figure 1.1, Darwin and Marx are compared with the leading neoclassical economist Léon Walras. Interest in Walrasian ideas did not become strong until after the Second World War, but throughout this period he remained overshadowed by Marx, despite energetic efforts by orthodoxy to exclude Marxism from the terrain of economics.

In *The Evolution of Institutional Economics* (Hodgson, 2004a), I examined the central role of Darwinism in the formation and early development of American institutional economics, particularly in the work of Thorstein Veblen. Darwinism was also a major inspiration for pragmatist philosophers and psychologists, including Charles Sanders Peirce, William James and John Dewey, who all influenced Veblen. With the exception of Chapter 3 and two sections in Chapter 2, the present book does not take a historical perspective. Instead it addresses contemporary concerns and themes.

In explaining both persistence and change in complex systems, Marx and Darwin emerge as two towering and enduringly relevant intellects. But in some fundamental respects their doctrines are antagonistic. Despite remaining strongly influenced by Marx, Veblen (1919) sensed this conflict in his essays. He proposed that Darwinism offered a superior philosophical outlook that was helpful in understanding the shifting mechanisms of institutional conservatism and change (Hodgson, 2004a). Veblen criticized Marxism as supporting the view that individuals were largely explained by their social circumstances. Such doctrines do not explain how social forces impel individual actors to think and act, and they lack a meticulous examination of the causal mechanisms at the micro and psychological level. By contrast, Darwinism focused on detailed analyses of the causes of change, including at the level of the individual. In contrast, Marxism does not descend to this level of detail and does not explain how social or cultural 'forces' affect individual dispositions or actions. Veblen (1901b, p. 76 n.) ironically described Marxism's 'theory of self-determining cultural exfoliation'. In contrast to views of the human agent as a mere receptacle of culture, Veblen emphasized that individuals created institutions and culture, just as individuals were moulded by them.

The enduring figure of Veblen emerges from the shadows of Darwin and Marx. Once the mutual importance yet divergence of the outlooks of Darwin and Marx are acknowledged, then we are led towards an institutional economics of Veblenian hue. Veblen proposed that the social sciences should be brought into a 'post-Darwinian' era. The elaboration of Darwinism within the social sciences leads inexorably to a form of institutionalism. Consequently, within this conception, 'evolutionary economics' and 'institutional economics' are two faces of the same coin.[3]

Part 1 here begins with a discussion of some aspects of Marxism and Darwinism. Therein I refute the notion, promoted today by both leftists and Christian creationists, that Darwin was a racist. Chapter 3 discusses the historical use of the term 'Social Darwinism' and produces some surprises concerning its past meaning and chronology. A major barrier to the incorporation of Darwinism into the social sciences is removed. Chapter 4 brings the Veblenian institutionalist perspective more to the fore, in a transcript of a debate with the Marxist social theorist Alex Callinicos.

Partly because this book addresses philosophical fundamentals, it includes some discussion of critical realism. Three essays on this philosophical approach are gathered together in Part 2.[4] Several leading critical realists are openly Marxist, and two of the essays here examine the connections between critical realism and Marxism. While some critical realist writings are inspirational, there are also disturbing and negative features.

Part 3 goes into more depth, by addressing issues fundamental to an institutionalist approach. Chapter 8 addresses the definitions of institutions and related entities, such as organizations, conventions and rules. Chapter 9 is

---

[3] Notably, in a masterly presentation of cutting edge developments in institutional and evolutionary microeconomics, Bowles (2004) acknowledges the inspiration of both Darwin and Marx. A 'kind of marriage of Marx and Darwin' has been discussed in anthropology (Sanderson 2001; Dawson, 2002).

[4] My unpublished essay 'Structures and Institutions' also focuses on critical realism. Some of the material in this essay made its way into Hodgson (2004a).

on the role of habit in institutional formation and evolution. Such aspects of institutional evolution are addressed in the agent-based simulation in Chapter 10. Finally, Chapter 11 addresses a prominent theme in modern evolutionary economics: the concept of a routine. It indicates how a Darwinian approach can be developed in the social sciences.

Ideology has always played a strong role in the social sciences. Even the most incisive of theorists is driven by motives to improve the world. Adam Smith wished to augment national wealth, David Ricardo promoted free trade, Karl Marx sought a socialist revolution, John Maynard Keynes railed against unemployment and Friedrich Hayek campaigned for individual liberty. Ideology is often the fuel of theoretical endeavour. But things go awfully wrong for science when:

(1) unwarranted policy claims are made for theoretical analysis;
(2) a jump is made from the theoretical to the normative without adequate consideration of questions of feasibility and mechanisms of implementation; or
(3) a particular scientific approach is evaluated by exclusively ideological considerations.

Examples of all three types of error, concerning the relationship between ideology and science, are criticized in this volume. Chapter 3 shows that 'Social Darwinism' was not simply used as a label for racist, militant, nationalist and other objectionable attempts to hijack Darwinism for political ends. It was also used to disallow the use of Darwinian theoretical ideas in the social sciences. This is a classic example of an error of type (3).

Errors of all three types are revealed in my discussion of critical realism below. Not all critical realists describe themselves as Marxists or socialists, but they remain amazingly tolerant of repeated ideological claims by leading critical realists, that their doctrine undermines social democratic politics, and points to an extreme version of socialism in which markets are entirely absent (Bhaskar, 1989b, p. 6; Collier, 1994, p. 195; Bhaskar and Collier, 1998, p. 392). I find these shallow arguments to be very worrying, and symptomatic of a deeper intellectual malaise within critical realism.

I am not saying that considerations of fact and value can, or should, be entirely separated. Values unavoidably infuse our preoccupations and priorities, even within science. The danger lies in the use of science as the uncritical instrument of ideology, rather than as the engine of enquiry.[5]

---

[5] This error is facilitated by attempts to see science itself as merely an ideological and institutional mechanism of social power (Aronowitz, 1988). There is no space to counter this debilitating reading of science here. Marxism, Darwinism and critical realism all commendably uphold a view of science as a search for truth, which is an

Just as many pro-market economists promulgate economic theory with the mistaken claim that it generally supports a free-market solution to policy problems, we find other social scientists making the unwarranted contention that their theoretical standpoint supports some type of socialism (Hodgson, 1999b). On the contrary, a deeper excursion into economic theory and realist philosophy leads directly to none of these ideological outcomes. Instead, they offer a much more open-ended agenda for the policy-inclined practitioner.

But academics are only human. We all prefer certainty to doubt, and simplicity to confusion. The appeal of an ideological solution with apparently strong theoretical underpinnings can be irresistible. Worriers and sceptics are not the obvious leaders of a distinctive and successful school of thought. Instead, the accolades go to the forthright, with their offers of clear solutions. But this is often the road to religion rather than science.

The world itself is muddled and uncertain. However, this is not an excuse for muddle and confusion in our own minds; instead it means that we must acknowledge the immense complexity of the real world, and be more cautious about our capacities to predict and to prescribe. It is here that the spirit of Darwin enters our discourse. It is a world of enormous variety, in which entities interact in rich and often unpredictable ways. In principle, we cannot disengage from this world, but any judicious intervention has to be cautious and experimental. The world is so complex that we will always be mystified by events. Yet if we can do anything to obtain greater understanding of the intricate mechanisms of human social life, then it will be worthwhile, especially if we wish to grope for improvements to the human condition.

---

anathema to the cultural relativist and other believers that science is merely a system of social power. Readers who believe that one person's truth-claims are simply as good as another's will find little comfort in this volume.

Part 1:

Marxism, Darwinism, Institutionalism

2. Darwin and Marx at the Crossroads

It is theory that decides what can be observed.

Albert Einstein

2.1 INTRODUCTION

A massive 1934 mural by Diego Rivera in Mexico City is entitled 'Man at the Crossroads'. To the colourful right of the picture are Diego's chosen symbols of liberation, including Karl Marx, Vladimir Illych Lenin, Leon Trotsky, several young female athletes and the massed proletariat. To the greyer left of the mural are sinister battalions of marching gas-masked soldiers, the ancient statue of a fearsome god and the seated figure of a bearded Charles Darwin. These conceptions of good and evil, progress and regress, and light and shade, were prominent in much of Western social science for the next fifty years.[1]

In 1999 the British Broadcasting Corporation asked their radio listeners to name the greatest men and women of the millennium. Ten years after the dismantling of the Berlin Wall and eight years after the collapse of the Soviet Union, Marx topped the poll. Einstein, Newton and Darwin followed in that order. Among these, Darwin and Marx stand out as the supreme theorists of structural change in complex living systems. They tried to understand the operative forces and processes of development in life and in human society, and both had a huge influence on our ideas.[2]

However, Marx is often neglected for ideological reasons and the contribution of Darwin is typically regarded as confined to biology. Even among 'evolutionary economists' the application of Darwinian ideas to the social sciences remains controversial. Only a tiny minority of sociologists appreciate the relevance of Darwin to social evolution. The original American institutionalists universally regarded themselves as 'evolutionary', but by Thorstein Veblen's death in 1929 most of them had abandoned Veblen's (1899, 1919) idea that Darwinism was relevant to understanding socio-economic evolution (Hodgson, 2004a).

[1] This chapter was first drafted for this volume, borrowing its first paragraph from Hodgson (2004d) and a small amount of material from Hodgson (1993, 1999a, 2004a).

[2] In July 2005 listeners to the BBC Radio Four 'In Our Time' programme voted Marx as the greatest philosopher ever.

Many Marxists follow the example of the late Stephen Jay Gould (1996) and others (Fracchia and Lewontin, 1999) and argue that Darwinian ideas do not apply to social, cultural or economic evolution. They divide the natural from the human sciences, with the theoretical maxim criticized by Peter Singer (1999, p. 30) 'of Darwin for natural history and of Marx for human history'. In this manner, Darwinism and Marxism are rendered as complementary but applicable to different scientific domains.

However, this division of influence is contestable: Darwinism offers a general theory of evolutionary systems. Darwinian ideas are too important to be restricted to biology. The leading biologist and philosopher of biology Ernst Mayr (1964, p. xviii) wrote: 'It has taken 100 years to appreciate fully that Darwin's conceptual framework is, indeed, a new philosophical system'.[3] Darwin had revolutionary ideas – addressed later in this chapter – concerning the nature of complex systems and their processes of change.

Despite the importance of Darwinian ideas to the social sciences, a rigorous and complete account of how Darwinian principles apply to socio-economic evolution is still lacking. It is not the purpose of this book to provide this, although some key steps are indicated. This chapter is concerned more broadly with the comparative worldviews of Darwinism and Marxism. Its aim, along with the two subsequent chapters, is to establish some key differences of outlook and to remove some prejudicial barriers to the incorporation of Darwinism in the social sciences.

2.2 CONVERSATIONS OF DARWIN AND MARX

Marx (1818–1883) and Darwin (1809–1882) were close contemporaries. Their paths must have crossed frequently in London but they never met personally (Colp, 1974). When Darwin's *Origin of Species* appeared, Marx and his friend Frederick Engels were both favourably impressed, although the idea that Marx went so far as to ask permission from Darwin to dedicate a volume of *Capital* to him turns out to be a myth (Feuer, 1975; Fay, 1978; Colp, 1982). Just as the personal trails of Marx and Darwin entwined in London's streets, their ideas have crossed and interacted ever since.

Shortly after the publication of the *Origin of Species* Engels wrote to Marx that it was 'absolutely splendid … Never before has so grandiose an attempt been made to demonstrate historical evolution in Nature' (Marx and Engels, 1983, p. 551). But the details of Darwin's theory were given inadequate attention in their writings. If the Marxian theory of socio-economic change is

[3] A survey of about one thousand academic philosophers organized by the *Philosopher's Magazine* put Darwin's *Origin of Species* as the third most important book in philosophy ever, after Plato's *Republic* and Kant's *Critique of Pure Reason* (*The Guardian*, 21 September 2001).

evolutionary, it is not so in the Darwinian sense of being centred on its central causal algorithm of variation, replication and selection (Hodgson, 1993). Claims to the contrary have downplayed the central, analytical message of Darwinism. The similarities between Marxism and Darwinism are chimerical rather than substantive (Ball, 1994).

Marx wrote to Engels in June 1862: 'It is remarkable how Darwin rediscovers, among the beasts and plants, the society of England with its division of labour, opening up of new markets, "inventions," and Malthusian "struggle for existence"' (Marx and Engels, 1985, p. 381). Marx and Engels characterized Darwin's doctrine as an inappropriate extension of the norms of capitalist competition to the natural world. Several writers have noted how Darwin's ideas bear the marks of the competitive market ideology of his time (Desmond and Moore, 1991; R. M. Young, 1985). Of course, Darwin was affected by his times, and the influence from the political economy of Thomas Robert Malthus was crucial (R. M. Young, 1969; Vorzimmer, 1969; Schweber, 1977; L. B. Jones, 1989). However, the scientific substance of Darwin's theory cannot be reduced to its intellectual or ideological context.

In defining the 'struggle for existence' Darwin (1859, p. 62) made it clear that it included interdependence and the rearing of offspring: 'I use the term Struggle for Existence in a large and metaphorical sense, including dependence of one being on another, and including (which is more important) not only the life of the individual, but success in leaving progeny'. Darwin was an apologist neither for capitalism nor imperialism. He extolled neither selfishness, competition, jingoism nor war (Loye, 1998).

Darwinism sustains altruism and cooperation, as well as competition (Kropotkin, 1902; Sober and Wilson, 1998). Darwin (1871, vol. 1, p. 162) wrote: 'Selfish and contentious people will not cohere, and without coherence nothing can be effected'. As elaborated in the next chapter, cavalier use of the term 'Social Darwinism' associates him with scientific and ideological doctrines that he never proclaimed.

Marx (1976a, pp. 461 n., 493 n.) mentioned Darwin in passing in two footnotes in the first volume of *Capital*. But mostly he left Engels to deal with controversies in the natural sciences. In the *Dialectics of Nature*, drafted in the 1873–1883 period, Engels devoted four pages to a superficial and critical discussion of Darwinism. Engels (1964, p. 313) described the 'whole Darwinian theory of the struggle for existence' as 'simply the transference from society to organic nature' of Hobbes's war of all against all, and 'the bourgeois economic theory of competition, as well as the Malthusian theory of population'. Engels (1964, p. 314) saw the idea of class struggle as much richer in content than the 'weakly distinguished phases of the struggle for existence'.

Engels (1964, p. 312) also made the amazing statement that the Ernst Haeckel's idea of '"adaptation and heredity" can bring about the whole process of evolution, without need for selection and Malthusianism'.[4] Engels thus belittled the importance of Darwin's principle of natural selection.

In his *Anti-Dühring* of 1878, Engels (1962, pp. 97–101) provided his fullest discussion of Darwinian theory. He gave a very brief outline of the theory of natural selection (p. 98), but went on to criticize Darwin for the 'blunder' of 'accepting the Malthusian theory so naively and uncritically' (p. 99) and for attributing 'to his discovery too wide a field of action' (p. 100).

Despite their initial enthusiasm for the *Origin of Species,* and their enduring public praise for Darwinism, Marx and Engels periodically upheld alternative contributions as superior to Darwin's theory. Engels's attestation that Haeckel's (1874) principle of 'adaptation and heredity' made Darwin's theory of natural selection redundant is one of several instances. After reading a book by Pierre Trémaux (1865), Marx declared to Engels on 7 August 1866 that 'it represents a *very* significant advance over Darwin' (Marx and Engels, 1987, p. 304). But Engels did not reciprocate Marx's enthusiasm, and the work of Trémaux faded into obscurity.

Engels wrote a long letter to Pyotr Lavrov in November 1875, in which he cautioned against Darwinism (Marx and Engels, 1991, pp. 106-9). Engels awkwardly described 'Darwin's method of verification' of evolution as involving the 'struggle for life' and 'natural selection'. Engels saw Darwin's work as 'merely a first, provisional, incomplete expression of a newly discovered fact' of 'evolution'. By 'evolution' Engels presumably meant the general idea that humans and other species have developed by descent with modification from common ancestors. Against several named 'bourgeois Darwinians' who acted as apologists for capitalist competition, Engels emphasized human solidarity and cooperation. But he failed to acknowledge that Darwin (1871, vol. 1, pp. 162, 166) had also upheld the positive role in the survival of human groups of 'fidelity', 'sympathy', social 'coherence', 'aid to each other' and individual sacrifice 'for the common good'.[5]

In a postcard to Engels dated September 1882, Marx referred briefly to the work of Rudolf Virchow, a German naturalist and opponent of Darwinism. Marx's judgement was that Virchow 'has again demonstrated that he is far and away above Darwin, he alone, in fact, being scientific' (Marx and Engels, 1992, pp. 317–18). Yet who knows of Virchow today, and who now would follow Marx's suggestion that Darwinism was unscientific?

---

[4] Haeckel was a professor of biology at Jena in Germany. Unlike Darwin, he professed racist, anti-Semitic and eugenic ideas (Gasman, 1971, 1998). As Gould (1978, p. 211) suggests, Haeckel was probably the source of some of Engels's ideas in his essay 'The Part Played by Labour in the Transition from Ape to Man'.

[5] Kropotkin, who understood and embraced Darwinism, later elaborated on the more general role of cooperation in nature in his famous book *Mutual Aid* (1902).

Ironically, six months later, as Marx was laid to rest in Highgate Cemetery, Engels famously declared in his graveside speech: 'Just as Darwin discovered the law of development of organic nature, so Marx discovered the law of development of human history' (Marx and Engels, 1989, p. 467). This public oration linking Darwin with Marx masked a deep scepticism of Darwinism, shared by Engels and his dead friend.

It seems that Marx and Engels publicly endorsed Darwinism for pragmatic reasons (Gould, 1978, pp. 23–8). They applauded its materialist erosion of religion, its rejection of the idea that species were created by God, and its support for the idea that humans had evolved from apes. In private they expressed strong but misguided reservations. They were very wary of the Malthus-inspired concept of natural selection. There is no evidence in their writings of any adequate understanding of, let alone detailed agreement with, Darwin's core arguments concerning the causal mechanisms of evolution. They saw Darwinism as tainted by bourgeois political economy.

For them, the legitimate explanatory scope of Darwinism was confined to nature, and excluded human society. Accordingly, Engels's oration partitioned the human from the natural world, seeing Marx as the theorist of society, with Darwin's contribution confined to nature. Many social scientists replicated this enduring division of scientific territory. As long as the implicit maxim of 'Darwin for nature, Marx for humanity' remained, there was little impetus for Marxists or other social scientists to get to grips with Darwinian ideas, or to consider their application to the social sciences.

Reacting from the rise of eugenics and fascism, by the 1930s Marxists and others were energetically re-enforcing the division between the social and the natural sciences. For many, Darwinism was tinged with racism. It acquired a negative hue, as in the Diego Rivera mural noted above.

I show below that Darwin himself held no countenance for racist ideas.[6] Unfortunately the same cannot be said for Marx or Engels, despite their strong egalitarian pronouncements. I also propose that the Darwinian vision of change through variety and selection is actually more feasible and progressive in the social sphere than the professed Marxian notion of a unified and comprehensive system of national planning. Darwinism has much more relevance for the study of modern human society than Marx and Engels ever admitted.

---

[6] However, his views on women reflected his times. He was no feminist and he opposed contraception. His sons received more formal schooling than his daughters. Darwin (1871, vol. 2, p. 316) proposed that: 'Man is more courageous, pugnacious, and energetic than woman, and has more inventive genius'. By contrast, and to their credit, Marx wrote a little on the oppression of women, and Engels addressed it extensively. However, they both reduced the problem of female subjugation to capitalist exploitation, and saw its resolution in the overthrow of that system.

2.3 WAS DARWIN A RACIST?

During the nineteenth century, racist ideas were widespread, even among intellectuals. Several followers of Darwin harboured racist, imperialist and sexist ideas. However, the false idea that Darwin himself was a racist reverberates today. American creationists and advocates of the anti-evolutionary credo of 'intelligent design' have associated Darwin with racism.[7] For example, Henry Morris (1974), the founder of the US Institute for Creation Research, blames Darwinism for racism, communism, fascism and 1960s radicalism. Several creationist websites associate Darwin with racism and fascism, despite the fact that Darwinism offers no scientific support for these ideas.

In May 2001 Sharon Broome, a black Democrat politician, proposed this resolution to the State Legislature in Louisiana: 'Be it resolved that the Legislature of Louisiana does hereby deplore all instances and ideologies of racism, and does hereby reject the core concepts of Darwinist ideology that certain races and classes of humans are inherently superior to others'. The state's House Education Committee approved this text by a majority vote, but fortunately the State Legislature subsequently removed all references to Darwinism from the resolution.

Many modern creationists uphold that God created all humans with equal rank and status. But belief in God neither excludes racism nor guarantees human equality. There are numerous historical examples of creationists and believers who have upheld that God created superior and inferior races. In fact, such arguments were widely used by Christians to justify slavery.[8]

Darwin wrote of 'civilized' and 'savage' peoples, but he saw the differences as much due to nurture and culture, rather than entirely a matter of nature. When in South America, Darwin (1845, pp. 561–3) was outraged by slavery and he strongly criticized the treatment of native peoples by the Spanish and Portuguese. In 1882 he signed a petition against the persecution of the Jews in Russia. Neither a jingoist nor a racist, by his own confession he was a radical and progressive liberal (F. Darwin, 1887, vol. 3, p. 178).

---

[7] In attempts to counter Darwinism in the USA education system, intelligent design is upheld as a sanitized and allegedly 'scientific' version of creationism that does not mention God. It contends that the complexities of earthly life cannot have emerged through haphazard evolution and must be explained by an intelligent designer. However, it cannot explain how the intelligent designer herself emerged, or how she possessed and used the requisite causal powers to construct her design in reality.

[8] Many believers regard Marxism and Darwinism as manifestations of the common atheistic enemy. The thematic opposition in this book between Marxism and Darwinism is thus enjoined by anti-scientific theism, forming a third point in a doctrinal triangle. I do not explore this third zone further here.

The full title of Darwin's path-breaking book is *On the Origin of Species by Means of Natural Selection, or the Preservation of Favoured Races in the Struggle for Life* (1859). Some have seen its reference to 'favoured races' as evidence of racism. But the *Origin of Species* does not refer explicitly to human races at all. Throughout the work, 'races' refers to 'varieties', and the terms are used interchangeably.

In one passage in *The Descent of Man*, Darwin (1871, vol. 1, p. 201) referred to the divergence between the human species and the apes being located 'at present between the negro and Australian and the gorilla'. He thus repeated the then widespread and highly regrettable belief by scientists that some human races are closer than others to apes. However, in the same volume, Darwin (1871, vol. 1, p. 104) emphasized the similarities in mental capacities between all human races: 'There can be no doubt that the difference between the mind of the lowest man and that of the highest animal is immense'. In this latter respect he was very close to his socialist co-thinker Alfred Russel Wallace (1870), who independently formulated the principle of natural selection and jointly published it with Darwin in 1858. Against the prevalent view of the time, Darwin and Wallace both stressed that the differences between the human races were much smaller than the differences between humans and apes.

In Chapter 7 of *The Descent of Man* 'On the Races of Man' Darwin considered two mutually exclusive hypotheses: that the races are sufficiently distinct to count as different species, and that they are sufficiently alike to count as one species with internal variation. Darwin (1871, vol. 1, pp. 231–2) demolished the separate species argument and proposed that humans are one:

> Although the existing races of man differ in many respects, as in colour, hair, shape of skull, proportions of the body, &c., yet if their whole organisation be taken into consideration they are found to resemble each other closely on a multitude of points. Many of these points are so unimportant or of so singular a nature, that it is extremely improbable that they should have been independently acquired by aboriginally distinct species or races. The same remark holds good with equal or greater force with respect to the numerous points of mental similarity between the most distinct races of man.

Darwin wrote that his contacts with other races during his voyage on HMS Beagle had convinced him 'how similar their minds were to ours'. In both his sentiments and his science, Darwin rejected any form of racial discrimination. He was not a supreme paragon of political virtue, but the accusation that he was a racist is way off the mark.

We now compare the true views of Darwin on race with statements by Karl Marx and Friedrich Engels. On the one hand, Marx and Engels called repeatedly for the solidarity of the international working class. Their appeal has been heeded by hundreds of thousands of Marxists who have fought, often at great personal cost, against racism and fascism. On the other hand, we find occasional racist statements in the writings of Marx and Engels that are simply unparalleled in Darwin's works or correspondence.

Marx was of Jewish descent, and he supported Jewish emancipation. However, in his 1844 article 'On the Jewish Question' he wrote: 'What is the worldly religion of the Jew? *Huckstering.* What is his worldly God? *Money*' (Marx and Engels, 1975, p. 170). Repeating such false, stereotypical and offensive descriptions, even in the rhetorical context of his argument, was highly provocative and dangerous, especially given that anti-Semitism was then widespread among intellectuals as well as the uneducated population.

Pandering to anti-Semitism was one thing. Advocating genocide was another. In the *Neue Rheinische Zeitung* on 13 January 1849 (edited by Marx and Engels) Engels proclaimed that 'the disappearance from the face of the earth … of entire reactionary peoples' such as the Slavs would be a 'step forward' (Marx and Engels, 1977, p. 238). Evidence of their racism also applies to those of African descent. In his letter to Engels of 7 August 1866, Marx with apparent approval cited a claim that 'the common negro type is only a degeneration of a far higher one' (Marx and Engels, 1987, p. 305).

Engels (1964, pp. 211–12, 309–12) approved of a book by Haeckel (1874), which has an unfortunate illustration depicting African people as close to apes.[9] This diagram was worse than Darwin's (1871, vol. 1, p. 201) brief and unfortunate endorsement of a hierarchy of races. In contrast to Darwin, who emphasized the greater difference between humans as a whole and apes, Haeckel pictured the absolute distance between Africans and apes as similar to the distance between Africans and Caucasians. Engels passed over Haeckel's obnoxious picture without comment.

Overall, however, racist statements are infrequent in the works and correspondence of Marx and Engels. But the point here is to compare the writings of Darwin with those of Marx and Engels. Many convict Darwin of racism, while Marx and Engels have been widely regarded as shining heroes of ethnic egalitarianism. Yet Darwin never made *any* statement that was remotely close to the phrases caricaturing the Jews, supporting Slav genocide and endorsing accounts of 'negro … degeneration' that are found in the writings of Engels and Marx.

Just as all these writers were creatures of their time, so too are we. The Soviet Union acquired its reputation as the major bulwark against rising fascism in the 1930s. This challengeable perception survived the Hitler–Stalin pact of 1939 and the horrific episodes of ethnic cleansing and mass

---

[9] The picture is reproduced and criticized in Gould (1978, p. 215).

extermination ordered by Stalin himself in his own territories.[10] Since the 1940s, the intellectual attitude to Marxism has been coloured by the ideological fallout from the alliance between the Soviet Union, Britain, France and the USA in the anti-fascist Second World War. The Soviet Union's status as an ally of Western democracies after 1941 gave it the false but enduring aura of an essentially emancipatory and egalitarian regime. At around the same time, as shown in the following chapter, Darwinism was tarred with eugenics and the notion of 'Social Darwinism' was used to diminish the influence of Darwinian ideas outside biology. The twin myths of Darwin as a racist and Marx as an unblemished anti-racist, were set in stone during the upheaval of the Second World War.

2.4 MARXIAN EVOLUTION VERSUS DARWINIAN ALGORITHMIC CHANGE

Inspired by Georg W. F. Hegel and others before, Marx and Engels regarded history as a series of pre-ordained, developmental stages. For them, historical progress was represented by a sequence of social formations, from 'primitive communism', through feudalism and capitalism to socialism and communism. Marxists see history as a struggle of contradictory forces, which may be resolved by moving beyond capitalism and towards communism, where harmony at last will prevail; all preceding history prepares the opportunity for this ultimate transformation. Within Marxism, there is a single, currently identifiable, final goal.

Also following Hegel, Marx identified the driving forces of change as largely within the system, and less through external shocks or through interaction with its environment. The logic of system development prepares the fateful collision of internal forces of production with internal relations of production. As Marx (1976a, p. 929) wrote in *Capital*:

> The centralization of the means of production and the socialization of labour reach a point at which they become incompatible with their capitalist integument. This

---

[10] Trotsky (1937) saw similarities between Stalinism and fascism. From 1939 to 1949 there were mass deportations and killings of Baltic, Caucasian, Polish, Slav and Turkic peoples, often with the aim of eliminating their culture (Pohl, 1999). The deliberately engineered famine in the Ukraine in 1932–1933 is estimated to have led to between six and ten million deaths (Conquest, 1986). Stalin's crimes rival those of the Nazis in scale and cruelty. Yet these episodes have been given much less attention than the Holocaust. Of course, we cannot convict a doctrine such as Marxism, Christianity or Islam simply by the sins of its adherents. Instead, the point here is to show that the awareness and ranking of such atrocities are framed by enduring but challengeable conceptual frameworks, acquired from an earlier history.

> integument is burst asunder. The knell of capitalist private property sounds. The expropriators are expropriated.

He thus saw capitalism as its own gravedigger. Marx (1981, p. 358) wrote of the 'immanent barriers' to capitalist development. In his theory of the tendency of the rate of profit to fall, the logic of capitalism's own internal development reduces the general potential rate of profit in the system.[11]

Joseph Schumpeter (1934, p. 63) was deeply inspired by Marx's writings on capitalist development and proposed a similar emphasis on 'such changes in economic life as are not forced upon it from without but arise by its own initiative, from within'. Marx and Schumpeter both emphasized the self-transformation of the economic system through its internal conflicts. Schumpeter (1942) proposed that capitalist commerce undermines the necessary foundation of loyalty and deference to authority, inherited from the feudal era. Although this theory is different from that of Marx, a Marxian and Hegelian emphasis on immanent change 'from within' remains.

By contrast, in biology, neither individuals, species nor even ecosystems are entirely 'self-transforming'. Evolution takes place within *open* systems involving *both* endogenous and exogenously stimulated change. Generally, evolution takes place through both internal changes and interactions with the (possibly changing) environment. Often the environmental context changes because of migrations and intrusions from another region. As observed by Darwin (1859), the isolation of groups of organisms and their adaptation to a particular environment have important effects on the evolution of species and ecosystems. Isolation gives new variation time to slowly evolve, but generally reduces the level of new variation that is being produced. Much change is due to introductions of species from other regions, which interact with their new neighbours and affect the course of evolution. Exogenous shocks, such as meteor impacts and climate change, are also believed to have had major influence on the evolutionary process, leading to the extinction of some species and the expansion of others.[12]

Likewise, in socio-economic evolution, exogenously stimulated change is sometimes of great importance. Organization theory thus recognizes a

---

[11] See the criticisms of Marx's theory of the falling rate of profit in Hodgson (1991) and Chapter 5 below. My 'impurity principle' (Hodgson, 1984, 1988, 1999a, 2001c) is in part an attempt to escape from a unilinear account of development, reduced to the mechanisms of the single dominant system. The existence of additional 'impurities' from a varied set of possibilities creates combinations with divergent paths of possible development (Hall and Soskice, 2001; Nicita and Pagano, 2001; Boyer, 2005).

[12] Another prevailing and important feature of Darwinian evolutionary processes is irreversibility. This is also a feature of thermodynamic systems. See Dosi and Metcalfe (1991) and Mani (1991).

distinction between *autogenic* changes, meaning that variation is self-generated or caused by forces within an organization, and *allogenic* changes, meaning that it is other-generated or caused by forces outside an organization (McKelvey, 1982, p. 77).

Exogenous shocks can sometimes overcome the cultural mechanisms of imitation and conformism that tend otherwise to reduce internal variety and lead to institutional ossification. Many historical examples illustrate the critical effects of exogenous forces. Ancient Greece was moulded by its conflicts with Sparta, Persia and elsewhere. The invasions of the Gauls into Italy in the fourth century BC hammered together Roman society. Invasions by Romans, Anglo-Saxons, Vikings and Normans have profoundly affected British institutions. The Mongol attacks of the fourteenth century AD cemented the Russian State. Mongol invasions of China from the thirteenth to the fifteenth centuries utterly transformed Chinese institutions. The modernizing seventeenth century revolutions in England were sparked by conflicts with Scotland. American warships in Tokyo Bay provoked the Meiji Restoration of 1868 and the subsequent rapid transition of Japan from feudalism to capitalism. The occupation of Japan and Germany by American and Allied troops in 1945 also led to major institutional changes. The course of institutional evolution has often been altered by the intrusion of new forces across the boundaries of national or regional socio-economic systems.

The Darwinian conception of change is very different from the Marxian view of historical evolution. Instead of the emphasis on change coming largely from within, Darwin emphasized the role of varied populations and their environment: individual organisms not only interact with one another but also – as groups and individuals – with their natural surroundings. In contrast to Marxism, the outcome of Darwinian evolution is not generally 'immanent' within the system or population itself.

Marxists identify possible future states of the world, including socialism and communism, while their timing is unknown and the route towards them is uncertain. They uphold that no other future options are compatible with full human emancipation. Hence the Marxist Rosa Luxemburg (1971, p. 368) wrote in 1915 of the choice between 'socialism or barbarism', thus partitioning the future into merely two basic options for humanity.

By contrast, Darwinism acknowledges much greater complexity in the pattern of future possibilities. Complex interactions between dissimilar elements make both the conception and prediction of future possibilities much more difficult. Additional dimensions of complexity emerge because evolution is not entirely a process of 'self–transformation' – interactions of components within a structure. It also involves interactions with changing environmental contexts. This high degree of context dependence and complexity means that the future is not partitioned into a few distinct alternatives.[13]

Not only are the real options multiple and complex, but also our ability to appraise them is limited. At best we have only a highly limited capacity to conceive of future outcomes or options, and an equivalently limited ability to evaluate their merits and demerits. Consequently, in these circumstances, politicians and social engineers have to rely on careful experimentation rather than bold revolutionary thrusts towards a single, allegedly superior future.

However, while Darwinism emphasizes complexity and warns of our limited powers of overall prefiguration or design, it does not belittle human capacities of forethought or prefiguration in dealing with practical problems at the level of the individual or group. Contrary to a widespread misconception, Darwinism underestimates neither human intentionality nor foresight. These capacities are real, but our ability to envision the future is nevertheless limited because of the complexity of the world.

The general processes of Darwinian evolution are not necessarily progressive. While discussing human social evolution, Darwin (1871, vol. 1, p. 166) wrote: 'we are apt to look at progress as the normal rule in human society; but history refutes this'. It is another common misunderstanding to regard Darwinism as proclaiming an automatic progression towards a superior state.

Darwinism rejects Hegelian and other teleological notions of destiny or inevitable progress. Instead of movement towards an identifiable outcome or goal, it focuses on the causal explanation of sequential, step-by-step developments. Causal explanations focus on processual algorithms. A key processual algorithm outlined by Darwin was natural selection.

Daniel Dennett (1995) emphasizes the algorithmic nature of the Darwinian explanation of change. Thorstein Veblen made a similar observation, although the word 'algorithm' was not then invented. Veblen (1919, p. 436) saw 'in the Darwinian scheme of thought … a continuity of cause and effect'. In an explicit comparison and contrast with Marxism, Darwinism for Veblen meant 'cumulative causation, in which there is no trend, no final term, no consummation'.

Similarly, Veblen (1919, p. 37) wrote of Darwinism creating a new emphasis 'whereby the process of causation, the interval of instability and transition between initial cause and definitive effect, has come to take the first place in the inquiry; instead of that consummation in which causal effect was once presumed to come to rest'. Consequently, science becomes

[13] See Hodgson (1999a) for a discussion of not only possible varieties of capitalism, but also possible futures that are neither capitalist nor socialist. I also argue that socialism is possible only if combined with markets and rapid dynamic innovation and technological change are sacrificed.

'substantially a theory of the process of consecutive change, realized to be self-continuing or self-propagating and to have no final term'. Veblen (1919, p. 192) referred to 'the field of cumulative change within which the modern post-Darwinian sciences live and move and have their being'. Again there is an explicit denial of teleological evolution towards an overall goal, and a clear contrast with Marxism.[14]

Accordingly, a Darwinian approach to social phenomena focuses on the causal details, and is sceptical of broad-brush accounts of 'economic forces', 'social forces' or 'cultural influences', which evade the detailed causal mechanisms of how economic, social or cultural circumstances affect the preferences, perceptions and decisions of real individuals. Veblen (1901b, pp. 76–81) thus derided broad-brush accounts of change through 'cultural exfoliation' and looked instead to a 'Darwinistic account of the origin, growth, persistence, and variation of institutions'.

The Darwinian conception of algorithmic change focuses on the conditional, rule-like dispositions that determine how each element in the system reacts to information or stimuli. Systemic change comes about through the repeated, cumulative effect of multiple, programmed responses. Change results from the repeated application of a multiplicity of interacting and relatively persistent rules.[15]

Darwinism suggests an ontology of structured algorithms and rule-like dispositions, interacting at the micro-level to create complex and unpredictable macro-outcomes. By contrast, the social ontology of Marxism is one of structures and forces at the macro-level, with inadequate attention to the micro-mechanisms. Consequently, Marxism underestimates the function of social rules, and fails to appreciate why rules of some kind are an indispensable feature of action and interaction in human society.

While Marxism rightly emphasizes social relations, their rule-like character is downplayed. The ontological image is of structures and flows rather than institutions and cognitively embedded rules. For example, at the level of productive activity, the Marxian labour theory invokes a questionable 'substance theory of value' that elevates physical (actual or embodied) labour

---

[14] By 'cumulative' causation Veblen referred primarily to cumulative sequences of cause and effect. Other authors give 'cumulative causation' the different meaning (in modern parlance) of processes of positive feedback (A. A. Young, 1928; Kaldor, 1985; Myrdal, 1939, 1957).

[15] Some writers have associated Darwinism with stochastic causality, but this is not necessarily the case. Darwinian evolution relies on ongoing variation, but it does not necessarily imply probabilistic causation as found in quantum physics. As chaos theory confirms, there are other possible sources of apparent randomness (Hodgson, 2004b).

inputs and outputs, rather than adaptive and relational knowledge, institutional linkages and social rules.[16]

2.5 MARXISM, DARWINISM AND THE HUMAN PSYCHE

With its inadequate treatment of micro-mechanisms, Marxism lacks any developed account of the psychological springs of human agency, including the role of habit. In Marxian theory, structures play the key explanatory role, but there is no explanation of the detailed causal mechanisms through which structures affect the dispositions and intentions of individuals. Structures bear the explanatory burden without the support of a detailed psychological theory.

In contrast, Darwinism brought not only the evolution of species but also a new understanding of the human mind and consciousness onto the agenda of science. Darwinians including William James (1890), Conwy Lloyd Morgan (1896) and James Mark Baldwin (1909) began to develop a Darwinian approach to psychology around the end of the nineteenth century (Richards, 1987; Plotkin, 1994).

Veblen noted this achievement, and it became an important part of his critique of Marxism. Veblen (1901a, pp. 225–6) observed that the theory of human motivation in Marxism is largely one of emerging rational appraisal of class interest, without any explanation of how the criteria and procedures of rationality themselves appear and evolve. Veblen (1906, pp. 581-2) emphasized that any rational appraisal of interests does not itself explain how people acquire their beliefs and seek particular objectives. The Darwinian outlook rules out a conception of human nature driven entirely by reasons or beliefs. This is because reasons and beliefs have themselves to be grounded in an evolutionary process. The emotional and impulsive grounding of our preferences and purposes have also to be taken into account. In acquired or inherited dispositions or sentiments, we carry the legacy of our pre-human origins, in organisms driven by dispositions and emotions, rather than by full, rational deliberation. As Veblen (1907, p. 308) put it:

> Under the Darwinian norm it must be held that men's reasoning is largely controlled by other than logical, intellectual forces; that the conclusion reached by public or class opinion is as much, or more, a matter of sentiment than of logical inference; and that the sentiment which animates men, singly or collectively, is as

[16] See Mirowski (1989) on the substance theory of value. Mirowski (1991) and Potts (2000) develop a notion of limited interconnectedness, leading to the vision in Dopfer (2004), Dopfer *et al.* (2004) and Parra (2005) of social systems as essentially composed of structures and processes of rules.

> much, or more, an outcome of habit and native propensity as of calculated material interest.

This crucial emphasis on habit, as a key mechanism by which social conditions affect individual preferences and beliefs, distinguishes Veblen from Marx. Veblen rightly argued that thc mere class position of an individual as a wage labourer or a capitalist tells us very little about the specific conceptions or habits of thought, and thereby the likely actions, of the individuals involved. Individual interests, whatever they are, do not necessarily lead to accordant individual perceptions or actions. As different capitalist cultures testify, the class position of an agent – exploiter or exploited – does not itself lead to a unique pattern of behaviour. Faced with such rival scenarios, Marxism lacks an adequate explanation of how structures or institutions affected individual purposes or inclinations.

For Darwinian psychologists such as James (1890), human agents possess instincts, habits and deliberative capacities. Our capacity to reason and appraise outcomes exceeds other organisms by far, but nevertheless depends upon the substrata of inherited and acquired dispositions. Darwinism embraces a 'doctrine of continuity' (Huxley, 1894, vol. 1, pp. 236-7) where consciousness and deliberation do not suddenly appear in the evolution of organisms. Hence Darwinism does not deny human intentionality but places it in an evolutionary context. Darwin (1859, p. 208) thus wrote in the *Origin of Species*: 'A little dose … of judgement or reason often comes into play, even in animals very low in the scale of nature'. Darwin (1871, vol. 1, p. 46) restated the idea in *The Descent of Man*: 'animals possess some power of reasoning. Animals may constantly be seen to pause, deliberate and resolve'.

Darwinism recognizes that human reason can neither appear nor function without inherited or learned dispositional supports. Just as earlier organisms have a smidgeon of reason, human rational capacities are built on subconscious mechanisms inherited from our pre-human ancestors. We retain instincts and unconscious mental processes that can function independently of our conscious reasoning. As some animal species developed more complex instincts, they eventually acquired the capacity to register fortuitous and reinforced behaviours through the evolution of mechanisms of habituation. In turn, upon these mechanisms, humans built culture and language. Our layered mind, with its unconscious lower strata, maps our long evolution from less deliberative organisms. Consistent with the evolutionary doctrine of continuity, habits and instincts are highly functional evolutionary survivals of our pre-human past.[17]

---

[17] Why didn't efficacious adaptive solutions all eventually become ingrained as instincts through natural selection? Veblen (1914, pp. 6–7) recognized this theoretical problem and argued that the capacity to form habits was retained, without

This Darwinian perspective of the human mind contrasts not simply with Marxism, but with much of social science. It is often taken for granted, or by definition, that 'action' is motivated exclusively by reasons based on beliefs. This proposition is undermined by modern psychology as well as the evolutionary outlook offered by Darwinism. Experiments since the 1970s show that conscious sensations are reported about half a second after neural events, and unconscious brain processes are discernable before any conscious decision to act (Libet, 1985, 2004; Wegner, 2002; Wegner and Wheatley, 1999). This evidence suggests that our dispositions are triggered before our actions are rationalized: we contrive reasons for actions already under way.

This undermines explanations of human action wholly in the terms of reasons and beliefs. This 'folk psychology' papers over a much more complex neurophysiological reality. These 'mind-first' explanations of human behaviour are unable to explain adequately such phenomena as sleep, memory, learning, mental illness, or the effects of chemicals or drugs on our perceptions or actions.[18]

Humans do act for reasons. But reasons and beliefs themselves are caused, and have to be explained. From a Darwinian perspective, reasoning itself is based on habits and instincts, and it cannot be sustained without them. Furthermore, consistent with the Darwinian doctrine of continuity, instincts and the capacities to form habits developed through a process of natural selection that extends way back into our pre-human past.

Mayr (1988, 1992) offers one of the clearest expositions of the importance of the Darwinian perspective for understanding human action. He fully acknowledges that human agents are purposeful, but places this in its evolutionary context. In contrast to teleological notion of an overall evolutionary goal, individual agents may be goal-driven. Mayr (1988, p. 45) defines 'teleonomic' or 'program-based' behaviour as that which '*owes its goal-directedness to the operation of a program'*. Such behaviour is governed by connected, rule-like dispositions, similar to a computer program. There remain enormous differences between a human mind and a computer, but they share this common, rule-driven or program-based characteristic.

---

all particular habits becoming instincts, because humans were faced with complex and varying circumstances (Hodgson, 2004a). A prominent and concordant contemporary view is that the human capacity to form sophisticated habits and transmit cultural information and norms was promoted by the experiences of survival during dramatic climate changes over the last million years (Richerson *et al*., 2001; Richerson and Boyd, 2001, 2004). Again this points to the importance of exogenous shocks in human evolution. Human culture did not evolve mostly 'from within'.

[18] See Bunge (1980); Stich (1983); P. M. Churchland (1984, 1989); P. S. Churchland (1986); Damasio (1994); Rosenberg (1995, 1998); Kilpinen (2000).

Viktor Vanberg (2000, 2002, 2004a, 2004b) elaborates Mayr's argument, and shows that it provides a powerful alternative to the idea – found in both Marxism and mainstream economics – that human agency can be explained essentially in terms of rational deliberation. The assumption that human behaviour is determined by emerging rational appraisal of interests (Marx), or a given preference function (neoclassical economics), lacks an explanation of the origin or operation of these rational capacities or preferences. The technology of rationality is assumed rather than explained.

By contrast, the program-based approach relies on evolutionary theory to explain the origin of systems of rule-like dispositions, which are either inherited as instincts, or acquired as habits in a historically specific cultural setting. Generally, the human problem-solving capacity that rational choice theory attributes to 'rationality', and Marxism to informed deliberation, is explained in the Darwinian terms by the knowledge of the world that is incorporated in rules or programs that guide behaviour. This knowledge has been accumulated through trial and error in the processes of human evolution and individual learning. Knowledge, in short, consists of adaptations that have emerged in an evolutionary process (Plotkin, 1994).

Accordingly, both customs and institutions are repositories of knowledge. This does not mean that all customs or institutions are efficient or desirable. Instead, relative to their environments, they embody more-or-less adaptive solutions, beneficial or otherwise. Humans have evolved to respect customs, because a society that completely destroyed its customary legacy would destroy its hidden knowledge of the past. This was the basis of Edmund Burke's (1790) famous criticism of the rationalist iconoclasm of the French revolutionaries. Marxists have dismissed such arguments as reactionary, without recognizing their inner core of truth.

While much human knowledge is embodied in institutions and transmitted by custom, humans have evolved to respect and follow customary practices, for good or ill. Whether good or bad, the role of custom is thereby an important element in the explanation of human behaviour. In contrast, in Marxism there is a 'failure to see the importance of custom' as John R. Commons (1925, p. 686) remarked. The Darwinian conception of the human agent restores the psychological role of habit, and the related roles of customs, routines and institutions, to their proper place. Darwinism places human rationality on an evolving foundation of instincts and habits, and situates this in its institutional, cultural and customary context. Its general ontology emphasizes algorithms, program-based behaviour and rule-like dispositions. All these issues are major themes in this book.

2.6 THE NEGLECT OF VARIETY IN THE MONOLITHIC MARXIAN FUTURE

The inadequate recognition within Marxism of the role of variety and systemic impurities leads to an underestimation of the role of different, coexisting, political or economic structures, and an insufficient emphasis on individual autonomy. Marxism claims to be an emancipatory, egalitarian and inclusive doctrine. However, Marxists have generally undervalued arguments from the liberal political tradition concerning individual autonomy and the legitimate limits to the power of the majority. This deficiency raises questions of economic as well as political pluralism

Marxists rightly argue that economic wealth and interests are the grounding of much political power: the economic 'base' profoundly affects the political 'superstructure'. However, this maxim also suggests that the abolition of private competition and the amalgamation of economic units into one integrated system would prepare the ground for a single-party state: a unified economic base would foster a monolithic political superstructure. Marx and Engels proposed an amalgamation of economic powers that would raise precisely such concerns. Yet this problem is largely ignored in the Marxian intellectual tradition (Hodgson, 1984, 1999a, 2005).

When challenged, Marxists say they believe in individual diversity and self-realization. But they do not embrace a variety of types of economic institution. How can political pluralism and individual autonomy be preserved, except within a system with multiple centres of economic power?

For Marx and Engels, communism meant a unified and harmonious social order, with neither conflict between classes nor a diversity of material interests. In 1848 Marx and Engels welcomed movements 'to centralize all instruments of production in the hands of the state'. They looked forward to a time when 'all production has been concentrated in the hands of a vast association of the whole nation' (Marx, 1973a, pp. 86–7). With the proposed 'abolition of private property' (Marx, 1973a, pp. 80–1) there would be no scope for private enterprise, even on a small scale.

This monolithic vision of communism persisted throughout their lives. It appeared, for example, in the second volume of *Capital* where Marx (1978, p. 434) wrote of the planned system of 'social production' where 'society distributes labour-power and means of production between the various branches of industry'. In one of his last manuscripts Marx (1976b, p. 207) advocated a 'social-state' that would 'draw up production from the very beginning'. Marx believed that this state would be subordinate to the will of the people, but his centraziling vision remained.

During the lifetimes of Marx and Engels, in contrast to their idea of nationalized property and national planning, the alternative idea emerged of a system of legally autonomous cooperatives or communes, explicitly linked and coordinated by contracts and exchanges. Philippe Buchez, a follower of Claude Henri de Saint-Simon, had proposed the formation of worker cooperative associations as early as 1831, and his ideas became prominent during the French Revolution of 1848 (Gide and Rist, 1915, p. 258; Reibel, 1975). Originally, like Marx and others, Buchez argued that the individual cooperatives should gradually merge into a single 'universal association'. However, and contrary to most contemporary socialists and communists, Buchez and his followers gradually recognized the need for multiple, smaller, autonomous worker cooperatives, linked by contracts and markets (Reibel, 1975, pp. 44–5). Consequently, writing in 1875, Marx (1974, pp. 353–4) described Buchez's developed ideas as 'reactionary', 'sectarian', opposed to the 'class movement' of the workers, and contrary to the true revolutionary aim of 'cooperative production ... on a national scale'.

Like Buchez, the anarchist Pierre Joseph Proudhon proposed an accommodation of contracts and exchanges within a permanent system of 'mutualist associations' involving groups of workers who would pool their labour and their property, holding and using these resources in common. Proudhon realized that without a decentralization of contractual powers, meaningful economic decentralization could not flourish. Hence he proposed that cooperative associations would be able to enter into contractual relations with one another. He also assumed that these contracts would be mutually defining and self-policing, dispensing with the need for a legal system, a government and a state. Proudhon was frequently criticized by Marx, for both his theory and his policy proposals. These statements show that Marx was hostile to any retention of commodity exchange or markets in a future socialist society (Moore, 1980, 1993).

Marx and Engels emphatically rejected the notion that contracts and competition should endure indefinitely after the proletarian revolution. In accord with most socialists and communists of their time, they proposed that all the means of production should be owned by society as a whole, not by small, autonomous communes or associations. Engels (1962, p. 388) thus wrote in the 1870s: 'With the seizing of the means of production by society, production of commodities is done away with ... Anarchy in social production is replaced by a plan-conforming, conscious organization'.

Marx supported worker cooperatives within capitalism because they demonstrate the benefits of cooperative labour (Jossa, 2005). They show that the workers are capable of managing production without capitalists. But he did not support their survival as independent local organizations. In his 'Inaugural Address of the International Working Men's Association' drafted in 1864 he praised the established producer cooperatives, but he did not see them as enduring in the same form under socialism. Instead, Marx (1974, p. 80) saw their salvation in their urgent development 'to national dimensions ... fostered by national means'. Marx argued that all worker cooperatives would have to grow into, or become part of, nationalized industries. For them, any form of common ownership of less than national scope would have to be subsumed into the unitary national 'association', which would be owned and controlled at the national level.

Throughout their lives, Marx and Engels gave no more than meagre hints of the form of organization of their proposed future society. It is thus all the more significant and remarkable that the singular notion of 'a vast association of the whole nation' involving collective production 'fostered by national means' reappears several times, without amendment or qualification, in their writings. Only a particularly blinkered Marxist could read the words of Marx and Engels on their proposed socialist future, and see no threat to a plurality of forms of common ownership and no antagonism to commodity exchanges, markets or a mixed economy. In their proposal 'to centralize all instruments of production in the hands of the state' they favoured a single, all-encompassing arrangement, subject to rational principles of overall accounting and control.

There is no evidence in the works of Marx or Engels that they saw any value in institutional and structural diversity, under capitalism or socialism. They did not appreciate that the only way of providing local production units with real autonomy over decisions concerning output levels or prices is to establish them as separate legal units, with the right to trade with one another.[19] By contrast, a 'vast association of the whole nation' means a single bureaucratic entity, notwithstanding the degree of internal participation or democracy involved. Key decisions within such an organization would be binding on all its members and departments. An advantage of a system of autonomous units, with the capacity to make contracts and exchanges, is that it preserves some autonomy from the central authorities. In a complex integrated economy, the capacity to exchange commodities is a precondition (but not guarantors) of genuine economic decentralization (Nove, 1983; Hodgson, 1999a). Marx and Engels never understood this.

Legal institutions protecting private property and permitting commodity exchanges are necessary but insufficient conditions of economic autonomy. Other institutions have also to be in place to sustain autonomy, but without some legally protected right to trade outputs, there is no chance of genuine local autonomy in production. Markets have many defects, including their trajectories of inequality and their exaggeration of pecuniary values. Nevertheless, commodity exchanges are indispensable in a complex society.

---

19 Ironically, many modern economists and sociologists fail to appreciate the importance of the status of the firm as a single legal person. They share with Marxism an epiphenomenal rather than constitutive view of law (Hodgson, 2002a, 2003c).

An important advantage of a system based on private property and commodity exchange is that within limits it can offer some scope for inventors or entrepreneurs with new ideas – which initially are often regarded as doomed or strange – to seek a market for their innovations and to benefit from any success. Many technological innovations depend on the promotion of a minority view that is not widely supported or acknowledged at the outset. The market-coordinated system of decentralized rights over property and decision-making is an important reason for the enormous technological dynamism of capitalism over the last 250 years. Alongside all its defects, the capitalist system has the capacity to retain diversity, accommodate innovation and stimulate immense increases in productivity.

Markets depend on competition between scarce resources. In response Marxists proclaim that humankind now has the technological capacity to overcome all scarcity and meet all human needs. This response ignores key questions of motivation and allocation at the individual level. It also skips over some pressing problems of limited physical resources on a planet with a rapidly expanding population. Furthermore, it ignores the difference between local and global scarcity. Because all organisms do not have access to all resources at once, the problem of local and immediate scarcity is omnipresent.[20] Abundance in some respects does not necessarily overcome scarcity. A pile of meat and vegetables does not constitute a cooked meal; time, planning, skill and energy are required to fill the table.

The omnipresent problem of local scarcity is the basis for Darwin's (1859, pp. 62–3) concept of a struggle for existence (which may involve cooperative activity to enhance survival). Accordingly, Darwinism focuses on individual strategies or cooperative arrangements for survival at micro level. Marxism gives insufficient attention to issues of organization and motivation at the micro level, by focusing more frequently on the macro rather than the micro picture and assuming that scarcity will entirely vanish in the future.

2.7 THE ESSENTIAL ROLE OF VARIETY IN DARWINIAN EVOLUTION

Darwin had much less to say than Marx or Engels about politics, and made no major statement concerning the desirability of any particular form of society. It is a big mistake to presume that a particular political stance can be

[20] The concept of scarcity is widely assumed by economists but rarely defined or discussed in detail. When Robbins (1932) regarded economics as the science of choice under scarcity, he defined scarcity loosely as a resource that is 'limited'. But there is a big difference between global scarcity and scarcity in a local and immediate sense. Many global resources are limited, but other global and useful resources such as skill, trust and honor do not face the same physical constraints.

derived logically from a scientific account of the mechanisms of biological evolution. Darwinism is neither a political creed nor an adequate guide to policy. However, there is a *Weltanschauung* in Darwinism that contrasts with that in Marxism. Darwin emphasized that biotic diversity provided natural selection with its evolutionary fuel. Without variation within a population, natural selection cannot work, because there would be no way of sorting the population according to degrees of adaptation to their environment.

Darwin took some further inspiration on this point from Malthus (1798, p. 379), who saw 'the infinite variety of nature' which 'cannot exist without inferior parts, or apparent blemishes'. A major motivation behind Malthus's *Essay on Population* (1798) was to criticize those radicals who believed in the perfectibility of society (R. M. Young, 1969; Hodgson, 1993, Ch. 4). For Malthus and Darwin, the existence of diversity, blemishes and impurities is essential to the vitality of the whole. A system relies on a variety of complementary mechanisms, rather than a single structural solution. Both Malthus and Darwin saw that error and failure could sometimes help to engender learning and favour future success. Their perspective is one of trial and error, rather than confident leaps into an imagined future. All this contrasts with both the absolute confidence of Marxists in a system of comprehensive planning, and the unwarranted faith of modern neo-liberals in a system that is *entirely* driven by markets. Both Marxists and neo-liberals reject the structural diversity of a mixed economy.[21]

In contrast to the Marxian and Hegelian emphases on immanent evolution, Darwin's theory focuses on selection working upon variety. Here also is a key difference between Darwin, on the one hand, and Jean-Baptiste de Lamarck and Herbert Spencer, on the other. Lamarck and Spencer argued that variation was largely a result of multiple adaptations to the environment. In contrast, for Darwin 'variation was present first, and the ordering activity of the environment ("natural selection") followed afterwards' (Mayr, 1982, p. 354). For Lamarck, the environment was the principal agent of change. In contrast, Darwin argued that change resulted from a combination of variation and environmental selection, which in turn might lead to a change in environmental circumstances.

Darwin made an important philosophical innovation with his ontological commitment to variety. Before Darwin, a Platonic and Aristotelian 'typological essentialism' prevailed, where species are defined in terms of a few distinct individual characteristics that establish their essence. All variations around the ideal type are regarded as accidental aberrations. Marx clearly was an Aristotelian in this respect. As evidenced in *Capital,* he

[21] The hostility of Marx and Engels to Malthusian ideas is noted above. It is remarkable that Hayek also ignored or belittled Malthus's significance (Hodgson, 1993, 2004c).

attempted to identify the essence of a system in terms of a few key characteristics, abstracting from variation and impurities.

In contrast, Darwin abandoned Platonic or Aristotelian essentialism to replace it by something very different. For Darwin, the essence of any type included its potential to exhibit or create variation. Accordingly, an understanding of an item must also consider the *population* of similar entities in which that variation is present or possible. Mayr (1964, 1982, 1985, 1988, 1991) called this 'population thinking', wherein species are understood in terms of a distribution of characteristics, whereas in typological thinking variation is a classificatory annoyance. Population thinking is of paramount importance for Darwinism, because it is upon variety that selection operates. This means that we cannot model an evolutionary system simply by focusing on the average or representative features of a population. Summarizing a complex system in terms of average or representative components neglects the variety that is essential to system behaviour and evolution.

After the Second World War, similar ideas concerning the importance of variety found their way into systems theory, which had been inspired in part by evolutionary biology (Bertalanffy, 1971). In this literature it is shown that sustained variety within a system is necessary to cope with unforeseen change (Ashby, 1952, 1956; Boguslaw, 1965; Beer, 1972; Luhmann, 1982; Hodgson, 1984, 1999a). Internal variety in structure and routine is the hallmark of a robust and innovative system. In stressing the importance of variety and innovation, the Darwinian *Weltanschaung* has survived and retained its relevance into the twenty-first century.

In establishing the meaning and viability of the Darwinian worldview, a case has been made for elevating Darwin from the zone of darkness on the left of Rivera's mural. Obversely, the dark side of Marxism has been downplayed, especially after the grand alliance of the Soviet Union with the West against the Nazis in the Second World War. An insufficiently critical view of Marxism has survived among liberal academics, while Darwinism has unjustifiably been regarded as the *bête noire* of the social sciences.

In the next chapter we focus on an aspect of this demonization of Darwinism: the use of the term 'Social Darwinism' to protect the social sciences from incursions from biology. It will be revealed that the actual use and frequency of the term was very different from the standard account in academic folklore.

3. Social Darwinism in Anglophone Academic Journals

Social Darwinism, as almost everyone knows, is a Bad Thing.

Robert Bannister (1979)

3.1 INTRODUCTION

Social Darwinism has been blamed for providing ideological and pseudo-scientific motivations for a number of twentieth-century horrors. These include eugenics, two world wars, Nazism and the Holocaust (Perry, 1918; Hofstadter, 1944; Crook, 1994; Hawkins, 1997). The majority of social scientists today would protest against racism, fascism, imperialism or sexism, and against any abuse of biology in support of these doctrines. I count myself as one of these protestors.[1]

This chapter differs from preceding accounts in that it is primarily a contribution to the history of the term itself, rather than of the impact of Darwinism on social science and political ideology.[2] I ask: who used the term and what did they mean by it? I trace the uses of the term 'Social Darwinism' within the academic journals of the Anglo-American academic community, whose scientific literature became dominant over all others by 1945.[3]

Of course, the study of the impact of Darwin's ideas on the social sciences is important, but it is full of traps for the unwary. Many authors have attributed to Darwin ideas that he did not hold. Others blame Darwin for any celebration of competition in the social sphere, examples of which are easy to find. In fact, Darwin himself saw benefits in cooperation as well as

---

[1] A version of this chapter first appeared as Hodgson (2004d).

[2] Klaes (2001) makes a strong argument in favour of investigations into the history of the use of key terms in discourse, alongside the history of the ideas that such terms may represent.

[3] Racist, sexist, individualist and imperialist notions were evident in other pre-1945 scientific literatures, including in Continental Europe. Darwin's ideas were also influential in Europe. But the connection between the two sets of ideas in the Continental literature is under dispute (McGovern, 1941; Gasman, 1971, 1998; Kelly, 1981; Benton, 1982; Bellomy, 1984; L. Clark, 1985; Weikart, 1993, 2002). No presumption is made here whether or not the conclusions that apply to Anglophone journals apply to other academic literatures as well. There is clearly a need for citation-based studies of these other literatures.

competition. The idea that competition brings economic benefits was widespread in the social sciences long before Darwin, and can partly be attributed to classical economists such as David Ricardo and Adam Smith. In addition, Herbert Spencer was much more vocal than Darwin in his support of market competition.[4]

Although earlier histories (Hofstadter, 1944; G. Jones, 1980) of 'Social Darwinism' also concentrate on the Anglophone community, they present as historical fact what has been and continues to be a pejorative, polemical label. To question this view does not in any way diminish the importance of attacking unfounded, reactionary or regressive ideas wherever they appear. Rather it will demonstrate that historical misrepresentation, and the use of 'Social Darwinism' as a term of abuse, have served not only partisan political ends, but have foreclosed discussion of the importance of ideas from biology in helping to understand human affairs.

Science is not separate from society or politics, but it has standards of openness, veracity and rigor. A worry is that the term 'Social Darwinism' has been used in the twentieth century to close down much of the discussion in the social sciences concerning the influence of human biology on human behaviour. Typically with inaccurate accounts of its past usage, it has forced an unwarranted division between conceptualizations of the natural and the social. The acute effects of these closures and divisions still endure in modern anthropology and sociology. They are particularly damaging at the present juncture, because we are experiencing an explosion in the application of Darwinian and other evolutionary ideas in the human sciences. The important philosophical and conceptual implications of Darwinism for social science are now widely acknowledged. Those misguided by the rhetoric of 'Social Darwinism' are less well prepared to engage with these developments.

The results of this enquiry into the nature and academic impact of Social Darwinism differ considerably from important accounts of Social Darwinism in Anglo-American academia (Hofstadter, 1944; Hawkins, 1997). Instead, the facts and arguments here sustain the broadly revisionist tradition of Robert Bannister (1979), Greta Jones (1980), Donald Bellomy (1984), Mark Pittenger (1993), Paul Crook (1994) and others who have shown that political appeals to Darwinism in Britain and America were most frequently associated with anarchists, liberals and socialists. The label was used primarily by leftists to pin upon their opponents.

There was no self-declared school of Social Darwinists. Rather the term 'Social Darwinism' originally appeared during a debate on the proper uses of

---

[4] 6989 articles and reviews including both the words 'competition' and 'efficiency' appear in journals in the JSTOR database from 1850 to 1949 inclusive. Only 234 of these 6989 items mention Darwin or Darwinism. 335 of them mention Spencer. 537 of them mention Adam Smith. 354 mention Ricardo.

biology for understanding society. In contrast, since the 1940s, it has been widely used to dismiss any use of biological ideas in the social sciences. The outcome is that 'Social Darwinism' is an ambivalent and misleading label.

Contrary to common supposition, it will be shown that the early use of the term 'Social Darwinism' in Anglophone academic journals was highly infrequent and sporadic, and almost entirely disapproving of what the label was supposed to describe. The term disappeared from the principal academic journals in 1925 and reappeared in 1932, when it was used prominently in an additional manner, to describe analytical and analogical links between sociology and biology. Subsequently its use became much more frequent, with the war against Nazism and the appearance of Richard Hofstadter's classic book on *Social Darwinism in American Thought* (1944).

Hofstadter identified Social Darwinism not in terms of any school that used the term to describe its own ideas, but in terms of the usage of key phrases such as 'natural selection', 'struggle for existence' and 'survival of the fittest'. After Hofstadter the term 'Social Darwinism' was used not only as a general description for abuses of biology by the Nazis and others, but also as a means of sustaining the established separation between the social sciences and biology. Despite the decisive defeat of fascism in 1945, the use of the term rose inexorably and exponentially for the remainder of the twentieth century. It acquired mythological attributes, referring to a pre-1914 era when its use was assumed to be prevalent. At least as far as the Anglophone academic journals are concerned, this assumption is false.

Scholars after Hofstadter have shown that not only conservatives and nationalists used Darwinian arguments. In addition, anarchists, socialists and liberals deployed them extensively. Despite this, a widespread opinion remains that Darwinism has intrinsic, intractable and ideological problems for social science, and hence it should be banished from social science altogether (Hawkins, 1997). Powerful counter-arguments to this opinion have been presented elsewhere. The aim of this chapter is to trace neither the implications of Darwinism in the social sphere, nor the impact of ideas described by others as 'Social Darwinism'. Instead, the aim is to trace the dissemination, use and meaning of the term 'Social Darwinism' as it actually appeared in the academic journals of the time.

This chapter takes advantage of JSTOR an electronic database of leading academic journals in anthropology, economics, general science, history, literature, philosophy, political science, population studies, sociology and other subjects, which became available in the 1990s. These journals are almost entirely in English, and several date back to the time of Darwin. A search was made for the terms 'Social Darwinism', 'Social Darwinist' or 'Social Darwinists' in articles or reviews.[5]

The appearance of the concept in a book rather than a journal would often be flagged, as long as that book was sufficiently influential to be reviewed in a leading journal, and the review actually cited 'Social Darwinism'. The JSTOR search thus allows a more complete picture of uses of the 'Social Darwinism' in Anglophone academic discourse than hitherto possible.[6]

When a journal article mentions 'Social Darwinism' it is important to determine whether it advocated or critiqued the doctrine that was given that label. In the case of a review, it is important to ascertain whether the author of the book under review advocated or critiqued such a doctrine, and whether the reviewer agreed or disagreed with the book author in that respect.

Section 3.2 of this article briefly reviews the historical background and those that might be associated with 'Social Darwinism', principally in the English-speaking world. This section should not mislead the reader into presuming that I am attempting an adequate or complete account of the impact of Darwinism in politics and social science. It simply provides a background to the main theme of this chapter, which is in Sections 3.3 to 3.7.

Section 3.3 analyzes uses of the term 'Social Darwinism' in the Anglophone academic literature up to 1914. Section 3.4 does the same for the period up to the Great Depression. Section 3.5 notes the changing meaning of the term in the period from 1932 to 1940. Section 3.6 shows how the Second World War gave an enormous boost to the use of the term in the academic literature. Section 3.7 briefly discusses sociobiology and Social Darwinism. Section 3.8 concludes the chapter.

---

[5] JSTOR user services can be contacted via jstor-info@umich.edu or jstor@mimas.ac.uk. The list of journals searched is in the appendix to this chapter. Hereafter in the text, any reported search for the term 'Social Darwinism' also involved the simultaneous search for the alternative terms 'Social Darwinist' or 'Social Darwinists'. With the kind assistance of Robert Bannister, additional electronic journal databases were searched at Cornell University (http://cdl.library.cornell.edu/moa/) and at the University of Michigan (http://moa.umdl.umich.edu/). The journals on these databases are not entirely academic in nature, and most of the material is from the nineteenth century. The term 'Social Darwinism' was not found in these additional databases, although by the 1880s there were several references to Darwin and Darwinism.

[6] The frequency claims made here are strictly limited to the journal literature. However, I know of no book in English of academic importance or impact in the 1890–1950 period in the social sciences that was not itself reviewed in a journal in the JSTOR database. If 'Social Darwinism' were a term used extensively in the book in question, then it would be likely to be mentioned in the journal review. Hence, the exclusive use of academic journals is not an excessive limitation here. However, a citation study of academic monographs is a project for another work.

3.2 SEARCHING FOR SOCIAL DARWINISM: SOME BACKGROUND ISSUES

Who were the leading academic 'Social Darwinists' in America and Britain in the nineteenth century? If we take the existing literature on 'Social Darwinism' as a guide, then the names that spring up immediately are Herbert Spencer and William Graham Sumner. If we put the phrase 'Social Darwinism' in a standard web search engine, then Spencer appears in profusion: he is regarded as the foremost 'Social Darwinist' with Sumner as his American Deputy. There is no denying their impact. Sumner was a prominent professor at Yale University. Spencer had no academic position, but he was enormously influential in Anglo-American academia.

The names of Spencer or Sumner are often cited, but their works are little read. In fact, neither Spencer nor Sumner used the term 'Social Darwinism'. It is only in retrospect and by association that they are deemed pioneers of an ill-defined creed given that name. It is true that Spencer promoted 'the survival of the fittest'. In fact, he originated the term. However, it was not until 1866, after the first edition of the *Origin of Species* had appeared, that Darwin was persuaded by Alfred Russel Wallace to use Spencer's phrase – rather than 'natural selection' – in key passages in that work (Waters, 1986, pp. 207–8). In truth, Spencer did not like being described as Darwinian because he believed that he had published a valid theory of evolution prior to Charles Darwin. Spencer (1893) argued that natural selection did not provide an adequate explanation of the evolution of species. In several key respects his doctrine was very different from that of Darwin and it was recognized as such at the time (Wiltshire, 1978; Hodgson, 1993).

Despite today being widely described as a 'Social Darwinist', there is relatively little Darwinism in Sumner's writings (Bannister, 1973, 1979; N. E. Smith, 1979). Sumner occasionally adopted Spencer's phraseology of the 'survival of the fittest' and less often Darwin's term 'natural selection', and used them in an imprecise exoneration of individualism, inequality and market competition. In his most important treatise, Sumner (1906) mentioned Darwin only once. Sumner's disciple Albert Galloway Keller (1923, p. 137) remarked that his teacher 'did not give much attention to the possibility of extending evolution into the societal field'. Again, it is mainly in modern rhetoric that Sumner appears as a leading 'Social Darwinist'.

Broadly 'evolutionary' ideas appeared in famous works of the 1860s and 1870s by Henry Maine, Edward Tylor, Lewis Henry Morgan and others. Some of these classic evolutionists distanced themselves entirely from Darwin's work. Passing references to 'struggle', 'fitness', and even 'natural selection' in their books showed the influence of Darwinian or Malthusian terminology but no deep commitment to Darwinism (Bowler, 1988).

Other social scientists took a different theoretical line, arguing that Darwin's core theoretical principles of variation, inheritance and selection could be used to analyze the evolution of social systems, without suggesting that social phenomena could be explained entirely or principally in biological terms. They saw Darwinian theory as a general tool for analyzing evolving systems – unconfined to biology – rather than an ideological or political doctrine.[7] Indeed, the political stances of many of these theorists happened to be quite different from what is today associated with 'Social Darwinism'.

The British economist Walter Bagehot (1872) was one of the first to apply the core Darwinian theoretical ideas to the social sciences. On the political side, Bagehot defended liberal democracy and social reform. Henry Drummond (1894) similarly embraced Darwinian theory and emphasized the role of the cultural environment in human development. In accord with Darwin in *The Descent of Man,* Drummond saw the positive evolutionary role of human altruism and cooperation. David Ritchie (1896) – a Scottish philosopher of Fabian and liberal political views – argued that social institutions could be treated as units of Darwinian selection. Similarly, Thorstein Veblen (1899) called for the application of Darwinian principles to economics, wrote of 'the natural selection of institutions' and argued that socio-economic evolution was neither an optimizing nor a teleological process. Notably, despite their resolute applications of Darwinian concepts to the theory of social evolution, none of these authors has been widely and subsequently described as a Social Darwinist.[8]

The Russian anarchist scholar Petr Kropotkin (1902) rigorously applied Darwinian principles of natural selection to the social domain. He argued that cooperation and mutual aid were exemplified among other species in nature, and thus they also apply to humankind. Furthermore, he attacked those that had used the term 'struggle for existence' to connote war or individualist competition. Kropotkin saw this 'struggle for existence' as broadly and generally 'a struggle against adverse circumstances'. Kropotkin thus

---

[7] These past applications of core Darwinian theory to social evolution are discussed in more detail in Hodgson (2004a).

[8] An exception is Coats (1954, p. 532) who saw Veblen as adopting 'an extreme form of Social Darwinism'. See also Keller (1915, pp. 10–11) and Note 16 below. Another exception is Hawkins (1997) who criticizes Ritchie as a 'reform Darwinist' but ignores Veblen. It is not clear why Bagehot, Drummond, Ritchie or Veblen have not been referred to more widely as 'Social Darwinists', other than the term before 1940 was extremely rare, and after 1940 it was more prominently associated with competitive individualists or racists. The idea that the core Darwinian theoretical principles might be applied to social evolution was discussed less frequently after the First World War, and has remained relatively neglected and misunderstood (Hodgson, 2002b, 2004a; Hodgson and Knudsen, 2006).

interpreted the concept in general terms, in a theoretical manner consistent with the authors mentioned in the preceding paragraph.[9]

Most of the early uses of the term 'Social Darwinism' emanated from Continental Europe, rather than from Britain or America. The earliest appearance of the term seems to be in an 1879 article in *Popular Science* by Oskar Schmidt, followed immediately by an anarchist tract published in Paris in 1880 entitled *Le darwinisme social* by Émile Gautier. Foreshadowing Kropotkin, Gautier argued that the true application of Darwinian principles to human society meant social cooperation rather than brutal competition. However, unlike Kropotkin, Gautier used the term 'Social Darwinism' to criticize those who claimed to use Darwinian ideas to support capitalist competition and laissez faire. Following Gautier, others popularized the term in France (L. Clark, 1985). In 1882 Giuseppe Vadalà-Papale published *Darwinismo naturale e Darwinismo sociale* in Italy and helped to proliferate the term in that country (Bellomy, 1984).

The once fashionable French sociologist Gabriel Tarde (1884) was one of the few in academic circles who used the term 'Social Darwinism' approvingly. Tarde (1890) attempted to apply Darwinism to an analysis of imitative behaviour in human society. But this usage was relatively primitive and innocent, without strong ideological connotations, and hence Tarde does not appear in modern demonologies of 'Social Darwinism'.

The early Continental European critics of misapplications of Darwinism were not tilting at imaginary windmills. In Germany, the respected academic biologist Ernst Haeckel was an enthusiastic advocate of a Darwinism mixed with strong racist sentiments (McGovern, 1941; Gasman, 1971, 1998). Haeckel was not alone: several American followers of Darwin harboured racist, imperialist and sexist ideas, including leading academics such as Joseph Le Conte (1892) and Daniel Shute (1896).

But such propositions are neither contained in, nor implied by, Darwin's own writings. What are arraigned today – mostly by critics – under the term 'Social Darwinism' are ideas that have either little connection with Darwinism or are not exclusively represented by it. As established in the preceding chapter, Darwin was no racist. He extolled neither selfishness nor competition. Darwin himself never used the term 'struggle for existence' as a justification for imperialism or war. The cavalier use of the term 'Social

[9] However, despite Kropotkin's erudite use of Darwinian views in social science, his political ideas were so remote from twentieth-century caricatures of 'Social Darwinism' that Hawkins (1997, pp. 178–80) attempted unconvincingly to exclude Kropotkin from his broad definition of 'Social Darwinism', which includes anyone who believed that principles of evolution in nature have something to do with human society. See Johnson (1998) for a critical review of Hawkins's book.

Darwinism' associates him with scientific and ideological doctrines that he never proclaimed.

Not only did Spencer coin the phrase 'survival of the fittest' before Darwin, but also Thomas Robert Malthus inspired the term 'struggle for existence'.[10] In this broad intellectual context, these phrases were used in a variety of ways. As Gertrude Himmelfarb (1959, p. 407) notes, Darwinian ideas were associated with every conceivable political stance, from pacifism to militarism, from socialism to individualism, and from liberalism to conservatism.

Social Darwinism has been linked with eugenics; but conservatives, liberals and socialists alike adopted eugenic policies. Eugenics – the policy of improving the human stock by controlling marriage and reproduction – found its advocates and its critics, but was infrequently described as 'Social Darwinism' until after the Second World War.[11]

If it were the case that the likes of Spencer or Sumner were regarded in Anglophone academia at the time as leading 'Social Darwinists', then we should expect some repetition or citation of this perception in the contemporary academic journals. In fact, no such citations are found. There is no clear evidence in pre-1937 Anglophone academic publications to support the current view that Spencer and Sumner were the acknowledged leaders of an ideological movement then described as 'Social Darwinism'.[12]

The academic citations in leading Anglophone journals prior to the 1940s tell a very different story, the narration of which is a principal purpose of this chapter. It is relatively easy to find examples of racist, sexist, individualist, competitive, nationalist and imperialist sentiments in Anglo-American academia. It is much more difficult to show that they were widely described – by supporters or opponents – as 'Social Darwinism' within those academic circles prior to the 1940s.

---

[10] Claeys (2000, p. 228) argues that 'the concept of "Social Darwinism," insofar as it focuses centrally on the idea of the "survival of the fittest," is to a significant degree a misnomer. Much of what we associate with the concept had been in formation for over half a century by the time the *Origin of Species* appeared in 1859'.

[11] An exception was Wells (1907), as noted below. Liberals and socialists such as E. Aveling, E. Bellamy, C. H. Cooley, J. B. S. Haldane, J. Huxley, J. M. Keynes, H. J. Laski, J. Needham, G. B. Shaw, C. P. Snow, B. Webb, S. Webb and H. G. Wells counted themselves as followers of eugenics (Paul, 1984). Critics included F. Boas, B. Kidd and L. F. Ward.

[12] However, some early Continental critics of what they described as 'Social Darwinism' after 1880 did associate this term with individualistic competition, and also criticized Spencer in this vein (L. Clark, 1985). But as shown below there is no evidence in the pre-1937 Anglophone journals searched here of any direct association of Spencer with the 'Social Darwinism' label.

Of course, the fact that 'Social Darwinism' is the wrong or missing label does not mean that there was no real substance to be labelled. Individualist, racist and imperialist ideas were evident in academia and elsewhere. However, the main burden of this chapter is to explore how these views became so labelled, the frequency of use of the label in the academic journals, how the meaning of the label changed, and to suggest on historical grounds that that the label is highly misleading.

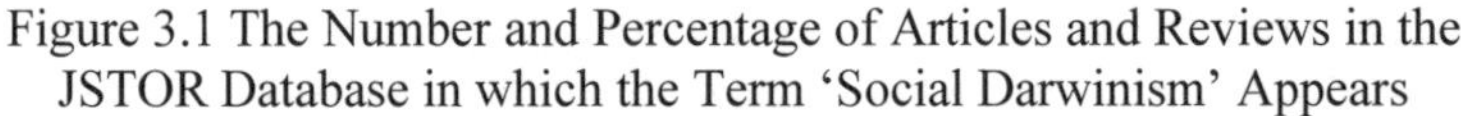

Figure 3.1 The Number and Percentage of Articles and Reviews in the JSTOR Database in which the Term 'Social Darwinism' Appears

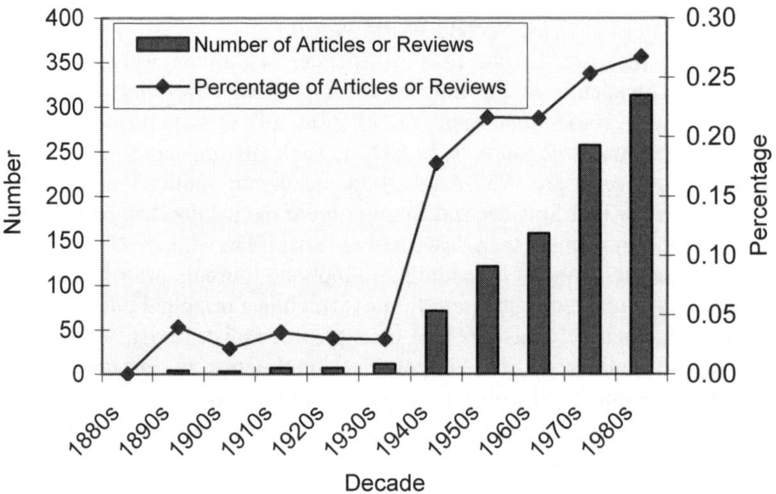

3.3 CITATIONS TO 'SOCIAL DARWINISM' BEFORE THE FIRST WORLD WAR

Having prepared the ground, we can now turn to the history of the term itself, as it appears in the academic journals. The overall picture is presented in Figure 3.1. Within the large JSTOR database of journals, references to 'Social Darwinism' appear in articles or reviews only *nine* times prior to the outbreak of the First World War in 1914.[13] This is a surprisingly low number,

[13] If the JSTOR search is extended to minor items other than articles and reviews, then there are a few further appearances of 'Social Darwinism'. The very first citation, in *Mind* in 1887, notes the appearance of the term as a chapter heading (in Italian) in De Sarlo (1887). De Sarlo defended Darwinism, but because of the possible triumph

especially as the JSTOR database dates from the 1850s. Over 42,000 articles and reviews appear in this database up to 1914. As shown in the Appendix, several leading journals were in existence by 1900, and several more were founded between 1900 and 1914.

By contrast, in articles or reviews in the JSTOR database up to and including 1914, there are 2,458 citations to 'Darwin' and 2,786 citations of the name 'Spencer'.[14] While Darwin, Spencer and Sumner were highly cited, the term 'Social Darwinism' was hardly ever used. Furthermore, its principal but rare usage was in books critical of that doctrine, emanating from Continental Europe and often in languages other than English.

The first of these nine JSTOR citations to 'Social Darwinism' was in an 1895 review by the Harvard economist Frank Taussig of a book by the Italian socialist economist Achille Loria (1895). Taussig (1895, p. 537) praised Loria's 'brilliant qualities ... wide learning ... skilful logic' and so on. He applauded Loria's critical chapter on Social Darwinism and its demolition of 'current misapplications of the theory of natural selection to social phenomena'. The next three appearances of the term 'Social Darwinism' in the JSTOR database were all in 1897, including two approving reviews of Loria's (1895) book and a very short review by the American sociologist Albion Small of a book in French by Louis Wuarin (1896). Wuarin's book was also critical of 'Social Darwinism' and Small did not dissent from this criticism. Hence all the four early appearances, up to and including 1897, endorse critiques of what two Continental Europeans described as 'Social Darwinism'.

In the next appearance in JSTOR articles or reviews, the influential American sociologist Edward Alsworth Ross (1903, p. 448) wrote briefly of the 'master error of the social Darwinists', namely the mistaken belief that economic struggles had to be similar to biological struggles. Again, this citation is critical of 'Social Darwinism'.

We have to wait until 1907 for the next appearance of 'Social Darwinism' in articles or reviews in the leading Anglo-American academic journals. The term 'Social Darwinism' was used infrequently, and up to that date there was

---

of human intelligence over struggle, he did not believe that it applied to social evolution. He thus rejected 'Social Darwinism' as misconceived. Also the *Economic Journal* in 1895 notes the publication of Loria (1895), discussed below. An 1896 article in French by Loria was abstracted in the *American Journal of Sociology* in 1897. A further JSTOR article of 1911 alludes in a footnote to Novicow's (1910) *La critique du darwinisme social,* without using the English term. Because these minor mentions are in neither articles nor reviews, they are not included in the bibliometric data presented here.

[14] This number drops to 887 if the phrase 'Herbert Spencer' is required in the citation. Given that there were several writers named Spencer, the number of citations to Herbert Spencer is likely to be greater than 887 but less than 2,786.

no single approving reference to any doctrine thus described. In addition, the (two Continental European) books that are reviewed were similarly critical of such an ideology. This is in remarkable contrast to some popular accounts of 'Social Darwinism' today.

The 1907 appearance of the term was in the *American Journal of Sociology* in an article by D. Collin Wells. Partly because the article itself is entitled 'Social Darwinism' it is worthy of more detailed discussion. This was the first use of the term in the title of an article in the JSTOR database. In addition, *it is the only article or review found in this entire database clearly and explicitly advocating 'Social Darwinism' in any sense whatsoever.* Wells (1907, p. 695) insisted, however, that by 'Social Darwinism' he did 'not mean those propositions of the doctrine of evolution which Darwin chiefly emphasized'! Instead, Wells broadly defined Social Darwinism as

> the general doctrine of the gradual appearance of new forms through variation; the struggle of superabundant forms; the elimination of those poorly fitted, and the survival of those better fitted, to the given environment; and the maintenance of racial efficiency only by incessant struggle and ruthless elimination.

The final clause above is clearly contestable, and it will find no endorsement in Darwin's writings. With the important exception of this final clause, the remainder of this definition of Social Darwinism is so vague and broad that it would be consistent with the views of most scientists. None would deny 'the gradual appearance of new forms through variation', or some struggle in the face of scarcity, or the sad demise of those less fit to survive. Wells also saw survival in a 'given environment', rather than making the mistake of seeing fitness as context-independent. Wells (1907) went on to use his invocation of 'rigorous selection' to argue for 'individualism' and against the collectivisms of trade unions and socialism. However, as Kropotkin (1902) and others have demonstrated, political individualism does not logically flow from Darwinism. In attempting to use biology to extol individualism, Wells was much closer to Spencer than Darwin.

The foremost American sociologist Lester Frank Ward had been invited to comment on Wells's paper when it was presented at the annual meeting of the American Sociological Society in 1906. Ward assumed that a paper entitled 'Social Darwinism' would be on the struggle among races and nations. To his surprise he found that Wells's paper was on eugenics. Ward (1907a, p. 709) wrote in a highly critical response:

> In Europe, especially on the continent, there has been much discussion of what they call 'social Darwinism'. Not all scholars there agree as to what it is, but certainly none of them use the expression in the sense that Dr. Wells uses it. … Over there the discussion of this topic relates to two problems: first, the economic

struggle, and, second, the race-struggle. Those who appear to defend this 'social Darwinism' are biologists mainly and not sociologists at all. Most of the sociologists attack it, as it is there understood. … The great writers on race struggles never use the term 'social Darwinism,' but a number of sociologists have called them 'social Darwinists' without knowing what Darwin really stood for.

Ward affirmed that Social Darwinism was a term that was most prominent in Continental Europe, where it was used principally by critics of attempts to justify race struggles or wars in terms of the 'survival of the fittest'. In an article on 'Social and Biological Struggles' published in the same year, Ward (1907b, pp. 289–90) argued that

the greater part of all that sociologists say on the subject is wide of the mark, and exhibits an almost complete failure on their part to understand the true nature of biological struggles. … The sociologists generally confound the so-called 'struggle for existence' with Darwinism, and very few of them have an adequate idea of what Darwin's phrase 'natural selection' means. … [T]he sociologists … have only a confused idea of the whole process which they imagine to constitute Darwinism.

Ward argued effectively that biology cannot be used to support *laissez faire*, race struggle or national belligerence. He also protested against the association of Darwinism with these ideological views. Ward (1907b, pp. 292–3) wrote:

I have never seen any distinctively Darwinian principle appealed to in the discussions of 'social Darwinism.' … I wish to protest in the strongest possible terms against the application of the term Darwinism to race struggle. I know of no ethnologist, historian, or sociologist among those who see the real effect of the struggle of races, who has accepted this designation for that law.[15]

The next appearance of 'Social Darwinism' in the leading Anglophone academic journals was in 1911 in a review of a book by the Russian-born liberal pacifist Jacques Novicow entitled *La critique du darwinisme social* (1910). Novicow himself identified a vague doctrine called 'Social Darwinism' and blamed it for imperialism and war, although he noted that Darwin's own views were different. The reviewer was sympathetic to

[15] Ironically, Ward himself has subsequently been lumped within Social Darwinism (Hofstadter, 1944). But Ward (1907a, 1907b) repeatedly attacked the abuse of biology for ideological causes and argued that the outcome of evolution, whether in nature or society, was rarely if ever optimal. He promoted women's rights and opposed racism. Ward (1913) referred disapprovingly to 'Social Darwinism', where he again criticized eugenics and drew attention to his 1907 remarks against Wells.

Novicow's anti-war sentiments. Novicow's text caused a flurry of further references to 'Social Darwinism' in the Anglophone journals.

We may summarize the position up to 1914, as evidenced by the leading Anglo-American academic journals:

- The use of the term 'Social Darwinism' was very rare in these journals.
- Generally, articles or reviews that mentioned 'Social Darwinism' in these journals disassociated themselves from the doctrines then associated with the term. The only exception was Wells (1907), who endorsed the term but used it in a distinctive manner, to refer to his version of eugenics. There is no cited evidence that advocates of race struggle or imperialist war widely used the term. No article or review that mentioned 'Social Darwinism' in leading Anglophone journals endorsed imperialism or war. With the single exception of Wells (1907), none promoted racist views.
- Instead, all the available evidence suggests that the predominant usage of the term 'Social Darwinism' was by Continental European socialists, anarchists, pacifists and radicals who were critical of ideologies of capitalist competition, imperialist war, or racial struggle. The works that had the most impact in promoting the term in leading Anglophone journals were by Achille Loria (1895) and Jacques Novicow (1910).
- Despite the influence of Spencer and Sumner in the Anglophone world, the term 'Social Darwinism' was not applied to their views in these journals.

3.4 CITATIONS TO 'SOCIAL DARWINISM' FROM THE FIRST WORLD WAR TO THE GREAT DEPRESSION

Twelve JSTOR citations to 'Social Darwinism' appeared in six articles and six reviews from the outbreak of the First World War in 1914 to the Great Crash in 1929. None supports any purported ideological content of the term 'Social Darwinism'. The twelve citations are dominated by the reality of war and a concern for peace. Witnessing the greatest human slaughter in history, progressive and radical academics reacted against the belligerent rhetoric of 'race struggle' and the 'survival of the fittest'.

Two 1917 reviews were of the book by the American pacifist George Nasmyth (1916), which criticized 'Social Darwinist' justifications of war. In the midst of nationalist jingoism and carnage in Europe, the reviewers were sympathetic to Nasmyth's pacifist sentiments. In an influential volume of that time, the American philosopher Ralph Barton Perry (1918) argued that ideas of racial superiority and the natural status of conflict had been used to justify the war. Perry attacked all associations between biology and the social sciences. Darwinism was accused of a circularity of logic and a 'strong tendency to favor the cruder and more violent forms of struggle, as being more unmistakably biological' (Perry, 1918, p. 145).

In a similar vein, S. J. Holmes (1919, p. 21) noted in an article the 'perverted Darwinism' that upheld 'that competitive struggle is necessary for the progressive evolution of men'. For him this was a fundamental error 'too commonly found in the writings of the social Darwinist school'. In promoting social reform, Holmes urged the importance of education. Holmes accepted eugenics but rejected Social Darwinism. He described the anti-eugenicist Benjamin Kidd as 'a prominent social Darwinist'. Holmes also cited Spencer, but did not describe him in the same manner. In another article, in the following year, Erville Woods (1920, p. 3) wrote that sociology

> has been extravagant in its professions of indebtedness to biology. Many absurdities in social theory have masqueraded in the borrowed trappings of biological conceptions. The so-called biological analogy is a case in point. Much more pernicious was the attempt to base an ethics of rapacity and greed upon what was ignorantly called social Darwinism.

This statement by Woods was prescient. He was fully aware that the label of 'Social Darwinism' was 'ignorantly' applied. Yet in worrying about the abuse of 'Darwinism' to support 'an ethics of rapacity and greed', Woods followed Perry (1918) by suggesting that the solution is not to correct such abuses and misconceptions, but to end all theoretical intercourse between sociology and biology. Eventually, the majority of sociologists adopted this strategy. It is akin to a policy of ending all conversation, simply because some people speak lies.

In 1921 Gregory Zilboorg (1921, p. 399) implausibly described Marxism as 'economic and social Darwinism'. Also the prominent American sociologist Harry Barnes (1921) noted without much further comment the attacks of Novicow and others on the 'so-called "social Darwinism"' of Ludwig Gumplowicz and Heinrich von Treitschke. Barnes's article was the first item in the JSTOR database to mention both 'Social Darwinism' and the name of William Graham Sumner. But Barnes did not then describe Sumner as a Social Darwinist.

A 1922 review briefly noted without disapproval a brief short attack on Social Darwinism. An article by Clarence Case (1922) criticized attempts to justify war as an extension of instinctive behaviour. A review of 1924 noted without dissent a criticism of 'Social Darwinism' in a book entitled *The Problem of War and Its Solution* (Grant, 1922).

Clearly, from 1914 to 1924, the issue of war and its aftermath dominated these twelve citations of 'Social Darwinism'. Then, remarkably, not long after the dust of the First World War settled, the term disappeared from the Anglo-American academic journals. In the years from 1925 to 1931, the term

'Social Darwinism' did not emerge in this literature, despite global economic strife and rising fascism and anti-Semitism in Europe. Its next appearance – in 1932 – is highly significant, not least because of its remarkable absence for the preceding seven years.

We may again summarize the position, this time from 1914 to 1931, in the leading Anglo-American academic journals:

- The term 'Social Darwinism' remained very rare, and it simply disappeared from these journals from 1925 to 1931 inclusive.
- All articles or reviews that then mentioned 'Social Darwinism' in these journals disassociated themselves from the doctrines they associated with the term.
- Critiques of 'Social Darwinism' in these journals prominently associated the term with doctrines of nationalism, imperialism or war. Strong anti-war sentiments prevailed in the academic literature that addressed this issue.
- Neither Spencer nor Sumner was then described as a 'Social Darwinist' in these journals.[16]

3.5 REVIVAL AND METAMORPHOSIS: 'SOCIAL DARWINISM' FROM 1932 TO 1940

The author of the re-appearance of the term 'Social Darwinism' in the academic journals was no less than Talcott Parsons (1932) – the most influential American sociologist of the twentieth century. His used the term as a tool within his grand project to rebuild his discipline, to help fix the supposed boundaries of good and bad sociology. In a long article on Alfred Marshall, Parsons mentioned Social Darwinism twice. Parsons (1932, p. 325) briefly noted the application of Darwinian concepts of variation and selection to social evolution. Then in a footnote he wrote: 'The whole line of thought uppermost in this "Social Darwinism," is closely identified with the "scientific" aspects of the doctrines of Natural Law. Its emphasis is on the

---

[16] Interestingly, when Sumner's student Keller (1915, pp. 10–11) mentioned once in a book the term 'Social Darwinism' he referred to some alleged proponents, but not in that context to Sumner. Furthermore, Keller's definition of 'Social Darwinism' was not as a political or ideological creed but in terms of attempts to 'extend Darwinian evolution into the field of the social sciences'. Keller named 'Ritchie, Kidd, and especially Bagehot' as pioneers of the application of Darwinian theoretical principles to the social sciences. Keller's book is exceptional for this period, both for a rare appearance of the 'Social Darwinism' term, and for his own attempt to apply Darwinian theoretical principles to social evolution, without explanatory reduction to biology. See the discussion of Keller in Campbell (1965).

inexorability of social determinism'. But Parsons failed to name any proponent of this 'line of thought'.

Despite the typically cryptic elusiveness of this passage, Parsons extended the usage of 'Social Darwinism' from its previous ideological associations to anyone who believed in 'the application of Darwinian concepts of variation and selection to social evolution'. But it is not clear whom he had in mind. As I have argued elsewhere (Hodgson, 1993, 2004a), rigorous attempts to apply Darwinian theoretical principles of variation and selection to socio-economic evolution are extremely rare. With its re-introduction by Parsons, following the precedents of Perry (1918) and Woods (1920), the meaning of the term Social Darwinism began to change. It was applied not exclusively to doctrines of race struggle or war, but to any application of Darwinism or related biological ideas to the study of human society.[17]

We shall quickly pass over Parsons's disapproving, clumsy and imprecise references to the 'scientific' aspects of 'Natural Law', and to 'the inexorability of social determinism'. What is being disapproved of, and what alternative may exist, is far from clear. In another footnote, Parsons (1932, p. 341) wrote: 'Pareto, like Marshall and Weber, sharply repudiates what he calls "social Darwinism."' But no textual references are given. We have to turn to Parsons's (1937) *Structure of Social Action* to find the relevant misgivings of Pareto and Weber. As for Marshall, there is no repudiation of Social Darwinism in his works, and Parsons (1937) cited none. Although Marshall (1890) mentioned Darwin a few times, it was not in repudiation. In fact, Marshall was an explicit devotee of the works of Spencer (Thomas, 1991; Hodgson, 1993; Laurent, 2000), who today is widely but wrongly described as a Social Darwinist! Parsons's standards of scholarship were somewhat defective, to say the least.

In the academic journals, two years later, Parsons returned to the fray, determined to depict 'Social Darwinism' as a living adversary of his brand of social science. He stretched the usage of the term to cover methodological as well as ideological views. Parsons (1934, p. 524) thus wrote: 'As the history of the great body of thought sometimes called "Social Darwinism" amply shows, the radical positivistic position leads directly to the view that these conditions are the decisive factors in social life'. By 'these conditions' Parsons (p. 523) meant 'man's non-human environment' as examined by 'biology and psychology'. However, as noted elsewhere (Hodgson, 2001b), Parsons's understanding of the term 'positivism' was highly idiosyncratic,

---

[17] Veblen (1899, 1919) was one of the few people (alongside Bagehot, Ritchie and Keller) to apply Darwinism theoretical principles to social evolution. As a student, Parsons read Veblen's writings, but in the 1930s he made a deliberate break from his own Veblenian past (Camic, 1987, 1991; Hodgson, 2001b). It is possible that Parsons was alluding to Veblen in this 1932 footnote.

and had little if anything to do with the concept as invented and defined by Auguste Comte. By 'positivistic' thought, Parsons (1934, p. 513) meant the notion of using the methodology of 'physical science … as a standard for the measurement of the rationality of human action'. The 'positivistic' approach was said to involve an 'emphasis on scientific "objectivism"' and the neglect of individual purposes or ends in explanations of human action. What Parsons seemed to be suggesting, in a rather convoluted way, was that 'Social Darwinism' over-emphasized natural conditions, to the exclusion of human society and individual intentionality. But again he gave no references to support this claim. Once again, Parsons used the rhetoric of 'Social Darwinism' to exclude or downplay insights from biology or psychology within social science.

The material from these two articles by Parsons (1932, 1934) was recast in his monumental *Structure of Social Action* (1937). This book mentions 'Social Darwinism' several times, and in a similar vein. It became clear that Parsons was trying to change the character and focus of sociology, and to establish strong barriers between sociology and other disciplines, particularly economics, psychology and biology (Camic, 1987, 1991; Hodgson, 2001b). In particular, Parsons wanted to prevent biologists from incursion into areas of research that should belong to his new sociology. Parsons was thus the most important inventor of the modern demonology of Social Darwinism in social science.

Another mention of Social Darwinism took a subtly contrasting line. In a sympathetic double review of a biography of Veblen (Dorfman, 1934) and a collection of Veblen's writings (Mitchell, 1936), Read Bain (1936, p. 486) approvingly referred to Veblen as 'the Darwin of economics … he made a Darwinian analysis of culture more radical (fundamental) than any achieved by the so-called "social Darwinists." They proceeded by specious analogy; he by intensive analysis'. But despite Veblen's explicit attempt to construct a 'post-Darwinian' economics, Bain did not describe Veblen as a Social Darwinist. Bain (1940, p. 257) warned briefly and vaguely of the dangers of 'social Darwinism and biological determinism'. But again, Veblen luckily escaped condemnation. Like Parsons, Bain saw Social Darwinism as a scientific as well as an ideological stance.

In the same year as Parsons's milestone article, the aforementioned University of California biologist Holmes (1932, p. 202) associated Social Darwinism with ideas of 'group selection … mutual aid, social sympathy, self-sacrifice and … cooperation'. This was redolent of Kropotkin, and very different from the usage by Parsons. Also in that year, Barnes (1932, p. 544) mentioned the contention of the 'so-called "Social Darwinists" that 'war had been the chief constructive process in the evolution of humanity'. Barnes went on: 'It must be pointed out, however, that Darwin himself never sanctioned any such sociological interpretation of his evolutionary theories, and the title "Social Darwinism" was appropriated by this group without the approval of Darwin himself'. As well as rightly challenging the Darwinian pedigree, Barnes (p. 548) also noted that 'Social Darwinism' and other 'interests and activities as characterized biological sociologists thirty years ago have now become thorough anachronisms in the field'.

This treatment of Social Darwinism as a thing of the past was evident in some other journal citations. Four articles and two reviews appearing from early 1936 to February 1940 briefly mentioned Social Darwinism in the context of historical discussions of the development of ideas in the late nineteenth century, in Germany, Japan, Yugoslavia and elsewhere. Unlike Bain and Parsons, but in accord with Barnes's (1932) proclamation of the earlier demise of Social Darwinism in academic sociology, they did not identify Social Darwinism as a present threat. But with the events of the next few years, and the intervention of Parsons and others, the situation was to change, as 'Social Darwinism' was perceived increasingly as a current menace.

A 1937 citation of 'Social Darwinism' is of some additional significance, because it is the very first description in the JSTOR database of Spencer as a Social Darwinist. In a book review, Leo Rogin (1937, p. 413) reported the view of the Russian Marxist B. I. Smoulevitch: 'While the doctrine of social Darwinism played an important part in Herbert Spencer's formulation, its combination, more recently, with the racial theories makes the latter type quite the most vicious'. In this manner, the description of Spencer as a Social Darwinist travelled into the Anglophone academic journals.

Clearly, with its re-appearance in the 1932-1940 period, the term 'Social Darwinism' assumed an additional and subsequently enduring connotation. Previously it had been associated with the ideologies of individualism, race struggle and imperialism. In the works of Parsons (1932, 1934, 1937) and a few others, it became additionally connected with work *within science* that proposed partial or complete explanations of social phenomena in biological terms, or used biological analogies, or found ideas from biology useful in the social domain.

Accordingly, in this context, Spencer became associated with Social Darwinism, alongside unwarranted conflations of the ideological with the scientific. Spencer himself had pioneered his own unjustified conflations of ideology and science. Note also that the first JSTOR cited description of Spencer as a Social Darwinist came from a Marxist source. The idea that all science comes with inherent ideological tags is commonplace in Marxian literature. So arose the myth that Spencer had promoted something that was widely described by him or his contemporaries as Social Darwinism. This myth was given an enormous boost in the next period, when Sumner's name was bracketed with Spencer's.[18]

3.6 'SOCIAL DARWINISM', THE SECOND WORLD WAR, AND THE SUBSEQUENT EXPLOSION

In May 1940 the Nazis invaded Holland, Belgium, Luxemburg and France. In the following months the Battle of Britain was waged in the air. Against Nazi belligerence, pacifist sentiments seemed less viable than in the First World War. Consequently, after 1940 the literature criticizing 'Social Darwinism' concentrated more on the ills of fascism and racism, and less on earlier 'Social Darwinist' attempts to justify war.

Evalyn Clark (1940) alleged that the German economist Adolf Wagner (who died in 1917) was one of the 'founders' of National Socialism. Wagner was described as a nationalist, imperialist, racist and Social Darwinist. William McGovern (1941) published a timely book entitled *From Luther to Hitler: The History of Fascist-Nazi Political Philosophy*. In JSTOR journals from 1941 to 1944, one article and four reviews noted approvingly its critique of 'Social Darwinism'.

In another citation, Joseph Gittler (1942, p. 383) wrote: 'Following Spencer, a group of thinkers who have been called "social Darwinists" formulated another theory of social evolution. Included in this group were Benjamin Kidd, Jacques Novicow, G. Vacher de Lapouge, and Otto von Ammon'. After its 1937 precedent, this is the second JSTOR description of Spencer as a Social Darwinist. Its author ignorantly described Novicow as a devotee of Social Darwinism. In fact he was a leading critic.[19]

Up to and including 1942, the maximum number of JSTOR citations to Social Darwinism in any single year was three. The annual average from 1895 to 1942 inclusive was 0.85 citations. The USA entered the War in December 1941, and after a year had passed the citation rate leapt upwards. There were five citations in 1943, twelve in 1944 and sixteen in 1945. This quantitative explosion prohibits detailed discussion of all references.

However, several of the citations to Social Darwinism during the Second World War still treated it as a historical phenomenon, existing principally before the First World War. But some warned of the dangers for the present.

---

[18] The first Anglophone suggestion that Sumner was a Social Darwinist that I have come across is by Stern (1933). Also Ellwood (1938, p. 505) argued that Sumner was 'much closer to the social Darwinists' than Spencer, thus significantly excluding the latter from this category.

[19] By contrast, the writings of Ammon and Lapouge were preoccupied with explanations of social phenomena in terms of alleged racial characteristics. Lapouge's studies of 'Aryanism' were fêted by the Nazis.

In such a vein, a reviewer noted 'the slashing assault on social Darwinism' in a work by Lewis Mumford (1944). Two reviews, by Raymond Nixon and by the American economist Frank Knight, commended the critique of Social Darwinism by Laurence Stapleton in his 1944 book *Justice and World Society*.

Subsequently the deluge. In 1944 Hofstadter published his classic *Social Darwinism in American Thought.* It had previously appeared as a Columbia University Ph.D. thesis in 1938. In his description of American Social Darwinism, Hofstadter lumped together a host of diverse figures, including Spencer, Sumner and Ward.[20] For Hofstadter, Social Darwinism was a reactionary creed, largely associated with the promotion of racism, nationalism and competitive strife. The skills of a great historian were deployed in the ideological war effort against fascism and genocide.

The first review of this influential treatise appeared in the academic journals in December 1944. In all, three reviews of this work appeared in 1944, seven in 1945, and two in 1946. The reviews were generally favourable. Ironically, Keller (1945) gave the book a positive review. Keller was a follower of Sumner, and like his teacher has himself since been dubbed a 'Social Darwinist'. Citations to Hofstadter's book were even more plentiful than its reviews, particularly in later years. It became the seminal treatise on Social Darwinism, and it has driven the discussion of the topic ever since.

The Second World War put the concept of Social Darwinism in a position of prominence that it had never previously attained. The menace of Nazism stimulated critiques of Social Darwinism. At the same time, Parsons's reconstruction of sociology gained influence and popularity (Camic, 1991; Hodgson, 2001b). He built a Chinese Wall with the social sciences on one side, and biology and psychology on the other.[21] Growing citations to the menace of 'Social Darwinism' helped to reinforce this wall, by pointing to the barbarian abuses of biology in recent memory.

As shown in Figure 3.1 above, references to Social Darwinism in the Anglophone literature grew exponentially after the 1940s. In terms of the percentage of all JSTOR articles and reviews, its appearance increased substantially after 1944. Hofstadter's (1944) work both expressed and sustained critical interest in this new version of the demon creed. From 1944 to 1969 inclusive, Hofstadter's book was mentioned in no less than 23.6 per cent of all JSTOR articles or reviews citing Social Darwinism. The book was revised and reprinted several times. In 1968 it reached its fifteenth reprinting. It remains by far the single most important reference on the topic. From

---

[20] After Stern (1933) and Ellwood (1938), Hofstadter (1941) was one of the first to propose in English that Sumner was a 'Social Darwinist'.

[21] Ironically, Parsons (1966, 1977) later made some use of biological analogies in his work.

Hofstadter (1944) to the present day, mentions of 'Social Darwinism' were plentiful but entirely dismissive and critical.

Another effect of the extension in meaning of Social Darwinism was to associate it much more strongly with the figures of Spencer and Sumner. As noted above, their work was rarely described as Social Darwinist until the 1930s. In the JSTOR literature, Spencer was first portrayed as a Social Darwinist in 1937, and Sumner was not so described before the appearance of Hofstadter's book. After 1944, the prevailing depictions of Spencer and Sumner changed dramatically. From 1944 to 1959 inclusive, Spencer was cited in 37.6 per cent, and Sumner in 23.6 per cent, of all JSTOR articles mentioning Social Darwinism.

Remarkably, neither Spencer nor Sumner was described in the JSTOR database as a 'Social Darwinist' prior to the 1930s. While they supported individualism and market competition, Spencer and Sumner were strong critics of militarism and imperialism. Especially around the time of the First World War, the majority of the rare uses of the term Social Darwinism associated it with militarism and war. Hence, even when criticized, Spencer and Sumner were placed in a different camp. Subsequently, however, with the rise of Nazism, intellectuals embraced the idea of an anti-fascist war. Consequently, critics of 'Social Darwinism' became less likely to adopt an anti-war stance. A barrier preventing the inclusion of Spencer and Sumner in the 'Social Darwinist' camp was removed. The fact that they were not Darwinians was simply ignored. Parsons's wide definition of Social Darwinism, which included anyone who applied biological ideas in the social sciences, also helped to admit them. They were labelled as Social Darwinists just prior to the explosion in use of the term in the 1940s, and the label stuck. Spencer and Sumner belatedly became 'Social Darwinists' as a result of mutating meanings, historical flukes and compelling events.[22]

We may again summarize the position, this time from 1940s to the present, in the leading Anglo-American academic journals:

- The Second World War greatly amplified the usage of the term 'Social Darwinism', to unprecedented levels.
- Articles or reviews that mentioned 'Social Darwinism' in these journals generally disassociated themselves from the doctrines they associated with the term.
- Following Parsons (1932, 1934, 1937) and others, the term 'Social Darwinism' became prominently associated with particular

[22] Although the proposition here that Spencer and Sumner were not described as Social Darwinists before the 1930s is strictly confined to the JSTOR journals, the present author has not discovered any earlier description of them as Social Darwinist in any publication. Evidence to the contrary would be welcomed.

methodological and scientific, as well as ideological views. In particular, it was used to exclude or downplay the use of insights or analogies from biology within social science.

- Strong anti-fascist and anti-racist sentiments pervaded the citations of 'Social Darwinism' in these journals. But, in contrast to the period before 1940, the term 'Social Darwinism' was less frequently associated with the advocacy of war. It was more prominently used to connote competition, racism and the use of biology in social science.
- Contrary to almost all earlier accounts in the Anglophone academic journals, Spencer and Sumner began to be widely described from the 1940s as leading 'Social Darwinists'.

3.7 SOCIOBIOLOGY AND SOCIAL DARWINISM

Figure 3.1 shows an increase in the percentage of articles or reviews citing Social Darwinism in the 1970s and 1980s. To what extent is the increase due to the publication of Edward O. Wilson's *Sociobiology* in 1975, and to the explosion of controversy over this new discipline?[23]

What concerns us here is the role that sociobiology, and the reaction against it, played in reinvigorating the phobia against Social Darwinism. Wilson (1975, 1978) himself rejected the label of 'Social Darwinism'. There is no evidence that he is a racist or a fascist, although he has been accused of these sins. Furthermore, his passionate environmentalism would not readily align him with exponents of unbridled capitalist competition (Segerstråle, 2000). Alarmingly, some neo-fascist groups in Europe have adopted sociobiology as a slogan, but fascism is not known for its pursuit of accuracy or truth.

The publication of Wilson's work created a storm of controversy. In America, the 'Sociobiology Study Group of Science for the People' entered the fray, declaring immediately that Wilson had opened the door to racism and other doctrines that they explicitly associated with 'Social Darwinism' (Allen *et al.*, 1976). Other authors, including in the JSTOR literature, have subsequently repeated this characterization of Wilson as a Social Darwinist.

If Social Darwinism simply means the application of Darwinian ideas to social phenomena, then Wilson stands condemned, along with Kropotkin, Ritchie, Veblen and many modern writers who have also applied Darwinian principles of variation, selection and inheritance to socio-economic change.

---

[23] It is not the purpose of this chapter to scrutinize the scientific content of sociobiology. Elsewhere it has been criticized for its over-extended attempts to reduce social phenomena to biological terms (Sahlins, 1977; Boyd and Richerson, 1980; Rose *et al.*, 1984; Durham, 1991; Hodgson, 1993).

In contrast, if Social Darwinism means the use of Darwinism to justify individualist, conservative or racist views, then Wilson must be acquitted. Alternatively, if Wilson is charged with claiming to explain human social phenomena *entirely* in biological terms, then he must also be acquitted, partly on the grounds of his explicit and repeated claims to the contrary. But if Wilson is charged with exaggerating the possibility of using biology to explain human behaviour then there still remains a strong case against him to be answered.[24] It all depends on the precise charge. The imprecise accusation of 'Social Darwinism' is of little help.

Using the methodology employed in this chapter, we can assess the impact of sociobiology on the use of the 'Social Darwinism' term. From 1975 to 1979 inclusive, seven JSTOR articles or reviews mention both Social Darwinism and sociobiology. In the 1980s, a further 33 articles or reviews mentioned both these terms. It seems that the appearance of sociobiology in 1975 can partly, but not wholly, account for the increase in usage of the term Social Darwinism in the 1970s and thereafter.

Inspecting these articles and reviews, it is clear that dismissals of sociobiology in terms of being described as a revived 'Social Darwinism' are in a minority. Nevertheless, a widespread ignorance of the true historical meaning of the term Social Darwinism still prevailed. Despite the scholarly contributions of Bannister and others, many are unaware of the way in which the term had actually been used before the 1930s.[25] The subsequent historical shifts in the meaning of the term are also unappreciated.

The influence of Parsons and others remains, in using the term to condemn any attempt to explain any social phenomenon in biological terms. The conflation of ideology with science greatly impaired the post-1975 debate concerning the merits or demerits of Wilson's sociobiology. If the problem with sociobiology is its biological reductionism, then the problem should be described as such. The description of sociobiology as Social Darwinist adds further confusion to an already enraged debate.

3.8 CONCLUSION: THE MYTHOLOGY OF 'SOCIAL DARWINISM'

I now summarize the key results of this study of the appearance of the term 'Social Darwinism' in the Anglophone academic journals. Its use, at least in

[24] Veblen could likewise be prosecuted for his sometimes unwarranted use of the concept of instinct, and Marshall for his invocation of flawed Spencerian biology (Hodgson, 1993, 2004a).

[25] Bannister's (1979) excellent book received 17 citations in JSTOR books and articles in the 1980s.

this context, was very rare up to 1924 and nonexistent from 1925 to 1931 inclusive. After some appearances in the 1930s, its frequency of use began to increase exponentially after 1940. However, with the single exception of Wells (1907), the phrase was used by critics who disassociated themselves from the doctrines then associated with the term.

Another result is that a shift in meaning has been detected by comparing its earlier and rare appearances up to 1924 with its more abundant profile after 1940. During the First World War, 'Social Darwinism' was used most frequently to describe ideologies of militarism, nationalism and imperialism. Accordingly, in the literature surveyed, neither Spencer nor Sumner was then described as a Social Darwinist. Despite their support for capitalist competition, these authors were anti-militarist and anti-imperialist.

The term re-appeared in the Anglophone academic journals in an article by Parsons (1932), who promoted a different meaning of the term, using it in part to describe any attempt by social scientists to utilize ideas from biology. Also in the 1930s, Spencer and Sumner began to be described as Social Darwinists in these journals.

During the Second World War the use of the term 'Social Darwinism' increased to unprecedented levels. In the context of the Allied war effort against fascism, Hoftstadter's (1944) classic critique of 'Social Darwinism' downplayed the previous association of the term with militarism and accented its other connotations. Hofstadter also added impetus to the argument of Parsons that the social sciences should sever all links with biology. He also portrayed Spencer and Sumner as leading 'Social Darwinists', and the description stuck. He lumped together all sorts of views under the vaguely defined label 'Social Darwinism' and failed to note the crucial differences in both analysis and orientation between Darwinism and Spencerism. In contrast to the period before 1940, the term 'Social Darwinism' was no longer prominently associated with the advocacy of war. It was more prominently used to connote competition, racism and the use of biology in social science.

These results are consistent with the revisionist accounts of Bannister (1979), Donald Bellomy (1984) and others. They support the verdict that the label of 'Social Darwinism' has harboured a number of myths. The label associated Darwinism with a number of particular ideological propositions that do not follow logically from this scientific theory. Such misinterpretations were aided by the limited assimilation of Darwinian theory prior to the First World War (Bowler, 1983, 1988).

Instead, if rarely, the term was originally and principally applied by anarchists, socialists and pacifists to varied political views that they opposed (Bannister, 1979). By the 1940s, widespread political sentiments, from anarchists such as Kropotkin, through liberal free traders such as Spencer and

Sumner, to more militant nationalists, and racists such as Haeckel, were all conflated together under the single, misleading label of Social Darwinism.

A theoretical position cannot itself be completely evaluated simply in terms of the political views of its proponents. On the contrary, no matter how distasteful (or attractive) the political views of individuals proposing a theoretical analysis, this has no bearing on whether the theoretical explanations of causes and effects are actually true or false. The choice of priorities for scientific research is partly and unavoidably a political decision. But the scientific evaluation of scientific theories or results is not.

Not only have multiple insights been rejected on the grounds of the obnoxious political views (perceived or actual) of their proponents, but also a whole tradition of attempting to apply Darwinian ideas to social science, or to gain insight from biology concerning the human condition, has been consigned to obscurity. This is despite the fact that the political views of many of the promoters of evolutionary ideas in the social sciences – Kropotkin, Ritchie, Veblen and Ward included – were far from individualist or conservative. All have been casualties of the ongoing campaign against 'Social Darwinism', and the attempt to remove any discussion of biology from social science.

Another, related myth was to see any close relationship between biology and the social sciences as inevitably negative or unsound. This myth gained strength in the 1930s when Anglo-American sociology tried to break entirely from biology. To consolidate and justify its independence and isolation from the natural sciences, it exaggerated and misrepresented the previous impact of Darwin's ideas on the social sciences. Given further impetus by the horrors of Nazism, the effect of the myth was to terminate much interdisciplinary conversation between the social sciences and biology. This had a dramatic and adverse effect on the development of the social sciences. For example, by simply assuming that it was all due to nurture rather than nature, psychologically-informed examinations of the nature and limits of human mental capacities on social behaviour were pushed to one side (Cravens, 1978; Degler, 1991; Weingart *et al.*, 1997). Furthermore, the early idea of applying Darwinian evolutionary principles to social evolution (in the manner of Ritchie, Veblen and others) was ignored for much of the twentieth century (Campbell, 1965; Hodgson, 1999b, 2002b, 2004a).

Overall, the label of 'Social Darwinism' is unhelpful and misleading. In its established context it serves the purpose of tolerating 'Darwinism' in biology but entirely excluding it from social science. It lumps together and dismisses a whole host of varied and important developments in the 1870–1914 period that in some way developed or maintained links between biology and the social sciences, including the careful use of biological analogies in the analysis of social evolution (Hodgson, 2004a). We should be critical of racist, sexist and imperialist ideologies, but these emanate neither from the act of linking biology with the social sciences, nor from the principles of Darwinism.

The woods can be dangerous. So we might tell children stories of woodland beasts or bogeymen, to warn them away from the forest. Similarly, prevailing accounts of 'Social Darwinism' have been invented as bogeyman stories, to warn all social scientists away from the darkened woodland of biology. We are told that any use of ideas or analogies from biology in the social sciences is unsafe. We are warned not to stray into that biological zone, for terrible things might happen, as they surely happened before. But scientists should not be treated like children. And some accounts of the history of 'Social Darwinism' are false or misleading in several crucial details.

It would be better if the use as a descriptive term of the highly ambiguous and imperfectly grounded phrase 'Social Darwinism' were discontinued. It would be clearer and more effective if authors criticized more directly the readily identifiable and less ambiguous ideological ills of racism, sexism, imperialism or eugenics. If biological reductionism is also to be a target, then let us describe it by its name. If some promoters of sociobiology or evolutionary psychology attempt to explain the social domain entirely in biological terms, then let us critically evaluate that methodology, and identify the irreducible properties of the social domain. Let us stop telling false histories, and henceforth call things by their proper names.

APPENDIX: LIST OF JOURNALS SEARCHED UP TO AND INCLUDING 1989, WITH DATE OF FIRST INCLUSION

Some of these journals changed their names, in which case both the old and the new names are listed.

Academy of Management Journal (1963), *Accounting Review* (1926), *Administrative Science Quarterly* (1956), *African Affairs* (1944), *African Historical Studies* (1968), *African Studies Bulletin* (1958), *American Antiquity* (1935), *American Economic Association Quarterly* (1908), *American Economic Review* (1911), *American Historical Review* (1895), *American Journal of Archaeology* (1885), *American Journal of Botany* (1914), *American Journal of International Law* (1907), *American Journal of Mathematics* (1878), *American Journal of Philology* (1880), *American Journal of Political Science* (1973), *American Journal of Semitic Languages and Literatures* (1895), *American Journal of Sociology* (1895), *American Literature* (1929), *American Mathematical Monthly* (1894), *American Midland Naturalist* (1909), *American Naturalist* (1867), *American Political Science Review* (1906), *American Quarterly* (1949), *American Slavic and East European Review* (1945), *American Sociological Review* (1936), *American Speech* (1925), *American*

Statistician (1947), *Annals of Mathematical Statistics* (1930), *Annals of Mathematics* (1884), *Annals of Probability* (1973), *Annals of Statistics* (1973), *Annals of the Association of American Geographers* (1911), *Annals of the Missouri Botanical Garden* (1914), *Annual Review of Anthropology* (1972), *Annual Review of Ecology and Systematics* (1970), *Annual Review of Sociology* (1975), *Anthropology Today* (1985), *Applied Statistics* (1952), *Archaeological Reports* (1954), *Asian Survey* (1961), *Australian Journal of Chinese Affairs* (1979), *Background on World Politics* (1957), *Biennial Review of Anthropology* (1959), *Biometrics* (1947), *Biometrika* (1901), *Biotropica* (1969), *Black American Literature Forum* (1976), *Botanical Gazette* (1876), *British Journal for the Philosophy of Science* (1950), *British Journal of Sociology* (1950), *Brittonia* (1931), *Bulletin of African Studies in Canada* (1963), *Bulletin of the American Geographical Society* (1901), *Bulletin of the School of Oriental and African Studies* (1940), *Bulletin of the School of Oriental Studies* (1917), *Bulletin of the Torrey Botanical Club* (1870), *Callaloo* (1976), *Canadian Journal of African Studies* (1967), *Canadian Journal of Economics* (1968), *Canadian Journal of Economics and Political Science* (1935), *China Quarterly* (1960), *Classical Philology* (1906), *Classical Quarterly* (1907), *Classical Review* (1887), *College Composition and Communication* (1950), *College English* (1939), *Comparative Literature* (1949), *Comparative Politics* (1968), *Comparative Studies in Society and History* (1958), *Contemporary Sociology* (1972), *Contributions to Canadian Economics* (1928), *Coordinator* (1952), *Current Anthropology* (1959), *Demography* (1964), *Ecological Monographs* (1931), *Ecology* (1920), *Econometrica* (1933), *Economic Geography* (1925), *Economic History Review* (1927), *Economic Journal* (1891), *Economica* (1921), *Eighteenth-Century Studies* (1967), *ELH* (1934), *English Historical Review* (1886), *Ethics* (1938), *Ethnohistory* (1954), *Evolution* (1947), *Family Coordinator* (1968), *Family Life Coordinator* (1959), *Family Planning Perspectives* (1969), *Far Eastern Quarterly* (1941), *Far Eastern Survey* (1935), *French Historical Studies* (1958), *French Review* (1927), *Geografiska Annaler* (1919), *Geographical Journal* (1893), *Geographical Review* (1916), *German Quarterly* (1928), *Greece and Rome* (1931), *Harvard Journal of Asiatic Studies* (1936), *Harvard Studies in Classical Philology* (1890), *Hesperia* (1932), *Hispanic American Historical Review* (1918), *Hispanic Review* (1933), *Historical Journal* (1958), *History and Theory* (1960), *History of Education Quarterly* (1961), *History Teacher* (1967), *Incorporated Statistician* (1950), *Industrial and Labor Relations Review* (1947), *International Affairs* (1931), *International Economic Review* (1960), *International Family Planning Digest* (1975), *International Family Planning Perspectives* (1979), *International Family Planning Perspectives and Digest* (1978), *International Journal of Ethics* (1890), *International Migration Digest* (1964), *International Migration Review* (1966), *International Organization* (1947), *International Studies Quarterly* (1967), *Isis* (1913), *Italica* (1926), *Journal of Accounting Research* (1963), *Journal of Aesthetics and Art Criticism* (1941), *Journal of African History* (1960), *Journal of American Folklore* (1888), *Journal of American History* (1914), *Journal of Animal Ecology* (1932), *Journal of Applied Ecology* (1964), *Journal of Applied Econometrics* (1986), *Journal of Asian Studies* (1956), *Journal of Black Studies* (1970), *Journal of British Studies* (1961), *Journal of Business* (1954), *Journal of Business of the University of Chicago* (1928), *Journal of Conflict Resolution* (1957), *Journal of Contemporary History* (1966), *Journal of Ecology* (1913), *Journal of Economic*

Abstracts (1963), *Journal of Economic History* (1941), *Journal of Economic Literature* (1969), *Journal of Economic Perspectives* (1987), *Journal of Educational Sociology* (1927), *Journal of Finance* (1946), *Journal of Financial and Quantitative Analysis* (1966), *Journal of Health and Human Behavior* (1960), *Journal of Health and Social Behavior* (1967), *Journal of Hellenic Studies* (1880), *Journal of Higher Education* (1930), *Journal of Human Resources* (1966), *Journal of Industrial Economics* (1952), *Journal of Inter-American Studies* (1959), *Journal of Latin American Studies* (1969), *Journal of Marriage and the Family* (1964), *Journal of Military History* (1989), *Journal of Modern African Studies* (1963), *Journal of Modern History* (1929), *Journal of Money, Credit and Banking* (1969), *Journal of Near Eastern Studies* (1942), *Journal of Negro Education* (1932), *Journal of Negro History* (1916), *Journal of Peace Research* (1964), *Journal of Philosophy* (1921), *Journal of Philosophy, Psychology and Scientific Methods* (1904), *Journal of Political Economy* (1892), *Journal of Politics* (1939), *Journal of Risk and Insurance* (1964), *Journal of Roman Studies* (1911), *Journal of Social Forces* (1922), *Journal of Southern History* (1935), *Journal of Symbolic Logic* (1936), *Journal of the Academy of Management* (1958), *Journal of the American Association of University Teachers of Insurance* (1937), *Journal of the American Geographical Society* (1859), *Journal of the American Mathematical Society* (1988), *Journal of the American Military History Foundation* (1937), *Journal of the American Military Institute* (1939), *Journal of the American Oriental Society* (1854), *Journal of the American Statistical Association* (1922), *Journal of the Anthropological Institute of Great Britain and Ireland* (1872), *Journal of the British Institute of International Affairs* (1922), *Journal of the History of Idea* (1940), *Journal of the Royal Anthropological Institute of Great Britain and Ireland* (1871), *Journal of the Royal Geographical Society of London* (1831), *Journal of the Royal Institute of International Affairs* (1926), *Journal of the Royal Statistical Society* (1887), *Journal of the Society for Industrial and Applied Mathematics* (1953), *Journal of the Statistical Society of London* (1838), *Journal-Newsletter of the Association of Teachers of Japanese* (1963), *Language* (1925), *Latin American Research Review* (1965), *Limnology and Oceanography* (1956), *Man* (1901), *Management Science* (1954), *Management Technology* (1960), *Marriage and Family Living* (1941), *Mathematical Tables and Other Aids to Computation*, *Mathematics Magazine* (1947), *Mathematics Newsletter* (1926), *Mathematics of Computation* (1960), *Memorandum of Institute of Pacific Relations* (1932), *Midwest Journal of Political Science* (1957), *Military Affairs* (1941), *Mind* (1876), *Mississippi Valley Historical Review* (1914), *Missouri Botanical Garden Annual Report* (1890), *Modern Asian Studies* (1967), *Modern Language Journal* (1916), *Modern Language Notes* (1886), *Modern Philology* (1903), *Monumenta Nipponica* (1938), *National Mathematics Magazine* (1934), *Negro American Literature Forum* (1967), *New England Quarterly* (1928), *New Literary History* (1969), *New Phytologist* (1902), *News Bulletin (Institute of Pacific Relations)* (1926), *Nineteenth-Century Fiction* (1949), *Nineteenth-Century Literature* (1986), *Notes and Records of the Royal Society of London* (1938), *Noûs* (1967), *Operations Research* (1956), *OR* (1950), *Osiris* (1936), *Oxford Economic Papers* (1938), *Pacific Affairs* (1928), *Past and Present* (1952), *Philosophical Perspectives* (1987), *Philosophical Quarterly* (1950), *Philosophical Review* (1892), *Philosophical Transactions of the Royal Society of London* (1776), *Philosophy and Phenomenological Research* (1940), *Philosophy and*

Public Affairs (1971), *Philosophy of Science* (1934), *Phylon* (1960), *Political Science Quarterly* (1886), *Population and Development Review* (1975), *Population Index* (1937), *Population Literature* (1935), *Population Studies* (1947), *Population: An English Selection* (1989), *Proceedings of the American Mathematical Society* (1950), *Proceedings of the American Political Science Association* (1904), *Proceedings of the Modern Language Association of America* (1886), *Proceedings of the National Academy of Sciences of the United States of America* (1915), *Proceedings of the Royal Anthropological Institute of Great Britain and Ireland* (1965), *Proceedings of the Royal Anthropological Institute of Great Britain and Ireland* (1965), *Proceedings of the Royal Geographical Society* (1857), *Proceedings of the Royal Society of London* (1854), *Public Opinion Quarterly* (1937), *Publications of the American Economic Association* (1886), *Publications of the American Statistical Association* (1888), *Quarterly Journal of Economics* (1886), *Quarterly Publications of the American Statistical Association* (1920), *Quarterly Review of Biology* (1926), *RAIN* (1974), *Renaissance News* (1948), *Renaissance Quarterly* (1967), *Representations* (1983), *Review of Economic Studies* (1933), *Review of Economics and Statistics* (1919), *Review of English Studies* (1925), *Review of Financial Studies* (1988), *Reviews in American History* (1973), *Russian Review* (1941), *Science* (1880), *Scientific Monthly* (1915), *Shakespeare Quarterly* (1950), *SIAM Journal on Applied Mathematics* (1966), *SIAM Journal on Numerical Analysis* (1966), *SIAM Review* (1959), *Slavic and East European Journal* (1957), *Slavic Review* (1961), *Social Forces* (1925), *Social Psychology* (1978), *Social Psychology Quarterly* (1979), *Sociological Methodology* (1969), *Sociology of Education* (1963), *Sociometry* (1937), *Soviet Studies* (1949), *Speculum* (1926), *Statistical Science* (1986), *Statistician* (1962), *Studies in English Literature* (1961), *Studies in Family Planning* (1963), *Studies in the Renaissance* (1954), *Systematic Zoology* (1952), *Transactions and Papers (Institute of British Geographers)* (1935), *Transactions and Proceedings of the American Philological Association* (1869), *Transactions of the American Mathematical Society* (1900), *Transactions of the Anthropological Society of Washington* (1885), *Transition* (1961), *Trollopian* (1945), *Twentieth Century Literature* (1955), *University Journal of Business* (1922), *Western Political Quarterly* (1948), *William and Mary Quarterly* (1892), *World Archaeology* (1969), *World Politics* (1948), *Yale French Studies* (1948), *Yearbook of Anthropology* (1955).

4. Institutionalism versus Marxism: A Debate with Alex Callinicos

Second Peasant: 'Oh there you go, bringing in class to it again'.
First Peasant: 'That's what it's all about! If only people would realize'.

Monty Python and the Holy Grail

4.1 INTRODUCTION

On 30 April 2001 a public debate was held at the University of Hertfordshire between Alex Callinicos from the University of York and Geoffrey M. Hodgson on the theme of 'Institutionalism versus Marxism'. An edited transcript of the two opening speeches is reproduced below.[1]

Both speakers acknowledged a degree of doctrinal agreement. However, the debate also illuminated some fundamental differences of analysis and outlook between institutionalism and Marxism, in contrast to attempts to reconcile these doctrines (Dugger and Sherman, 2000; O'Hara, 2000).

4.2 IN DEFENCE OF INSTITUTIONALISM
GEOFFREY M. HODGSON

4.2.1 This is not primarily a debate about political ideology

When I say that this is not a debate about political ideology, my Marxist opponents will immediately quote from Marx's eleventh *Theses on Feuerbach* of 1845 'the philosophers have only *interpreted* the world in various ways; the point is to *change* it' (Marx and Engels, 1976, p. 5). Let us accept the importance of this statement: we are all dissatisfied with some aspects of the world and most of us want to change it in some way. But if we are going to change the world then it is important to understand it too. It is the role of social theory and the social sciences to obtain a scientific understanding of social structures and forces, before any attempt to change the world can be effective. Hence, instead of politics and policy, I want to focus primarily on questions of theory.

[1] I wish to thank Alex Callinicos for kindly participating in the debate and making his text available for this volume.

Institutionalism in its original form (as distinguished from the 'new institutional economics' of Oliver Williamson and others) was a movement that flourished in the United States, particularly from the beginning of the twentieth century through to the Second World War. It has continued since, in a relatively marginalized form. But there have been institutionalist Nobel Laureates, such as Gunnar Myrdal and Simon Kuznets.

Another reason why it would be a little embarrassing for an institutional economist to talk just about political ideology concerns the history of that school. Within institutionalism there is a wide diversity of political views – far greater than that found within Marxism. Political viewpoints among institutionalists have ranged from conservative though social democratic to socialist and anarcho-syndicalist. So this is another reason why I am not going to focus so much on politics as on social theory and social science.

I would like also to recognize the theoretical achievements of Marxism. Marxism is one of the great systematic social theories. *Capital* is one of the social science classics of the last two hundred years. Other great works that could be mentioned include John Stuart Mill's *Principles*, Léon Walras's *Elements*, Alfred Marshall's *Principles*, Vilfredo Pareto's volumes on economics and sociology and so on. These are some of the classics, in both economics and sociology. *Capital* ranks as one if not the best of these. There is no equivalent great tome in institutionalism. Against a Marxist, this puts an institutionalist at a disadvantage. Above all, Marxism has an impressive historical scope and a powerful analysis of the capitalist system, which I think we should acknowledge as being relevant even today. However, while within institutionalism there is a lack of a consensus over a number of issues, I will try and draw out some unifying points.

4.2.2 Where institutionalism and Marxism agree

So, in theoretical terms, where do institutionalism and Marxism agree? Both institutionalism and Marxism recognize the problem of structure and agency. This is one of the central problems of social theory. My opponent Alex Callinicos will acknowledge this, because he has published several articles and books on the key question of agency and structure (Callinicos, 1999). The question concerns the relationship between the individual and social structure and how this relationship is to be theorized. Both institutionalism and Marxism share this concern, and both schools of thought see agency and structure as irreducible to one another. They are both against the extreme positions, where everything becomes explicable simply in terms of structure, or simply in terms of individuals. (Although some institutionalists and some Marxists have sometimes veered too much towards one or other of these extremes.)

Both institutionalists and Marxists agree on another issue. This is one of the under-estimated problems of social science, which nevertheless in my view is extremely important. This is the recognition of historical specificity. Unlike much in the physical world, the socio-economic world changes dramatically and structurally through time. Accordingly it may be necessary to change the theory to deal with the changes in social reality. This is not true for the physical sciences, because the laws of physics have been constant since a few milliseconds after the Big Bang. But the social sciences deal with a changing subject matter. One theory may not adequately fit all social forms. This is strongly recognized in Marxism and explicitly in *Capital*, which focuses just on capitalism. It is recognized also in Marx's methodological writings in the *Grundrisse* and in his *Contribution to the Critique of Political Economy*. The same point is also recognized by institutionalism and the German historical school (Hodgson, 2001b).

4.2.3 A critique of the Marxist theory of human agency

Now I come to some points of disagreement. I focus first of all on the question of agency. What I don't want to do is to slip in to a standard critique of Marxism as being deterministic. I am not trying to caricature Marxism or to replace it with some of its versions, like the Marxism that prevailed in the Second International, which has been criticized for being deterministic or overly structuralist. Louis Althusser would be another example of an overly structuralist version of Marxism. I wish to deal with neither extremes nor caricatures. I want to deal with Marx. I could quote you many similar statements, but I think that this is quite a symptomatic passage from the *Resultät,* published in the Penguin edition of the first volume of *Capital*:

> The capitalist functions *only* as personified capital, capital as a person, just as the worker is *no more* than labour personified. (Marx, 1976a, p. 989, emphasis added)

I think that there are problems with this statement. Marx recognizes the individual. Marx also sees the capitalist system as a set of structured relations. But what is doing the work analytically here is the structure alone. Capitalists and workers are seen as simply expressions of social structure. Thorstein Veblen, the founder of American institutionalism, reacted to this aspect of Marxism with the following words:

> The materialistic [or Marxist] theory conceives of man as exclusively a social being, who counts in the process solely as a medium for the transmission and expression of social laws and changes; whereas he is, in fact, also an individual, acting out his own life as such. Hereby is indicated not only the weakness of the materialistic theory, but also the means of remedying the defect pointed out. With

> the amendment so indicated, it becomes not only a theory of the method of social and economic change, but a theory of social process considered as a substantial unfolding of life as well. (Veblen, 1897, p. 137)

For Veblen, in contrast to the above statement from Marx, both the individual and the social relations and structures interact and interpenetrate and mutually constitute each other. By contrast, in Marxism, the supreme analytical work is done by the structure. Marxists try to explain individual agency by a notion of the structure acting as a constraint. People try to do the best they can, but within structural limits. Within these they try to work out certain outcomes. The individual is subsumed within a structural explanation. In Marxism, the connection between social structure and individual action is made by the presumption of rational reflection upon individual interests acting under the constraints of social structures. Individuals act rationally in the sense they try and do their best they can to achieve their own objectives, but the structures bear down upon them and force them to do certain things. The capitalist is forced to be greedy, the worker is forced to struggle for higher wages and so on.

Accordingly, in Marxism we find the notion that once the working class realizes their true situation, once they are no longer duped by ideology or religion, or 'false consciousness', and once they reflect rationally on their situation, then they will struggle for outcomes that lead to revolution. They will strive for better working conditions, a shorter working day and higher wages. These struggles, unsatisfied within capitalism, will lead to a revolutionary outcome. Veblen took a very different view. Veblen (1919, p. 441) wrote that

> the sentiment which animates men, singly or collectively, is as much, or more, an outcome of habit and native propensity as of calculated material interest. There is, for instance, no warrant in the Darwinian scheme of things for asserting *a priori* that the class interest of the working class will bring them to take a stand against the propertied class.

Veblen argues that what is required is a theory of what animates people, including why they take up particular objectives. This would be a cultural theory of their circumstances. One cannot assume that material interests, the basic class relations, always impel people towards certain outcomes. As Veblen put it, nothing *a priori* leads the working class to take a stand against the propertied class. They can go in another direction: they can be racist by seeing other ethnic groups as the source of their problem; they can be nationalistic and seek salvation in national symbols or adventures; they can become fascists. We see many tragic examples of these developments in the history of the working class movement. Repression is not turned into a revolt against the system but into some other ideology. The missing link in Marxism is a theory of what impels people to do specific things. This theory has to be in part a cultural theory. It has to take on board the cultural circumstances as well as the basic material relationships.

The mention of Darwinism in the above passage might be perplexing. Veblen believed very strongly in the importance of Darwinism for social science: I will address later some of his reasons. But Veblen did not propose a biological reductionism. He did not argue that the social sciences had to be reduced to biology. He actually criticized those that relied exclusively on biological explanations of social behaviour. Veblen was not following a sociobiological line. What he believed is that Darwinism provided a theory of change and a philosophical conception about the world, which had enormous implications for the social sciences.

4.2.4 Teleology *versus* evolution

Concerning the issue of teleology versus evolution, there is a contrast between Veblen's Darwinian conception, on the one hand, and the Marxian notion, on the other. If you believe that the circumstances in which people are placed will inevitably lead them to struggle against their oppression, whatever the cultural circumstances, or the ideology, or the political mediations involved, then you harbour a notion of an immanent, teleological development of society. Due to perceived mechanisms and constraints, society is impelled down a particular road towards a particular outcome. Marx also argues that the development of the 'productive forces' at any point of time is consistent with a particular set of social relations. For him, highly developed productive forces imply communism, and communism only. History may not be rigidly determined but it has an ultimate destination, whether or not the destination is actually achieved.

This teleological theme in Marxism is evident, for instance, in the notion that capitalism is the last class society, and that after a revolution (which is not necessarily regarded as inevitable) the next stage will be socialism and then communism. Implicit here is the idea of a perceived destination to history. History is driving (not necessarily with certainty or inevitability but) towards an immanent end which is itself pre-ordained.

This type of teleological thinking is totally alien to Veblen's absorption and interpretation of Darwinian evolution. The whole point of Darwinism, which even today is not widely understood, is that evolution has no destination or goal. Darwinism is neither essentially about progress nor about the perfectability of society. At the deepest theoretical level, it is about evolutionary mechanisms and detailed causal explanations. Evolution is a sequence of particular, connected causes. In Darwinism there is no particular endpoint, and no finality. Veblen rejected the idea that the Marxian process of class struggle had an immanent end. Veblen (1919, p. 416) favoured 'the unteleological Darwinian concept of natural selection' against 'the Marxian notion of a conscious class struggle as the one necessary method of social progress'. Veblen (1919, pp. 416–17) rejected the idea of

> the assumed goal of the Marxian process of class struggle, which is conceived to cease in the classless economic structure of the socialistic final term. In Darwinism there is no such final or perfect term, and no definitive equilibrium.

An evolutionary process is continually at risk of being upset by external events or internal contradictions. It can lead in principle in all sorts of different directions. It can be path dependent and locked into particular lines of development. Such tracks of evolution are sometimes highly sensitive to initial conditions. At some crucial points, the path can be disturbed and evolution can go in one of many different directions. Against the idea than history has a (perhaps not inevitable, but nevertheless) pre-ordained goal, evolution can go in an infinite number of possible directions. There is a great contrast between these two conceptions.

4.2.5 Non-deliberative action and tacit knowledge

Another important issue I want to raise here is the conception of knowledge. One of the greatest contributions that Veblen made – which is in fact has a highly modern ring – is the importance of knowledge to economic growth and development. It is not simply that knowledge and information are important. Veblen also emphasized that habitual knowledge is crucial. He wrote about the importance, in economic development, of 'the accumulated, habitual knowledge of the ways and means involved ... the outcome of long experience and experimentation' (Veblen, 1919, pp. 185–6).

This is the kind of knowledge which takes a long time to build up, much of which is tacit in individual habits like learning languages or learning to ride a bicycle. This is not codifiable knowledge that is written down in books. Economic development is very much about building up this knowledge in individuals, and also building up routines that inter-lock this knowledge between individuals, to unlock it in appropriate circumstances. Veblen (1919, p. 328) thus wrote:

> The complement of technological knowledge … is, of course, made up out of the experience of individuals. Experience, experimentation, habit, knowledge, initiative, are phenomena of individual life, and it is necessarily from this source that the community's common stock is all derived. The possibility of growth lies in the feasibility of accumulating knowledge gained by individual experience and

> initiative, and therefore it lies in the feasibility of one individual's learning from the experience of another.

So knowledge is also social. But notice the emphasis here on circumstance, experience, ongoing process, acquiring knowledge by doing. These are things which are very much context dependent. This is not knowledge in the sense of books or information on the Internet. It is knowledge that is actually highly contextualized, highly specific to circumstance and indeed highly localized in its nature despite the fact that it is also social. Veblen (1914, p. 176) referred to

> the body of knowledge (facts) turned to account in workmanship, the facts made use of in devising technological processes and applications, are of the nature of habits of thought.

Hence engrained habits in individuals are the stuff of knowledge and the stuff of economic skills and potentialities. We find a contrast here with Marx. But I do not want to isolate or accuse Marx in particular here, because Veblen's notion of knowledge as habitual adaptations is so modern that its very few people in the history of ideas in the last two hundred years have made similar points. Looking at most writers in the social sciences in the nineteenth century, including Marx, they had a very limited notion of knowledge. They had a sort of post-Enlightenment view that knowledge is made up of ideas. These ideas are transmitted and enter people's heads. Ideas are communicated and ideas drive action.

What this post-Enlightenment view ignores is that ideas come out of, and are constrained by practice, as much as practice comes out of ideas. Furthermore, as Veblen and others emphasized, habit is essentially the basis of knowledge and belief. In particular, ingrained habits are the springs of technological knowledge and of economic activity.

By contrast, there is no developed concept of habit in Marx. In a famous passage in *The German Ideology,* Marx and Engels extolled the possibility under communism of switching readily from one skilled activity to another: hunting in the morning, fishing in the afternoon and criticizing after dinner. What is neglected here is the immense amount of learning that it required to acquire any developed skill and the impossibility of being competent in anything more than a few of them. Because skills are made up of ingrained habits, Marx's idea of the dissolution of the division of labour is untenable.

Another expression of the consequences of his nineteenth-century view of knowledge is his discussion of deskilling in the first volume of *Capital*. This deskilling idea was latter developed by Harry Braverman in *Labor and Monopoly Capital* (1974). Marx (1976a, p. 788) wrote:

> the development of the capitalist mode of production ... enables the capitalist ... to set in motion more labour ... as he progressively replaces skilled workers by less skilled, mature labour-power by immature, male by female, that of adults by that of young persons or children.

For the progressive replacement of the skilled by the unskilled in the above manner, Marx has to assume implicitly that the kind of benefit that labour is giving is largely mechanical and physical. There is very little recognition here of embodied knowledge and habits, which is trained up in individuals, and in teams. Also Marx doesn't explain why the skilled workers are going to be replaced by less skilled. After all, it would seem obvious that if machines were going to take over some of the jobs, then it would be the less skilled jobs that would be more easily taken over by machines. Furthermore, activities that involve tacit skills would be the activities that are more difficult to replace by programmable machines. In all, Marx's deskilling argument is highly problematic and to some extent it reflects a different conception of knowledge from that held by Veblen.

4.2.6 The impossibility of complete collectivist economic planning

This discussion of knowledge has important implications concerning Marx's and Engels's discussions of comprehensive planning. Marx and Engels did actually want to centralize ownership and control of the means of production in the hands of some kind of nation state.[2] They believed that it would be possible to plan everything from the centre, through the organs of this 'vast association' or 'social-state'. Of course, they wanted this state to be democratic and believed that it would be different from a capitalist state. But the key problem here lies in their belief that some kind of wholesale comprehensive planning is possible.

But this option disappears once we adopt a Veblenian view of knowledge. If much knowledge is tacit and bound up with activities, then it cannot be gathered together by the central planners. Although he held this conception of knowledge, Veblen himself did not develop this critique of central planning. Veblen himself seemed to believe in some vague form of anarcho-syndicalism. However, from a very different political point of view, a similar conception of knowledge formed the basis of the famous critique of central planning by Friedrich Hayek (1988). Whatever our political viewpoint, we have to take this criticism seriously. There is an insurmountable problem of centralizing relevant knowledge.

How can the state (or some other similar body) control all these things when the knowledge involved in production is contextualized, localized,

---

[2] See their statements cited in chapter 2 above.

particularistic and idiosyncratic? These problematic aspects of knowledge were emphasized by both Hayek and Veblen. It is impossible to gather together all that knowledge into some rational planning central apparatus because of the nature of knowledge itself.

We have to draw a distinction between, on the one hand, completely centralized and comprehensive planning and, on the other hand, other forms of partial planning, such as indicative planning, or planning of some core productive activities. While Hayek was antagonistic state planning, many institutionalists have traditionally been in favour of some degree of partial planning from the centre. The idea of getting all knowledge and making rational decisions about the whole of society from the centre is rendered impossible as long as you accept the Veblenian conception of knowledge that I outlined earlier. But, contrary to Hayek, some form of partial planning, such as within a mixed economy, is not ruled out by this conception of knowledge.

However, in the *Communist Manifesto*, Marx and Engels seemed to rule out any kind of mixed economy, in which planning, markets and some private ownership were combined. There they applauded unreservedly the 'abolition of private property'. They were not inclined to reinstate even 'the property of the petty and of the small peasant' on the spurious ethical grounds that 'to a great extent' it was 'already destroyed'. But it is not an ethical justification to fail to reinstate something simply because it has already gone. If the peasantry has lost their property then perhaps the argument should be that it should be restored. They wished for an order in which 'capital is converted into common property, into the property of all members of society'. This is an unqualified, unlimited, unbounded notion of common ownership of capital that is difficult to reconcile with a modern complex economy. They advocated the abolition of 'bourgeois freedom' including the 'free selling and buying' of commodities (Marx, 1973a, pp. 80–81). This statement seems to exclude all forms of market or trade. Perhaps with the benefit of hindsight, this is all economically as well as politically naïve. These statements in the *Communist Manifesto* do not stand up to critical examination. They are inconsistent with an institutionalist understanding of the necessary role of markets.

We can consider whether markets should be dominant or subordinate. Those that take a relatively *laissez-faire* view and want a relatively free market system would advocate a wider role for markets. Others, like myself, would give them a more limited scope. There are all sorts of possibilities and combinations. But the essential point is this: to some extent markets are always necessary to deal with conflicting individual plans and economic complexity. Particularly in a modern economy, it is impossible to bring all knowledge together in one central planning agency, and make that (democratic or undemocratic) institution do the main work of planning the economy. No agency can cope with all the knowledge, and centralize it all together. Marxists have never really shown how such a centralization of knowledge involved in complete social planning is possible (Hodgson, 1999a).

Finally, I would like to tie in another thread. As argued above, Marxism reinforces its teleological view of history by seeing its destination as some kind of completely socialized planning. I have argued that this an impossible outcome. An institutionalist would also respond from a Darwinian standpoint, by arguing that history has multiple possible outcomes. The goal of complete socialization is not viable, but there is an infinite variety of alternative possible routes to take.

This is not only true for the grand sweep of history. It is also true for the here and now. This is extremely important in terms of one's attitude to political developments. For example, I can remember in the late 1970s and early 1980s there was a debate on the left about Thatcherism. Many (but not all) Marxists took the view that Thatcherism was the only possible outcome for British capitalism. Thatcherism was seen by many Marxists as the only rational response by the capitalists to the crises of the 1970s. Hence the viable choices were either Thatcherism or a worker's revolution to overthrow capitalism.

This view was profoundly anti-institutionalist. An institutionalist would argue that there is no reason to presume that Thatcherism is (or was in Britain at that time) the only viable version of capitalism. There are other versions of capitalism, and these can begin to develop at any point in time. After all, there are manifest varieties of capitalism throughout the world. The consequence is that we do face very real choices, even within capitalism. We are not confined to these rather narrow political alternatives proposed by many Marxists: either socialist revolution or accept an extreme and exploitative version of capitalism.

In contrast, there is the possibility of a politics that engages with the present more directly. It talks about real, immediate alternatives and opens up areas for discussion. These areas would include, for example, about different kinds of market, different degrees to which the market may operate, different kinds of planning, the role and limits of the state, different planning agencies, a pluralism of structures and agencies operating at the economic level, different types of mixed economy and so on. This debate becomes possible once you escape from the false dichotomy of accept *either* the most rapacious version of capitalism *or* socialist revolution. This dichotomy disables serious discussion and analysis about what is possible in the present. On this practical issue the difference between institutionalism and Marxism is illustrated most clearly.

4.3 IN DEFENCE OF MARXISM
ALEX CALLINICOS

4.3.1 Some points of agreement

In some ways I feel a bit embarrassed because I am not an economist and I should disclaim any pretensions to expertise on the subject of economics. By intellectual training I am a philosopher and I am also a political activist, so I try both to interpret and to change the world. Probably not very well at either, but I am going to talk more about economics than Geoff did, which is odd.

Let me start with what I think are the most important points of agreement between Marxism and institutionalism. A key point of agreement is that both Marxism and institutionalism recognize the bankruptcy of neoclassical economic orthodoxy. Concretely, what that means is both Marxism and institutionalists agree that it is impossible to construct an adequate economic theory on the basis of the idealized rational actor. We agree that every form of economy depends crucially on institutional conditions, which are partly to do with culture and partly to do with forms of political organization, and so on and so forth. We also agree that the economy must be understood as part of an evolving historical process. This is common ground between more than just Marxism and institutionalists; it would also be common ground (if there were any remaining) with any supporters of the nineteenth-century German historical school, whose most important product was Max Weber. It is also implicit in Keynes, although his training in neoclassical economics obscures it.

I also think important points of agreement are the importance of disequilibrium, chaos (in the scientific sense) and complexity, in understanding how capitalist economies work. A lot of what we find in contemporary analyses of complex systems in nature and society, someone who espouses Marx's historical dialectic can take on board with great comfort. And all this I think is not just a matter of relatively obtuse philosophical and methodological arguments. It is of critical political importance in the modern world.

Inasmuch as there is an ideology that in practical terms rules the word today, it is the so-called Washington consensus: the neo-liberal orthodoxy of de-regulation, privatization, spending cuts and so on. Imposed on large parts of the world via the IMF and the World Bank, it is also what governs the general approach to managing the economy of Gordon Brown,[3] however much he may try and distance himself from it, from time to time to suit his political career.

[3] The UK Chancellor of the Exchequer from 1997

So I am going to take for granted that Marxism and institutionalism are part of a common critique of the neoclassical orthodoxy that is really important politically. That seems to me the critical points of agreement, but I think that Marxism has much more to offer than institutionalism does. Critically it involves a general historical theory of modes of production and in particular it has a very rich and developed analysis of the capitalist mode of production.

4.3.2 The logic of capitalism

Just let me remind you very briefly. I am sure you all know that according to Marx's general theory of history we have in the course of human history, in a more or less rapid more or less slow way, the development of the productive forces, that is to say humanity's productive powers. From time to time, however, this development of the productive forces runs into conflict with the prevailing relations of production, where these relations of production are critically the relations of effective control over those productive forces. So we have a conflict, this is putting it extremely crudely, between the prevailing state of technology and the prevailing social relations of production that produces a crisis in the economic system, what Marx calls the mode of production. At this point, to which I want to return to because it is very important, we have either the transformation of the economic system, what Marx calls the social revolution or we have stagnation or retrogression.

Now let me note in passing that, since I have been reading up what Geoff says about Marx in one of his voluminous writings, Geoff says that Marx does not explain why the productive forces tend to develop over time. Now I do not think there's a general answer to that question but I think Marx does have a very clearly stated explanation of why the productive forces develop under capitalism. Its competition between capitals, it's the competitive struggle between rival capitalists each seeking to maximize their share of the market and maximize profit which leads to technological innovation and the development of productive forces.

This leads me then in to Marx's theory of capitalism. Now I think this is really the most important issue. I am going to deal with some of the broader philosophical and methodological points that Geoff made, but I think a lot of those involve misunderstandings and misrepresentations. I think they are in some ways less interesting than the critical question of Marx's analysis of capitalism, so bear with me if I say a certain amount about that.

For Marx the peculiar thing about capitalism is that it is abstract; it is driven by a logic that is independent of any particular human or natural characteristics. Marx does not regard this as a virtue. He does not claim that this kind of peculiar logic is inherent in human history or society or whatever.

It is one of the key defining characteristics of capitalism as an economic system that the workings of the economy, the great variety of economies that exist say in the contemporary world, is subject to this remorseless abstract logic, a logic that is based upon two key features.

First of all the exploitation of wage labour: again this is something that I am sure you are all familiar with and I do not need to waste your time elaborating any more. The central claim that Marx makes that the profits of capital are dependent upon a process of exploitation of workers variously organized within different kinds of processes of production. The second key feature is the competitive accumulation of capital, that individual capitalist actors (as Marx puts it, individual capitals) are caught up in a process of competition in which they are presented or confronted with a series of choices, all of which turn around the necessity of accumulating or re-investing the bulk of the profits that they have extracted from workers in further and generally more technologically advanced production, which will allow them to keep up in the competitive game. So capitalism is essentially a remorseless process of the self-expansion of capital, what Marx calls the self-expansion of capital. Capitalism is capital constantly adding to itself through the extraction of profits, constantly seeking to expand itself.

Marx says that the purist form of this process is what it calls a circuit of money capital, what we these days call financial markets, which reduces capitalism to its barest structure, which is simply money seeking to expand itself without going through the intermediary, or apparently not going through the intermediary, of involvement in any kind of productive process. I think it is quite striking, if one reads Marx's analysis of the circuit of money capital in volume three of *Capital*, it is amazing how much light it throws on reality. One has a sense of instant recognition of the world of derivatives, long-term capital management and the whole Wall Street bubble, that is slowly and potentially catastrophically deflating.

Of course, this abstract logic is dependent on various institutional conditions, the process of what is commonly known as economic globalization, that is going on at the present time. It is critically dependent upon state policies of financial de-regulation in countries such as the United States and Britain, which dramatically altered the institutional context in which financial markets operated. Without this, the whole process of economic globalization would have been a non-starter.

I think that this is a common point, between Marxism and institutionalism to insist on the institutional context that enables certain economic processes to develop in the form in which they actually do. So this abstract logic of capitalism is interwoven with specific institutional contexts and state policies. Nevertheless capitalism as an economic system cannot be equated with any specific institutional complex. If we look at the history of capitalism over the last two hundred years we see a variety of different sets of institutions that sustain different types of capitalism, involving for example greater or lesser degrees of *laissez-faire*, greater or lesser degrees of state intervention. In the major capitalist countries today we see a variety of arrangements interconnecting, for example, the state corporations and the banking system.

But what it is also important to see, is that the logic of capitalism can break up any of these existing institutional complexes. What we are seeing at the present time is a very dramatic, long drawn out, crisis-ridden process, in which some of the major more nationally organized capitalisms are being restructured. We can see this happening in different forms, in fact more or less catastrophic forms. In the case of Japan and Germany at the present time under the pressure of global competition so that capitalism cannot be identified with any specific set of institutional conditions. It co-exists with but also destroys a whole variety of different institutional complexes.

Now, Veblen (as Geoff says) stresses the inertia, the resistance to change, that is generated by specific institutional conditions. Looking at the very complex process through which, say, Japanese capitalism is being restructured at the present time, it is necessary to understand that fact of institutional inertia. But simply to focus upon that the way in which certain structured habits filter the pressures of global competition would be to miss out on the dynamic forces operating these days on a world scale to drive economic change. I think as Geoff touched on towards the end of his presentation, here again we run into political implications. Globalization which is crucially a matter of political not just economic forces, its not just an economic juggernaut that operates like a natural force independent of institutions and political actions, not at all.

Nevertheless globalization is bringing into existence a particular pure form of capitalism, the new economy. On this topic there is much nonsense and ideological noise. But inasmuch as the idea of the new economy has any economic reality, it represents a form of capitalism in which the dependence of the capitalism economic system on production and exploitation are systematically accounted.

This is then related to a political diagnosis. Institutionalism, as Geoff put it very clearly, can lead us to seek reforms that will try and bring into existence and perhaps in a British context one might say bring back into existence, a more benevolent form of capitalism. Geoff's references to a mixed economy seem to me to involve precisely that sort of claim. Marx by contrast locates the source of the problem in, as I have tried to bring out, in the logic of capital itself and therefore the solution and the achievement of a different kind of social logic based upon the democratic organization of the economy in order to meet human need.

4.3.3 Planning, socialism and the state

This then takes us to the question of planning. There is clearly an enormous scope for debate about planning. I have to say, I am a very loyal Marxist, but I do not think that Marx himself is a great help in this debate. I think Geoff was being a bit counter-Marx when he attributed to Marx a theory of centralized planning: I do not think there is very much discussion of planning, full stop, in Marx. He reads too much into some passages in the *Communist Manifesto*, which were written before Marx developed his mature economic theory through a systematic engagement, in particular, with Ricardo's version of classical political economy. But it seems to me that whatever the case then we are on our own. I mean that the classics of socialism are not of any particular help. But there is an important debate to be had about the extent to which democratic collective regulation of the economy can supplant the kind of abstract logic of competitive accumulation that I have sought briefly to outline and which I think is central to Marx's analysis.

There is work that has been written on this subject. There is an interesting book for example by Pat Devine called *Democracy and Economic Planning* (1988) in which he tries to outline in some detail what kind of institutions would be required to organize a democratically planned economy. Much of this discussion unfortunately has been cut short by the kind of despair induced in many left intellectuals by the collapse of the Soviet Union. I think happily now that this mood, that there could be no alternative to pro-market capitalism, is beginning to evaporate. But this is an important area where debate, discussion and analysis need to continue.

I do not think it will do in that context however to misrepresent Marx's conception of socialism. I mean I do think it is just nonsense to attribute to Marx the theory of state socialism. He is very explicit about this in the *Critique of the Gotha Programme*. In this, one of his last major theoretical texts, Marx (1974, p. 354) wrote in 1875: 'Freedom consists in converting the state from an organ superimposed on society into one thoroughly subordinate to it'. Marx's conception of socialism is about partly liberating people from the imperious logic of capitalism but it is also about liberating people from the oppression of the centralized bureaucratic state. These are the two kinds of requirements that any Marxist conception of socialism would have to meet.

4.3.4 Teleology and political action

Let me now move on to what Geoff said about teleology and agency and so on. I have to say I did not recognize much of Marx in all that. I mean I thought the passages that he cited from Veblen were very interesting. I can point to very important passages in Marx, which say more or less the same thing. For example, the very famous beginning of the *Eighteenth Brumaire of Louis Bonaparte*, Marx (1973b, p. 146) wrote in 1852:

> Men make their own history, but not of their own free will; not under circumstances they themselves have chosen but under the given and inherited circumstances with which they are directly confronted. The tradition of the dead generations weighs like a nightmare on the minds of the living.

So I think Marx knew a bit about the power of tradition and didn't simply treat structures as the sole explanatory fountain in accounting for society. I think it is true in *Capital* his explanations involve referring both to the structures of capitalism and to the strategies of individual agents. It is true that he does tend to concede economic actors in *Capital* as rational actors – that is a kind of simplifying assumption that he makes to continue to get the argument going. But it is absolutely wrong to say that Marx had no understanding of tradition, tacit knowledge and all that.

There is a very interesting discussion of what Marx calls practical consciousness and language in the *German Ideology* – only a series of undeveloped hints but nevertheless a discussion which points towards the kind of analysis of language and consciousness that we find for example in the later Wittgenstein. So I simply do not think that this is a set of issues of which Marx is unaware.

Marx's conception of history is one that posits a constant interaction between human beings and social structures in which human beings both derive power from but also are constrained by those structures and in this interaction what Geoff calls cultural circumstances are clearly tremendously important. Key Marxist thinking in this respect is by Antonio Gramsci, where the whole project of transforming the working class into a self-conscious political subject involves very careful analysis of institutions, organizations, ideologies and so on. There are institutions, organizations and ideologies that inhibit the working class developing into a self-conscious subject but also those that could help it to become such a subject. So I think Geoff is wrong about all that.

Equally wrong is this idea that Marxism is committed to a teleological conception of history striving towards a pre-ordained end. It is true that Marx has a different conception of evolution from Darwin's. Critically for Marx it is the contradictions inherent in particular sets of social structures that form the context in which historical change develops. Darwin has quite a different conception of evolution. It does not follow that Marx's conception of history is a teleological one.

Again if I cite Geoff's writings rather than anything he said in his talk, he attributes to Marx the view that the communist society that Marx hopes will replace capitalism eventually involves harmony and the absence of variety. Now I think this is completely untrue. In the *Communist Manifesto,* Marx says that a communist society is one where the free development of each will be the condition of the free development of all. In other words a communist society is one that will be governed by the goal of individual self-realization. Now why make this the quite self-conscious goal, in a non-problematic way I think, of a communist society if individuals are all the same, if there's no variety, it would be quite nonsensical. Elsewhere Marx says that a socialist revolution will bring the end of social antagonism, in other words antagonism routed in exploitative relations of production but not of individual antagonism. In other words, surprise, surprise, even in a communist society individuals, thank God, will differ. There may be conflicts among them and it is precisely the differences between and sometimes the conflicts among individuals and groups of individuals that will be a critical driving force of progress in a communist society.

Unfortunately the workings of a communist society are not the most immediate and urgent political question confronting the left of the present time. But what is a critical issue is whether human beings can change history. I think here is an area where Marx is ambiguous but nevertheless I want to insist that his theory of history does not require any notion of historical inevitability. A teleological conception of history requires that change will occur in order to bring about the final goal. Marx's theory of history does not commit him to any such thesis of historical inevitability. In the *Communist Manifesto,* in the famous opening paragraphs, we have Marx and Engels explicitly offering a picture of human history as involving alternative solutions to great crises. They say that each past crisis of a major production involves 'either in a revolutionary reconstruction of society at large, or in the common ruin of the contending classes' (Marx, 1973a, p. 68). In other words each great historical crisis involves either the over-throw of the old mode of production, the establishment of a new mode of production which will permit further development and productive forces and so on, or if change does not occur, if the old classes remain locked in a conflict with neither side able to decisively beat the other then what we have is stagnation or retrogression.

In other words, what Geoff talked about, multiple alternative outcomes, is built into Marx's theory of history, and it has to be if Marx's theory of history is to found a coherent view of political action. Because if history is simply about the iron workings of certain historical laws operating according to natural necessity, then what is the point of political action, what is the point of changing the world, what is the point of all the effort that Marx and other great Marxists put into building political organization, engaging in great historical struggles, leading revolutions and so on? What is the point of all that, if it is all going to happen anyway? And therefore Marx's conception of history as a theory of alternatives of great historical junctures is the necessary foundation for any socialist political practice that is to take its inspiration from Marx.

So to conclude, what I would say is that I do not think that the kind of philosophical and methodological criticisms that Geoff has made actually hit the core of the Marxist tradition. Second that there's lots of scope for debate about alternatives to capitalism. Since the mass demonstrations in Seattle in 1999, we now are in a political context in which there is a willingness to debate the question of alternatives to capitalism. But finally if we want to understand capitalism itself, if we want to understand the nature of the beast under which we currently live, then we cannot do it without Marx.

Part 2:

Three Essays on Critical Realism

5. The Uncritical Political Affinities of Critical Realism

> The resulting impression is one of pulling global salvation out of the critical realist hat.
>
> Andrew Sayer, 'Critical Realism and the Limits to Critical Social Science' (1997).

5.1 INTRODUCTION

Critical realism has established a substantial following, leading to the formation of the International Association for Critical Realism in 1997 and the subsequent launch of its *Journal of Critical Realism* in 2002.[1] In particular, the works of Roy Bhaskar have attracted widespread interest, his ideas being adopted by leading social scientists, including Margaret Archer, Andrew Collier and Tony Lawson. To some degree, this reputation and following is deserved. Critical realism addresses some core issues in the philosophy of science and carries some important insights concerning the nature of scientific endeavour.[2]

Critical realism also makes persistent claims concerning its practical applicability and policy implications, which are often portrayed as radically socialist in character.[3] This chapter scrutinizes three of the more prominent of these political claims: that critical realism (*A*) is emancipatory, (*B*) shows that

---

[1] A version of this chapter first appeared as Hodgson (1999c). Since then I have come across Sayer (1997), which similarly argues that attempts to derive normative conclusions on the basis of explanatory critiques of social phenomena are flawed. Nielsen (2002) notes a tension between the highly politicized version of critical realism promoted by Bhaskar and the contrasting accounts of others such as Lawson and Fleetwood.

[2] The modern 'critical realism' of Bhaskar, Archer, Lawson, Collier and others should not be confused with the earlier tradition in American philosophy describing itself as 'critical realism'. See Sellars (1908, 1916), Bode (1922), Moore (1922) and the brief discussion of this phase of American philosophy in Hodgson (2004a).

[3] See, for example, Archer *et al.* (1998), Bhaskar (1989b, 1991, 1993) and Collier (1989, 1994). Bhaskar (1994) uses the term 'eudaimonistic society'. In other important critical realist works, including Archer (1995), Lawson (1997, 2003b), Downward (2003) and Lewis (2004), socialist or Marxist rhetoric is absent or downplayed. However, they have failed to distance themselves from the political claims made for critical realism by Bhaskar and Collier.

a genuine, democratic socialism is possible, and (*C*) shows that social democratic or Fabian politics are flawed.

Bhaskar, the founder of modern critical realism, has promoted all three propositions. Collier follows him on all counts. Lawson stresses the first. Archer, by contrast, does not emphasize any normative claims. Yet all three claims are found in an extensive anthology of *Essential Readings* in critical realism, of which all these four authors – plus Alan Norrie – are editors (Archer *et al.*, 1998). No editor takes this opportunity to disown any of the three propositions, or to warn of the problems involved in making excessive normative claims for critical realism.

Critical realists attempt a link between critical realism and a 'eudaimonistic society' of 'universal human flourishing' in which 'the free flourishing of each is the condition for the free flourishing of all' (Bhaskar, 1993, pp. 284, 202). Such repeated statements are unsatisfactory and vague because the economic and structural conditions under which 'flourishing' can supposedly take place are not elucidated, and 'flourishing' itself is very loosely defined. Such discourse is often juxtaposed with socialist or Marxist rhetoric. However, 'socialism' is not defined clearly, and the propositions concerning emancipation and human flourishing are so vague as to be consistent with numerous political philosophies. Such inadequate arguments are unworthy of serious philosophy.

A group of critical realists have produced a volume entitled *Critical Realism and Marxism* (Brown *et al.*, 2001). They considered the state of the 'marriage' between the two doctrines, and promoted it with the policy blurb that the book 'makes a contribution towards the eliminating of barbarism in contemporary capitalism'. While critical realists sometimes deny that their philosophy leads to any particular political or theoretical position (e.g. Collier 1994, p. 200), they show remarkable consistency and enthusiasm, documented abundantly throughout their writings (e.g. Collier 1994, p. 195; Collier 1989, pp. ix–x), to deploy critical realism in support of specific 'policy implications', generally of a strongly socialist, Marxist and anti-Fabian flavour.

Critical realists cannot have it both ways. If they wish to deny that their philosophy leads to any particular political position then they should separate Marxist ideology from their philosophy. In practice, however, critical realists seem very keen to explore 'practical implications' and draw 'policy conclusions'. They treat many policies, particularly concerning 'socialism', as decided by critical realism. If they wish to show that critical realism leads to socialist or Marxist policy conclusions then more detailed attention should be devoted to establishing the alleged links. If they do not believe that there are any such links, then their forthright denial would be welcome. It has not yet been forthcoming.

The point of this chapter is neither to criticize emancipation, socialism nor any other policy doctrine, nor to support any alternative ideology. Neither is it to provide a critique of critical realism as such. Instead, the point is to show that the claimed political implications of critical realism do not follow from its philosophy, and an inadequate case has been made for them.

5.2 IS CRITICAL REALISM EMANCIPATORY?

Some of the titles of Bhaskar's works (e.g. *Scientific Realism and Human Emancipation* (1986); *Dialectic: The Pulse of Freedom* (1993)) and much of their content betray a driving concern with the topic of human emancipation. The same theme is found in works by Collier (1989, 1994) and to some extent in Lawson (1997). Indeed, the claim to contribute to the meritorious project of human emancipation is one of the most striking and persistent of the claims made by critical realists.

The issues raised by Bhaskar, Collier and Lawson are complex and serious. They concern, in part, the age-old discussion within philosophy about the relationship between (positive) judgements of fact and (normative) judgements of value. As much as possible I am going to avoid this complicated controversy. Nevertheless, some discussion of Bhaskar's attempt to relate statements of fact and value is unavoidable.[4]

'My core argument', Bhaskar (1989b, p. 101) writes, 'is relatively simple. It turns on the condition that the subject matter of the human sciences includes both social objects (including beliefs) and beliefs about those objects'. So far so good. Many social theorists would endorse this statement. Critical realists then go on to note that within society there are different ideas and beliefs concerning specific social phenomena. For instance, as Collier (1994, p. 171) points out 'in Britain in the 1980s, a large number of people believed that unemployment was the result of the fecklessness of the unemployed'. These beliefs were a part of the social reality, and perhaps they also contributed to the perpetuation of unemployment itself. However, as critical realists assert, the 'fecklessness' theory of unemployment is generally false, and the true explanation of mass unemployment lies elsewhere. A

[4] Lacey (1997, p. 238) has exposed some problems in Bhaskar's claim that 'there is a quick rational move from coming to accept theories in the social sciences to adopting value judgements partial to emancipation'. Lacey argues persuasively that 'the proposed quick move' depends on 'the mediation of value judgements' or on 'value-impregnated theoretical terms'. Accordingly, 'any sound moves from theory to value judgements are mediated in the way that Bhaskar hoped to avoid'. Lacey also doubts whether 'Bhaskar's argument (even when modified to acknowledge the mediation) is applicable to theories in the social sciences in which social structures are posited to play key causal roles'.

social scientist finding the true explanation would not only be challenging the false theory, but also the social situation of which it is a part. Collier (1994, p. 172) explains this clearly:

> Particular institutions and false beliefs about them may be in a *functional* relation, such that the false beliefs serve to preserve the institutions that they are about ... to propound the truth is not just to criticise, but to undermine the institution.

I agree with this statement. But note that it contains no clear normative evaluation, and it does not raise the issue of emancipation. To achieve this, Bhaskar (1991, pp. 155-6) has to push the argument further:

> If one is in possession of a theory that explains why false consciousness is necessary, then one can pass immediately, without the addition of any extraneous value judgement, to a negative evaluation on the object that makes such consciousness necessary and to a positive evaluation on action rationally directed at removing it.[5]

I have no objection to this formulation, provided it is accepted that it requires the prior value judgement, that falsehood is bad and truth is good.[6] Clearly, the pursuit of truth will undermine support for those social institutions that are sustained by false beliefs. If the truth is an overriding moral good then it should be pursued, even if the result is a challenge to the existing social order. This, according to Bhaskar (1986, p. 169), is the 'essential emancipatory impulse' of the social sciences. Critical realists describe this as an 'explanatory critique'.

This critical realist argument boils down to the following: (x) some social institutions promulgate false beliefs which help to sustain these social institutions, (y) in confronting false beliefs and their explanations we are not only challenging these beliefs but also confronting the institutions that are sustained by them. Collier (1994, p. 172) asserts: 'To say that some institution causes false beliefs is to criticise it'.

The main problem with these arguments is not that they are wrong but that they contain no operational criterion as to what is a 'false' or what is a 'true' belief. Without such a criterion, any statement in the social sciences, from

---

[5] See also Bhaskar (1986, p. 177; 1989a, p. 63) for similar statements.

[6] However, the universal goodness of truth is not self-evident. If we lived under a totalitarian regime then it would not necessarily be morally acceptable to proclaim to the authorities the names of those that are working clandestinely to restore democracy. And if someone was dying, would it be morally good to tell her all sorts of unpalatable truths about her loved ones? In some circumstances, other moral values, such as democracy, or the personal feelings of a dying person, may outweigh the moral good of truth.

whatever perspective, might be emancipatory by this reasoning. Emancipation by this logic requires criteria of truth and falsehood. Critical realism offers little further detailed guidance on this. Furthermore, we are given no clue as to how one could 'explain' the basis or origin of false beliefs in social institutions, or how such institutions can 'cause' false beliefs. Critical realists should admit that this argument does not, as it stands, lead in any particular political or emancipatory direction. As an extreme illustrative case, consider the following quotation:

> To have the effect of action among men, it is necessary to enter into the process of reality and to master the forces actually at work. … And if liberty is to be the attribute of the real man, and not of the scarecrow invented by the individualistic Liberalism, then Fascism is for liberty … the Fascist State … interprets, develops and potentiates the whole life of the people.[7]

These words were written by Benito Mussolini and published in the *Enciclopedia Italiana* in 1932. I do not approve of them and that is not the reason I quote them. Emphatically, I do not believe, nor wish to suggest, that critical realists are witting or unwitting fascists. I wish to show, rather, that other people have started from analyses of what they claim to be social reality, attacked what they believed to be 'false' beliefs and drawn conclusions concerning what they sincerely understand to be the route towards human emancipation. I am not saying that critical realism has fascist implications. Instead I propose that there is nothing at the core of Bhaskar's 'emancipatory' argument that would convince a fascist to abandon their fascism. Likewise, a whole host of very different political philosophies are compatible with Bhaskar's 'emancipatory' argument.

Critical realism also fails to define adequately what emancipation means. Bhaskar (1991, p. 145) makes much of the alleged difference between 'emancipation' and 'the amelioration of states of affairs', where the former involves structural transformation. Likewise, Lawson (1997, p. 277) emphasizes '*emancipation* through *structural transformation*' and argues that emancipation is highlighted by critical realism because it points not to the '*amelioration* of events and states of affairs' but to the humanly beneficial transformation or replacement of underlying social structures.

Again, the problem with this is not that it is necessarily wrong but that it seems to ignore the fact that almost anyone waving the flag of 'human emancipation' – including fascists, conservatives, social democrats, anarchists and neo-liberals – has also attempted to replace or transform underlying structures. (Below I make the particular case that social democrats have changed structures.) Critical realism brings the ontology of structures to

---

[7] Translated in Department of Philosophy University of Colorado (1952, p. 10).

the debate, but it fails to exclude any of the major rival contending doctrines of human emancipation. Bhaskar (1986, p. 171) tries to explain the content of emancipation in passages such as the following:

> It is my contention that the special qualitative kind of becoming free or liberation which is *emancipation*, and which consists in the *transformation*, in self-emancipation by the agents concerned, *from an unwanted and unneeded to a wanted and needed source of determination*, is both causally presaged and logically entailed by explanatory theory, but that it can only be effected in *practice*. Emancipation, as so defined, depends upon the transformation of structures, not the alteration or amelioration of states of affairs.

Emancipation involves, in short, what is 'wanted and needed'. But we are given no other criterion to help us at this point. Being in favour of what is 'wanted and needed' is almost like being in favour of motherhood and apple pie. As a result, once again, we could find agreement with this broad definition of emancipation from a wide variety of political viewpoints. Even the modification of the term to 'self-emancipation' does not narrow it down much. Anarchists and neo-liberals, as well as Marxists, and even some fascists are allegedly in favour of 'self-emancipation'. The trouble is: what do these words mean?

It is not being suggested here that the task of a philosophy, such as critical realism, is to legislate for science. Contrary to the impression given by several critical realists, philosophy on its own can only take us so far. Hence, it is not being proposed that critical realism should make still more attempts to link itself to specific theoretical or normative approaches. On the contrary, the suggestion here is that the emancipatory claims of critical realism should be scaled down. It should be admitted that Bhaskar's emancipatory argument does not, on its own, lead to any particular political philosophy. My basic charge against the proposition that critical realism is emancipatory is that it is a rhetorical exaggeration. All discourse in social science that claims to overturn falsehoods that sustain – or are sustained by – institutions can equally make such an emancipatory declaration.

By focusing on underlying structures, critical realism goes beyond the ameliorative. But at the same time it has to be recognized that few contending major political philosophies are content with altering or sustaining 'mere appearances'.

5.3 DOES CRITICAL REALISM SHOW THAT A GENUINE, DEMOCRATIC SOCIALISM IS POSSIBLE?

Laced with leftist rhetoric, the emancipatory discourse in critical realism gives the false impression that it is well established that socialism is the only viable form of human emancipation. This argument can be made, but critical realists have done little to make it.

The specific claim that the emancipatory argument in critical realism has *socialist* policy conclusions is directly challengeable. We may simply and arbitrarily define 'socialism' as 'that which is emancipatory'. In this case the second proposition readily collapses into the first, and becomes equally ill-defined. However, this weak and nebulous definition of socialism would be open to multiple objections, including from socialists and critical realists themselves.

Historically, the term socialism has assumed a variety of different meanings. Nevertheless, some common threads of egalitarianism and collectivism run through them all. These ideas are clearly controversial, and if the 'socialist' claims of critical realism are to be meaningful and substantial then they must signal some informed engagement with this controversy.

The word 'socialism' emerged in popular discourse in France and Britain in the 1830s. For over a century after its appearance it was used to signify some type of widespread common ownership of the means of production. Socialists differed on the form of common ownership – whether it meant ownership by the state, by the municipality, by the community or by the workers – but they generally agreed on it as a goal. This central motif pervaded the writings of socialists as diverse as revolutionary communists, state socialists and Fabians. By the time socialist ideas had established a significant influence in Europe in the 1880s, the word socialism was almost universally defined in terms of common ownership of the means of production (Beer, 1940; Landauer, 1959; Hodgson, 1999a).

Furthermore, a general hostility towards competition and markets was thematic for socialism as a whole. This remained the case at least until the very different ideas of 'market socialism' or a 'mixed economy' took hold in some quarters after the Second World War. Since the 1950s, most major social democratic parties have adopted the notion of the mixed economy, combining private and public ownership. Nevertheless, most Marxists have retained the traditional hostility to the market that defined the socialism of Owen, Fourier, Marx and others at its inception.

Two lessons immediately emerge from this brief historical excursion. First, given past changes in its meaning, it is always necessary to define what one means by the term 'socialism'. Nevertheless, and second, the common collectivist and anti-market sentiments that have pervaded the socialist tradition do not make any arbitrary redefinition of the term viable. It has to be defined, but feasible definitions have to recognize its historical legacy.

Critical realist discussions of the nature of socialism still bear the marks of this history. Significantly, Bhaskar and Collier (1998, p. 392) declare:

> Critical realism shows the fallacy of several of the classical arguments against socialism and supports the *possibility* of a form of socialism which is neither a market economy nor a command economy nor a mix of the two, but a genuine extension of pluralistic democracy into economic life.

The form of socialism envisaged here is consistent with some traditional socialist thinking. However, it is a highly restrictive version of that doctrine. Many socialists, while being hostile to markets, have proposed that they be tolerated at the fringes of the economy. Bhaskar and Collier go further, attempting not merely to marginalize markets but to exclude them entirely. For them, no 'mix' of a market and a planned economy is acceptable. Evident from the quotation is the anti-market mentality that has marked much of socialism from its inception.

It is not clear whether 'a genuine extension of pluralistic democracy into economic life' involves a plurality of types of economic unit or structure, such as a mixture of worker cooperatives, municipal enterprises and so on. Or does it refer a pluralistic system of organized industrial democracy within a multiplicity of (perhaps relatively homogeneous) economic structures?

In any case, how would this collection of economic units be coordinated, so that decisions concerning outputs and prices could be made? In two centuries of economic thought no alternative solution to this coordination problem, other than markets or collective planning, or a combination of them, has ever been outlined in any detail. Bhaskar and Collier reject markets, so it seems that their solution to the coordination problem would be some form of collective planning. Their 'genuine extension of pluralistic democracy into economic life' must be subordinate to a collective plan.

Strangely in this context there is very little discussion by critical realists of the Austrian school critique of socialism. Critical realists such as Steve Fleetwood (1995, 1996) and Tony Lawson (1994, 1997) have written extensively on the work of Friedrich Hayek, even to the point of expressing considerable sympathy for his analysis. Lawson (1994, p. 154), for example, credits Hayek for supplying 'an embryonic transcendental realist account' of the relationship between actor and structure. Despite this, there is negligible discussion of Hayek's (1935, 1948, 1988) contribution to the socialist calculation debate and of the possibility that his critique of collective planning may carry some weight.

Perhaps the gambit here is to assert that the collective planning that is criticized by Hayek 'has nothing to do with socialism'. There are two problems with such an assertion. First, such collective planning has *everything* to do with the meaning of socialism advocated by socialists from the 1830s to at least the 1940s, including the short statement quoted above from Bhaskar and Collier, and the notable proposals of Patrick Devine (1988) and of W. Paul Cockshott and Allin Cottrell (1993). Devine, Cockshott and

Cottrell all admit no more than a marginal and reluctant role for markets. In different ways they propose an extensive role for collective planning over key sectors of the economy. Bhaskar and Collier deny markets entirely. The Austrian critique has devastating implications for *all* these proposals.[8]

Second, if socialism is to be defined in a different way, then such a definition is lacking in the critical realist literature. It is simply not good enough to repeat endlessly that critical realism has 'socialist' implications and fail to define what socialism means. Furthermore, since the traditional conception of socialism has been subjected to a strong challenge by the Austrian school, it is important to show how the 'socialism' advocated by critical realists is somehow invulnerable to such an attack. This defence must necessarily involve a detailed description of the *underlying structures and causal mechanisms of the proposed socialist system.* The canons of critical realism concerning causes and structures must be applied to critical realism itself. How are innovation, production and allocation decisions made in the proposed socialist system? How, and within what institutions, are these processes organized? Not least in this domain, it is necessary to be both critical and realistic. Unless there are answers to these questions, the identification of critical realism with 'socialism' must be abandoned.[9]

Collier (1989) has written a book linking critical realism with socialism. Bhaskar attempts the same connection in several places, sometimes switching from philosophical discourse to leftist desiderata. In one work, for example, no more than four sentences into a preliminary section titled 'philosophical

---

[8] See Lavoie (1985), Steele (1992), Boettke (2000). Adaman and Devine (1996) attempt to rebut any Austrian critique of their position. Hodgson (1999a, 2005) argues that this defence fails, largely as a result of their misunderstanding of the character of tacit knowledge. Nevertheless, Hodgson (1999a) also attempts to show the limitations of the Austrian defence of free markets, and proposes a mixed economy that would be excluded by Bhaskar and Collier, on the one hand, and by Austrians such as Hayek and von Mises, on the other. As Steele (1992, p. 22) concedes, it is possible to acknowledge the devastating power of the Austrian critique of comprehensive planning without accepting the neo-liberal policies often associated with it.

[9] Critical realists may refer approvingly to Devine (1988), Cockshott and Cottrell (1993), or Wainwright (1994). However, unlike Bhaskar and Collier, neither Devine nor Cockshott and Cottrell wish to exclude markets *entirely* from their system. Wainwright (1994) offers support for the socialist proposals of *both* Elson (1988) *and* Devine (1988), being seemingly unaware of their incompatibility. She does not acknowledge that, in contrast to Devine, Elson (1988) supports the idea of an extensive 'socialised market'. Wainwright fails to see the difference, or to accept unequivocally that *some* use of the market mechanism is unavoidable. But, to their credit, the difference between the Devine and Elson proposals is recognized by Adaman and Devine (1997).

underlabouring', there is a sudden shift to a vague, incongruous and overly normative aspiration of 'what we can hope to aspire to is the dawning of a new enlightenment, a socialist enlightenment which will stand to some future order of things, as the eighteenth-century bourgeois enlightenment stood to the American Declaration of Independence, the French revolution and the overthrow of colonial slavery' (Bhaskar, 1989b, p. 1).

A few pages later Bhaskar (1989b, p. 6) argues for 'needed, wanted and empowering sources of determination. This might include, for example, a switch from a situation where production is determined by the pursuit of profit and subject to arbitrary fluctuation, to one where it is subject to democratic negotiation and planning'. It is not explained why 'democratic negotiation and planning' is not also subject to 'arbitrary fluctuation', or why such fluctuation is deleterious, or why the absence of such fluctuation or the pursuit of profit is 'empowering'. The possibility that those participating in the planning process might also be subject to 'false consciousness' is not considered.

The contrast between Bhaskar's insightful philosophical arguments and his nebulous and superficial socialist flag-waving must amaze any thoughtful and questioning reader. I am sure that Bhaskar and other critical realists are sincere in their political views. But the use of superficial and inadequately defined 'socialist' normative statements in serious philosophical discourse is both unworthy and irresponsible.

Some critical realists seem to think that the advantages of socialism and the disadvantages of capitalism are self-evident. Collier (1994, p. 10) writes that it is 'inconceivable that permanent full employment or the vital degree of care for the environment could be achieved in a free market economy'. On the contrary, several economists have conceived precisely that full employment and care for the environment can be achieved in a free market economy.[10] Personally, I think that they are misguided, but it is no good taking the answers to these questions as obvious. If critical realists wish to make such evaluative statements then they have to substantiate them.

No detailed analytical link between critical realism and any form of socialism has been demonstrated. Critical realists have not shown that socialism is emancipatory, and socialism for them remains inadequately defined. Despite invoking Hayek, they have not answered the Austrian critique of collective planning. They have not shown how markets or the profit motive can be marginalized or abolished and replaced by alternative structures and mechanisms. They have neither explained the outline and structure of their proposed 'socialist' system, nor yet cited any literature making such a depiction and explanation.

---

[10] For example, Block (1989) and Furubotn and Pejovich (1974).

Contrary to the statement of Bhaskar and Collier, critical realists have not shown the fallacy of 'several of the classical arguments against socialism'. Indeed, they have failed even to discuss seriously any of these 'classical arguments against socialism' in any of their works. The *Essential Readings* mentions neither von Mises, Hayek nor the socialist calculation debate. The critical realist discussions of Hayek, by Fleetwood and Lawson, persistently avoid engagement with Hayek's argument that socialism is unworkable. The claim that critical realism has refuted the classical arguments against socialism is simply bogus. No such argument has been raised in the critical realist literature, let alone refuted.

Notice also the precise form of words that are used in the statement by Bhaskar and Collier quoted above. They claim that the readings to which they refer support the '*possibility*' of a specific form of socialism. In fact, no attempt is made to establish the possibility of *any* form of socialism, however defined. More specifically, no attempt is made to explain the possibility of a 'socialism' that is devoid of markets. Critical realists may claim, more broadly, that the 'possibility' of 'emancipation' is demonstrated. On the contrary, without a detailed explication of the nature of emancipation and the structural form of society in which people can be emancipated, they have demonstrated no such thing. Bhaskar and Collier either duck this question of detailed explanation or come out with extreme and implausible notions of 'socialism' in which markets are entirely absent.

We are presented with the peculiar combination of insightful philosophical discourse with crude and superficial political posturing. Of course, Bhaskar and Collier are entitled to their socialist views. However, their habit of mixing them within their philosophy, especially in such an unsubstantiated and undefined manner, does critical realism no good as an academic doctrine.

It seems that we must understand critical realism not merely as a philosophical or academic discourse, but as a sociological and political phenomenon. It is an attempt, perhaps, to find an intellectual and academic home for the lingering revolutionaries of the 1968 generation. It is a means for Marxist academics to make political postures while simultaneously earning their crust doing serious academic work.[11]

To their credit, there are other critical realists who are keen to give critical realism a much broader appeal, unconfined to socialism. But they are not helped by Bhaskar's and Collier's narrow socialist rhetoric. Bhaskar and

[11] The suspect practice of sneaking in a preferred political ideology into a supposedly scientific and academic discourse is not confined to critical realism. Regrettably, it is also found in the works of Friedman, Hayek and many others. Both the Austrian school and Chicago economists are notorious for their attempts to use academic discourse as clothing for their preferred ideology. Reckless and ungrounded policy stances are regrettably all too common throughout social science.

Collier seem to take it for granted that their audience is composed of no more than the most extreme anti-market type of socialist.

The thrust of the argument here is not against socialism, however defined. This work does not address the questions of its possibility or desirability. These questions have been addressed elsewhere (Hodgson, 1999a). The point being made here is that critical realists have not demonstrated the connection between their philosophy and their socialist politics. They have not demonstrated the possibility of socialism nor even engaged with arguments against its feasibility. The allegedly 'socialist' policy conclusions of critical realism are entirely unsubstantiated.

5.4 DOES CRITICAL REALISM SHOW THAT SOCIAL DEMOCRATIC OR FABIAN POLITICS ARE FLAWED?

Not only do Bhaskar and Collier associate critical realism with 'socialism', they also make repeated and pre-eminent efforts to distance it from political philosophies closest to socialism, namely social democracy or Fabianism. Bhaskar (1989b, p. 6) explains this rejection of social democracy:

> From the critical realist perspective, contrary to the tradition of contemporary social democracy, socialist emancipation depends on the transformation of structures, not the amelioration of states of affairs.

The suggestions here are that: (i) capitalist social structures are not conducive to emancipation; (ii) 'socialist' emancipation depends upon the transformation of structures rather than more superficial outcomes; and (iii) social democracy aspires to such superficial and ameliorative outcomes rather than to structural transformation of the system.

Critical realists have not demonstrated proposition (i). As noted above, they simply take for granted that neither markets nor the profit motive are conducive to human emancipation. They fail to explain why. Neither do they give any argument why any alternative system could be more emancipatory. Some of them praise authors such as Hayek, who proposes that capitalism is emancipatory, without showing why Hayek is wrong in this regard. Critical realists are critical of capitalism, but they have no developed critique of capitalism that connects explicitly with critical realism itself.

Having failed to demonstrate proposition (i), the burden then passes to proposition (ii), linking 'socialist' emancipation to the transformation of structures. Fair enough. But not all 'transformations of structures' are emancipatory for critical realists: they disapprove of some radical structural transformations. Accordingly, Collier (1994, p. 196) claims that the events in Eastern Europe of 1989–90 'for the most part led to economic and social developments which are the opposite of emancipatory'. But again, no further explanation is given. It is not explained in detail what 'the opposite of emancipatory' means. It is not shown why the post-1989 developments were a setback for human emancipation. Collier is also silent on whether Eastern Europe prior to 1989 was 'emancipatory' or not. Proposition (ii) fails to identify both the meaning of emancipation or the particular structures that are necessary for its fruition.

Let us then move on to proposition (iii). Clearly, it is important at this stage to ask what is and what is not a structural transformation. More fundamentally, what is a structure? We find within critical realism some answers to this question. Bhaskar (1989b, p. 4) writes of 'social structures – for instance the economy, the state, the family, language'. Archer (1995) discusses at length a demographic structure as an example of a social structure. Lawson (1997, p. 57) considers that 'the obvious candidates for social structure' include 'rules, relationships, positions and the like'.

So far, so good. Structure is an important concept in social theory. Quite reasonably, it is defined broadly within critical realism and elsewhere. Critical realists have made a major contribution to our understanding of structures. However, when they switch from socio-theoretical to normative political mode, they confuse matters or contradict themselves by narrowing down the concept of structure. For example, on the one hand, Bhaskar (1989b, p. 4) declares that language is an example of a structure, but, on the other, Collier (1994, p. 195) says 'linguistic reforms' will not 'transform structures'. One may ask if Collier's definition of structure is different from Bhaskar's?

If we stick to a broad and reasonable definition of structure, consistent with the statements of Archer, Bhaskar and Lawson, then genuine structural changes would result from factors affecting demography, such as birth control and health care, and from laws affecting such matters as work regulations, trade union rights, political decentralization, minimum wages, rent control and so forth.

Whatever the failings of social democratic governments in Europe and elsewhere – and there are many – it would be improper to suggest that they have not made major net improvements historically concerning such issues as health care, work regulations, minimum wages, gender rights, ethnic rights and political decentralization, to name a few. As a result, social democratic governments have achieved major *structural* reforms, and more than merely the 'the amelioration of states of affairs'. On this point, Bhaskar and Collier are inconsistent and wrong.[12]

---

[12] One is reminded of the type of politics satirised in *Monty Python's Life of Brian*. Reg, the leader of the Peoples' Front of Judea, addresses a meeting, declares the Romans as oppressors, and asks: 'And what have they given us in return?' Members

Critical realists may respond with the statement that social democratic governments have concerned themselves mainly with ameliorating capitalism – merely tinkering with the system rather than carrying out radical and fundamental reforms. In response, note first there is as yet no clear distinction in the critical realist literature between fundamental and superficial structural reforms. Second, Bhaskar and Collier do not make any such distinction in their rejection of social democratic and Fabian politics. Third, whether fundamental or superficial, social democracy must be credited with the achievement of important structural reforms, albeit within capitalism. Accordingly, if social democrats are to be criticized, it cannot be on the critical realist grounds that they fail to transform structures.

In an attempt to show that Fabianism and reformism are less effective that Marxian socialism, Collier (1989, p. 69) writes that the

> laws of economics and politics in a capitalist society ... trap the would-be reformers inside circles of constraint ... Marxian economic theory explains the mechanisms of this constraint, and socialist politics offers a means to their abolition: it is explained how an optimum use of resources could be made, and why this is not possible under capitalism.

However, while Marxian economic theory does indicate some constraints acting on would-be reformers, it does not elaborate how pressing those constraints are. Critical realism adds nothing on this issue. Neither Marxism nor critical realism gives any reason why the constraints under socialism would be more or less pressing than the constraints under capitalism. Contrary to Collier, in the writings of Marx there is no detailed account of the targets or mechanisms of resource allocation under socialism.

The critical realist claim that 'structural transformation sits easier with Marxist than with Fabian politics' (Collier, 1994, p. 195) is empty rhetoric. It is unsubstantiated in the critical realist literature and unworthy of critical realism as a philosophy.

Not only do critical realists wrongly argue that social democracy has not achieved structural reforms, but also they ignore the fact that there are other, quite different, political philosophies whose implementation would also involve substantial (and possibly radical) structural reforms. For example, Hayek's (1944, p. 31) proposal that the mixed economy should be replaced

---

of the meeting interrupt in turn: 'The aqueduct … And sanitation … Remember what the city used to be like … And the roads … Irrigation … Medicine … Education … And the wine … Public baths … And its safe to walk in the streets at night …' Reg retorts after each interruption and concludes: 'All right, apart from the sanitation, the medicine, education, wine, public order, irrigation, roads, the fresh water system and public health, *what have the Romans done for us?*'

by a wholesale market system, would be a major structural change. Whether progressive or regressive, it is also notable that neo-liberal governments have implemented important structural changes. For example, the government of Margaret Thatcher in Britain in the 1980s brought in punitive laws against the trade unions and greatly diminished their power. The democratically elected Metropolitan County Councils in London, Manchester and elsewhere, were simply abolished. The disastrous invasion of Iraq in 2003 by George W. Bush and Tony Blair has also overturned previous institutions. These are all structural changes, not merely 'the amelioration of states of affairs'. Critical realists may reply that these are examples of regressive structural changes, not those consistent with democracy and human emancipation. However, as we have seen, critical realism provides us with no clear criterion for deciding what is, and what is not, emancipatory or regressive.

I emphasize that I am not taking a position here for or against social democracy, for or against socialism, for or against capitalism, or for or against neo-liberalism. The point is to show that the claimed rejection by critical realists of social democratic or Fabian politics does not follow from critical realism itself.[13]

5.5 CONCLUSION

I have shown that three prominent political implications put forward in major works on critical realism are overblown or insufficiently substantiated (*A*), or simply false (*B* and *C*). The attempts of critical realism to make a 'quick move' from theory to policy are largely ineffective. The establishment of such policy positions would require a level and extent of enquiry hitherto largely unexplored in the critical realist literature. The emancipatory claims of critical realism are somewhat deflated by its inability to provide adequate criteria to assess different types of policy.

Would critical realism be strengthened or weakened by the abandonment of these normative propositions? I have no doubt that, as a scholarly contribution to our understanding, it would be strengthened. False claims weaken a doctrine. Their abandonment would help to broaden the appeal of critical realism beyond a narrow circle of revolutionary Marxists, sharing hostility to social democracy as much as to anything else. The removal of unsubstantiated ideological decorations would enhance the scholarly credentials of critical realism. It would not prevent individual critical realists believing in socialism or being hostile to social democracy. But they would have to abandon the claim that such political stances are supported or

---

[13] My own political position is irrelevant to this argument. Those interested in my normative views are directed to the final chapter of Hodgson (1999a).

justified by their critical realism. Critical realists would take the more reasonable position that their philosophy, instead of leading directly to specific policies, has some autonomy from the policy realm.

My worry, however, is that critical realism is not simply an academic doctrine but also an ideological movement, with its own institutional identity and characteristics, both within and beyond its academic sanctuary. A cultist trace to critical realism is regrettably evident in its unsubstantiated hostility to social democracy and by its narrow and repeated proclamations of an undefined and equally unsubstantiated 'socialist' alternative. Critical realists tell me that theirs is an essentially 'emancipatory' project. If critical realism is less of a scholarly doctrine and more of an ideological movement, then its political posturing may help it to gain more followers. But this will not add to its scientific credibility. I hope that these excesses are mere aberrations, and that my worries will prove unfounded.

6. Contestable Claims by Critical Realism in Economics

> Philosophy is a battle against the bewitchment of our intelligence by means of language.
>
> Ludwig Wittgenstein

6.1 INTRODUCTION

Critical realism has been widely debated.[1] It is not the primary goal of this chapter to discuss its core ideas. Instead, the aim here is to examine some of the theoretical claims made on behalf of critical realism, when used as guidance for economics as a discipline.

Two 'critical realist' examples are chosen and compared, one taken from the work of Andrew Collier (1989) and the other from the work of Tony Lawson (1997). Differences in stance within critical realism become immediately apparent. On the one hand, Collier argues that critical realism directly supports a particular theory – Marx's law of the tendency of the rate of profit to fall. On the other hand, Lawson is more circumspect. He explores only one 'illustration' of critical realism. He suggests that it is 'illustrated' by the theory that a prevalent form of workplace organization in Britain helped to bring about Britain's relative industrial decline. Lawson (1997, pp. 247, 326) claims that such a theory seems 'broadly consistent with critical realism' but adds a significant qualification in a footnote to the beginning of his 'illustration' chapter:

> Substantive explanations, then, even when serving illustrative purposes, ought not be tagged 'critical realist'. Nor, incidentally, should they be interpreted as constituting evidence by which the critical realist explanatory framework is itself to be assessed. ... In short, the examples and discussion which follow merely provide ... an indication that explanatory endeavours consistent with critical realism are feasible in the social realm.

This is a welcome qualification concerning the theoretical impact of Lawson's methodology. Collier is more definitive; he sees critical realism as

---

[1] See for example Baert (1996), Brown *et al.* (2001), Faulkner (2002), Fleetwood (1998), Lewis (1996, 2004), Nash (2004), Runde (1998), Walters and Young (1999). An earlier version of this chapter appeared as Hodgson (2004b).

positively supporting at least one specific theory. In contrast, Lawson sees the association between theory and critical realism as largely negative, in that critical realism is used to reject some theories, leaving a sizeable set of different theories that are compatible with critical realism. A purpose of the present chapter is to argue that while Lawson's position is preferable to Collier's, the set of remaining theories is even larger than suggested by Lawson, and critical realism has even less discriminatory power at the theoretical level than Lawson suggests. This is because at least one of the important rival theories of British industrial decline rejected by Lawson is in fact consistent with critical realism.

The 'critical realist explanatory framework', as such, is not assessed here. Nevertheless, positive claims have been made by critical realists: that (a) critical realism supports Marx's theory of the falling rate of profit (Collier, 1989), and (b) critical realism is 'illustrated' by the workplace organization theory of the relative decline of the British economy (Lawson, 1997). There are two additional negative claims, namely when (c) Collier (1989) and (d) Lawson (1997) *reject* some alternative theories or explanations, seeing them as inconsistent with critical realism.

Critical realists range between (i) making claims concerning 'implications' or 'illustrations' of critical realism of the above type, and (ii) stressing that no philosophy (critical realism included) can provide detailed or substantial theoretical or policy implications. I believe that philosophy can only bc a guide on such matters; it cannot generate theory or policy on its own. Lawson himself seems to take this view, but then in the name of critical realism he rejects some theories and associates his philosophical argument with one particular theory taken from economics. In contrast, as shown in the preceding chapter, Bhaskar and Collier make more exaggerated theoretical and policy claims on behalf of critical realism.

If Lawson is right in his assertion that a whole range of possible theories is consistent with critical realism, then a number of important questions still remain. Among these are the following: why do these authors choose and concentrate upon these particular examples in critical realist writings? In what sense can such examples 'illustrate' critical realism? And why are some particular alternative theories or explanations rejected?

Rather than attacking critical realism directly, this chapter focuses on the four claims (a), (b), (c) and (d), as well as the questions raised above. A crucial part of the argument here is to show that alternative theories, rejected respectively by Collier and Lawson, are *also consistent with critical realism*. In particular, contrary to the arguments of Collier and Lawson, it is argued that an (untenable) 'law of the tendency of the rate of profit to rise' (implicitly countered by Collier) and the (plausible) 'management failure thesis' (explicitly rejected by Lawson) are both consistent with critical realism, when suitably formulated.

While no overall verdict is pronounced here on critical realism as a philosophical approach, these case studies provide some insights concerning critical realism as a 'movement' or 'project'.[2] Accordingly, after looking at the two case studies, some observations are made in the concluding section concerning the character of critical realism, especially as it is presented to academic economists.

6.2 DOES CRITICAL REALISM SUPPORT MARX'S THEORY OF THE FALLING RATE OF PROFIT? OR COULD A THEORY OF A *RISING* RATE OF PROFIT BE CONSISTENT WITH CRITICAL REALISM?

In his *Scientific Realism and Socialist Thought*, Collier (1989, pp. 66–7) refers to Marx's 'law of the tendency of the rate of profit to fall' as an illustration of his philosophical approach. According to Collier, my arguments against this alleged Marxist 'law' are wrong, and inconsistent with critical realism. I claim the contrary, on both counts.

In chapters 13–15 in the third volume of *Capital*, Marx (1981) tried to reveal a tendency, rooted in the structures of the capitalism, for the rate of profit to fall. Marx defined the general rate of profit as the total amount of profit (or 'surplus value') divided by the total value of the fixed and circulating capital advanced by the capitalists.[3] The general rate of profit is the rate of return on investment for the capitalist class as a whole. Marx argued that capitalism has a tendency, as capital accumulates and technical progress advances, to substitute machinery for labour. In other words, production becomes more machine-intensive. In turn, Marx assumed that this results in a tendency for the value of capital goods (or 'constant capital') per worker-hour to increase. He argued that the denominator in the expression for the general rate of profit would tend to increase more rapidly than the numerator. According to Marx, there is a consequent underlying tendency for the general rate of profit to fall within capitalism.

---

[2] Such terms are employed by critical realists themselves, e.g. Lewis (2004).

[3] The reader may choose whether 'value' is defined in terms of money or in terms of 'socially necessary embodied labour time', and whether or not they are equivalent. To resolve this question would raise the controversial issue of the labour theory of value, which in fact we do not need to discuss here. Although I am a critic of this theory (Hodgson, 1982b), the reader may prefer to assume that the labour theory of value is valid. Alternatively, one may assume otherwise. For the purpose of this discussion of the falling rate of profit, nothing of immediate importance hinges on this question.

He clearly believed that this tendency would eventually be manifest empirically. Marx (1981, p. 337) wrote: 'In practice, the rate of profit will fall in the long run'. It was not simply an 'underlying tendency' that never surfaced in the actual world. For Marx, in critical realist terminology, the law ultimately operated at the 'empirical' and 'actual' levels. However, Marx was rightly aware that any economic 'law' is a propensity, rooted in economic structures, rather than a sequence of empirical events.

Marx (1981, pp. 339–48) went on to discuss some 'counteracting factors' or 'counteracting influences' that would supposedly delay or ameliorate any fall in the rate of profit. One of these is the 'cheapening of the elements of constant capital'. Alongside a supposed tendency of capitalism to increase the physical quantity or complexity of machinery per worker, Marx also recognized the tendency for the physical quantity of output per worker to increase. In other words, by some appropriate measure, labour productivity has a tendency to increase.

As a result of these productivity increases, the (monetary) value of (or socially necessary labour time embodied in) each physical unit of capital goods would decrease. Consequently, this 'cheapening of the elements of constant capital' means that the physical mass of capital goods per worker might increase but this may not necessarily result in an increase in the (monetary or labour) *value* of that constant capital. As Marx (1981, p. 343) put it: 'In certain cases, the mass of the constant capital elements may increase while their total value remains the same or even falls'.

In other words, the denominator of the expression of the rate of profit may not increase, and the 'counteracting factors' may nullify a fall in the rate of profit. Marx accepted that the 'counteracting factors' might be sufficiently strong to maintain or increase the rate of profit for a while. Nevertheless, he upheld that 'the rate of profit will fall in the long run'. Marx discussed the interaction between the 'the law of the tendency of the rate of profit to fall' and the labelled 'counteracting factors' at length. Sometimes he considered cases where the 'counteracting factors' hold sway. But he still proclaimed falling profits and crises as the outcome (Marx, 1981, p. 375).

To draw his conclusion, Marx had to assume that the 'tendency of the rate of profit to fall' eventually dominates the 'counteracting factors'. Critical realists might interpret Marx as saying that the 'tendency' has some kind of eventual causal dominance over the 'counteracting factors'.

Marx's supposed 'law' has been criticized by a number of authors.[4] There are several key arguments against the law. One of the principal counter-arguments is quite simple: there is no reason given by Marx why the

---

[4] See Sweezy (1942), Okishio (1961), Hodgson (1974), Steedman (1977), Van Parijs (1980) and Bowles (1981). Blaug (1980, pp. 43–7; 1997a, pp. 235–40) provides incisive summaries of the debates.

'tendency of the rate of profit to fall' will eventually win out over the 'counteracting factors'. There is no reason why one has causal priority, is more fundamental than, or dominates the other.

In addition, the tendency of capitalism to increase labour productivity is also likely to cheapen the elements of constant capital. This cheapening of capital goods may overwhelm the forces acting on the rate of profit in the opposite direction, and the rate of profit may thus rise. There are forces acting in both directions, and we have no reason to assume that the downward acting forces will have a tendency to win out over those acting in the opposite direction. There is no basis to claim a principal tendency for the rate of profit to fall, or a principal tendency for it to rise.

After the brief post-1968 revival of Marxism, the debate over Marx's law reached a peak in the 1970s. Subsequently, the debate subsided after the supporters of the law failed to refute the counter-arguments. The defenders of the law failed to provide a single reason why there should be a tendency – manifest empirically or otherwise – for the denominator in the rate of profit equation to increase faster than the numerator. They failed to provide a single argument to show why the alleged principal 'tendency', depending on a sufficiently rapid increase in the value of the capital goods per worker, was more fundamental or important than the alleged 'counteracting factors', including the cheapening of those capital goods. Accordingly, Philippe Van Parijs's (1980) careful summary of the debate was appropriately entitled 'an obituary' for Marx's law.

Some years later, Collier (1989) enters the fray, bringing critical realism into the dispute. Strangely, he does not identify any of the critical works against Marx's law that are cited above. Remarkably, he chooses just one critic as an adversary – myself. But he does not cite my 1974 article, which is my only work devoted entirely to criticism of Marx's law. Instead, he addresses a later essay of mine (Hodgson, 1982a) that does not enter into detailed discussion over the law, and concerns itself instead with other issues. In other words, among a host of works critical of Marx's law, the work chosen as the object of Collier's critical realist counter-attack, is a single article that is not even principally devoted to criticizing that law.

Collier (1989, p. 67) rightly argues that 'there is a multitude of generative mechanisms at work' and says quite reasonably that 'science must necessarily *abstract from* some of them to formulate laws, while remembering that the concrete situation is always a *conjuncture* … of several interacting processes'. Fair enough. But that does not give us a law of the rate of profit to *fall* any more than it gives us a law of the rate of profit to *rise*.

Collier seems to think that simply by mentioning the magic concept of abstraction that he has clinched the matter. But there is no justification to simply jump from the statement that there are 'several interacting processes' and the outcome 'is multiply determined' to the statement that 'there is a mechanism in capitalism which necessarily generates a tendency of the rate of profit to fall' (Collier, 1989, p. 68). What Collier seems to be arguing – although it is far from clear – is that the economist must (for some unspecified reason) focus on the forces acting in a downward direction, leaving the upward-acting forces out of vision, so as to derive 'the law of the tendency of the rate of profit to fall'.

But abstraction can cut both ways. In contrast to Collier, one could choose to focus on the tendency of capitalism to increase labour productivity and to thereby cheapen the elements of constant capital, thus 'abstracting from' the forces with an opposite result on the rate of profit. In this case, to use another useful critical realist phrase, increasing labour productivity in the production of capital goods is the 'generative mechanism' upon which I choose to focus. Neither Marx nor Collier gives any reason why these forces, which tend to cheapen the value of capital goods, should be regarded as less deeply rooted in the structures of capitalism. Neither Marx nor Collier gives any reason why one set of tendencies results from a 'generative mechanism' and the other does not. Marx focuses arbitrarily on one set, abstracting from the other. My alternative 'abstraction' in this paragraph is equally arbitrary. I here describe the tendency to cheapen constant capital as resulting from the 'generative mechanisms' of increasing productivity, and 'abstract from' those forces tending to bring down the rate of profit.

Hey presto! According to the same critical realist methodology, I formulate 'the law of the tendency of the rate of profit to rise'. The basic structure of the 'abstraction' argument in the last two paragraphs is identical. The conclusions are equally phoney. None of them proves a 'law' that has any special status over tendencies working in the opposite direction.

It is reasonable to ask why Marx and his defenders give the downward pressing forces the description and implied status of a 'law' and those that press in the opposite direction are labelled 'counteracting factors'. It is not enough simply to *describe* forces pushing downwards as 'laws' or 'tendencies' and those pressing upwards as merely 'counteracting factors'. This is an arbitrary, unwarranted and misleading labelling. In an equally unjustified and arbitrary manner, the labels in Marx's theory could be switched, giving the 'cheapening of the elements of constant capital' a higher status, calling those acting to push down the rate of profit 'counteracting factors'. This would also result in 'the law of the tendency of the rate of profit to rise'. Given that Marx's labelling of one as the 'law' and the other set of forces as 'counteracting' is entirely arbitrary, by the same canon we can arbitrarily switch the labels, giving the opposite result (Hodgson, 1974, p. 76). I made this label-switching argument over thirty years ago. No defender of Marx's law has ever given an adequate reply.

To show why 'there is a mechanism in capitalism which necessarily generates a tendency of the rate of profit to fall' Collier needs to show why the 'downward' set of forces dominates the forces acting in the reverse direction. Only then will the choice of 'abstraction' cease to be arbitrary. But no text from critical realism gives any guidance on this particular question. To use the language of critical realism: we have two sets of 'generative mechanisms' or forces. There are 'generative mechanisms' acting to push *down* the rate of profit. In addition, there are 'generative mechanisms' – resulting from a tendency within capitalism for labour productivity to increase – acting to push *up* the rate of profit. Concerning the rate of profit, why give one set of 'generative mechanisms', any higher (or lower) ontological, law-like or explanatory status than the other? Critical realism has not yet provided an adequate methodology to help us to find an answer.

But I hear a possible critical realist response to this – the sound of falling leaves. It might be argued that the law of gravity acts to make the leaf fall, but this outcome might be suspended or countered by wind wafting it upwards. However, falling leaves are not the same things as falling profits, and they involve different types of causal mechanism. In particular, in the physical world, gravity and the wind are not the same kind of causal mechanism and they operate on different ontological levels. Wind is an emergent property of huge collections of gas particles, whereas gravity applies to every single particle in the universe. In this sense, the law of gravity acting on a leaf is more fundamental than the wind wafting it upwards. This is because the forces of gravity, while varying, are always present whenever two or more masses are in proximity. On the contrary, a wind depends on the existence of an atmosphere and the direct collusion of the atmospheric particles with the object. Accordingly, physics has developed a theory of the motion of a body in a vacuum, prior to amending it to include any contingent atmospheric forces.

In contrast, in the economic domain, there is no basis whatsoever to give those forces that would lead to a fall in the rate of profit any higher law-like, causal or explanatory status than the increases in the productivity of capital goods that tend to increase the profit rate. Critical realism does not tell us which has priority over the other. Its method of abstraction can lead just as much to 'the law of the tendency of the rate of profit to rise'. Critical realism does not support the 'law of the tendency of the rate of profit to fall' neither does it show that the criticisms of the law are invalid.

The error in Collier's account is to jump from the valid proposition that tendencies are not always realized at the level of events to the arbitrary choice of one particular tendency among several. He fails to show that other countervailing tendencies – whether or not realized at the level of events – are unimportant. The ontology of tendencies does not give us licence to choose some tendencies and ignore others. But Collier, following Marx, gives just one tendency unwarranted law-like status.

There is a finale to all this. Immediately following his attempted rebuttal of my criticisms, and in concluding his discussion of the falling rate of profit, Collier writes: 'nor does it mean that that we can't forecast with some degree of confidence that capitalism will collapse'. This is a curious and symptomatic double negative. It seems that Collier would like to assert that we *can* forecast with some degree of confidence that capitalism will collapse. When critics, such as myself, point out that we are unable to predict the actual tendency of the rate of profit we are then lectured about scientific method. We are told that we should ignore empirical manifestations and focus on the deeper 'generative mechanisms'. In contrast, Collier himself is seemingly allowed to move to the empirical level and invite a 'forecast with some degree of confidence that capitalism will collapse' without giving any valid reason for such a forecast.

Collier is wrong about 'the law of the tendency of the rate of profit to fall'. And critical realism, *per se*, gives us valid arguments neither for nor against this alleged 'law'. At the crucial point, in deciding which set of forces might have priority over the others, it gives us no guidance. Additional arguments would be required, extraneous to critical realism, at least as we know it so far. In sum, contrary to Collier, critical realism offers no support to Marx's theory on this question.

6.3 IS CRITICAL REALISM ILLUSTRATED BY THE WORKPLACE ORGANIZATION THEORY OF THE RELATIVE DECLINE OF THE BRITISH ECONOMY? DOES CRITICAL REALISM LEAD TO A REJECTION OF THE MANAGEMENT FAILURE THESIS?

In his *Economics and Reality*, Lawson (1997) presents a major statement on critical realism and its significance for economics. In an era when many economists have lost their way in mathematical puzzles, forgetting that their science should be principally concerned to understand and explain economic phenomena in the real world, Lawson's book comes as salutary reading. But it is not my concern here to assess this volume overall. What I am concerned to do is to look at the implications of the approach that Lawson attempts to develop for the practice of economic science. Apart from making a case against mathematical formalism in economics, Lawson makes some illustrated claims concerning the application of critical realism as an adjudicator in theoretical disputes.

However, there are several remarkable omissions from his discussion of the possible implications of critical realism. There is no consideration, for example, of different theories of price or value, of monetarism versus Keynesianism, of the causes of economic growth, or of many of the prominent theoretical questions that have concerned economists in recent decades. To move beyond criticism of the mainstream to the construction of an alternative, we are left asking how critical realism may, more specifically, guide the choice or construction of economic theory.

I sympathize with Lawson, because he is in a difficult position here. As I know from my own attempts to criticize aspects of mainstream economics, the response is typically: 'What, then, are the implications of *your* approach? What do *you* propose instead?' The critic is then seemingly faced with the impossible task of rebuilding economic theory single-handed. In practice, the most that can reasonably be expected is a few illustrations of the implications of the proposed alternative approach.

When Lawson (1997) turns to such illustrations, he chooses just *one* application of critical realism to a theoretical controversy in economics. This is the debate concerning the causes of the long-term relative decline of the British economy. Lawson's choice of this example is understandable: some time ago he himself made a major contribution to this debate. But it may be unwise to stake all on just one (challengeable) illustration.

In a major formulation of the workplace organization thesis, Andrew Kilpatrick and Tony Lawson (1980) argue that worker resistance to technological and workplace change in Britain, based largely on the strength of trade union organization and the decentralized nature of collective bargaining, contributed substantially and cumulatively to Britain's loss of its world lead in several of its manufacturing sectors. There is much evidence in support of this argument and it has considerable plausibility. Similar or related arguments have been put forward by Andrew Glyn and Robert Sutcliffe (1972), David Purdy (1976) and G. Bernard Stafford (1983), among others. In his 1997 book, Lawson argues that this account is rooted in the social structures of work organization and conforms to the explanatory requirements of critical realism. His claim is that the workplace organization thesis is an 'illustration' of critical realism because it is an 'empirically grounded' explanation of a social phenomenon that is 'couched in terms of structures and mechanisms that are reproduced overtime, where that reproduction is itself explained' (Lawson, 1997, p. 247).

The first problem is that there are *several* competing explanations of Britain's relative industrial decline from the nineteenth to the mid-twentieth century. Some theories may be rejected on the grounds that they are implausible, misconceived, denied by the evidence, or internally logically inconsistent. Some of the remaining multiple explanations may be mutually incompatible. In which case some further explanations have to be rejected, on the basis of their false assumptions or whatever. But, after these processes of filtering, we still may be left with a substantial number of plausible theories. The remaining set will contain theories which are potentially complementary, leading to the possibility of multiple and logically compatible explanations of a single complex phenomenon (Mäki, 1997).

Consider some prominent alternative explanations of the British relative decline. Studies have pointed to low investment and productivity in manufacturing (Kaldor, 1966), the institutional schism between the City and industry (Hobsbawm, 1968; Ingham, 1984), the low skill levels in British management (Caves, 1980; Landes, 1969; Wiener, 1981; J. F. Wilson, 1995), or the sclerotic nature of British economic and political institutions (Choi, 1983; Elbaum and Lazonick, 1986; Hodgson, 1989, 1996).

In assessing these different explanations, we may ask, first of all, is a plausible causal explanation offered? Even if the answer is in the affirmative, the problems of theory choice do not end there. We may end up with several viable causal explanations. We may not be able to exclude any more of them. They may be mutually compatible. We may reach the conclusion that the remaining explanations may *all* be causally operative. The problem, then, is how do we decide among them: which are the more important? We have a number of causal arrows. The problem is to determine which are the strongest and thickest in the circumstances.

This problem of comparative causal assessment among potentially compatible theories is ubiquitous in economics. Take the problem of unemployment as an example. Collier (1994, p. 171) rightly rejects the 'fecklessness' theory of unemployment. However, some individuals may in fact be unemployed because they are feckless. Some may be too lazy to get a job – that being a major reason for their idleness. But this does not mean that the fecklessness theory of unemployment is generally correct. The theory remains generally invalid partly because it points only to a very minor causal arrow. Some unemployment *is* caused by fecklessness, but the fecklessness theory is wrong as the principal explanation of unemployment. It fails to explain the sudden increases in unemployment in recessions and the durability and scale of this mass phenomenon. We do not refute the fecklessness theory of unemployment because it fails to identify any causal link. We refute it because the causal link is of relatively little significance.

A similar problem arises, for example, in the debate between monetarist and rival theories of inflation. I am not aware of any economist who has denied that an expansion in the money supply can have inflationary consequences. No one has denied the possibility of a causal link between the supply of money and the price level. Instead, the debate between monetarists and Keynesians is over whether the money supply is, or is not, *the most important causal mechanism* involved in forcing up prices.

Jochen Runde (1998) usefully discusses the problem of assessing causal explanations from a critical realist perspective. Judiciously, he does not claim too much. From a realist viewpoint, Runde is clearly able to dismiss causal explanations that depend upon unreal idealizations 'that have no existence other than in the minds and discourse of scientific investigators' (p. 159). He further argues that candidate factors should be 'causally effective', be 'sufficient' and have 'causal depth'. These are important arguments, but they do not take us as far as some may wish. Runde admits that the 'the prospects for a universal method of assessing causal explanations are … poor' (p. 165) and the 'principles used to assess causal explanations … will often not have sufficient bite, to discriminate unambiguously between competing causal explanations. … there will always be situations in which it is not possible to identify one explanation as unambiguously superior to its rivals' (p. 168). His paper does not show that critical realism has very much more to add here. This is not necessarily devastating for critical realism, but it should encourage some much needed modesty from some other critical realists on what can be claimed for their philosophy.

Critical realism rightly emphasizes the importance of causal mechanisms, but it gives us little guidance to assess the importance of one causal link compared with another. It emphasizes underlying social structures, but even this does not clearly indicate what is more important or fundamental. It can be argued that this is not the task of critical realism: philosophy cannot legislate for science. If so, then in what sense is Lawson's single chosen example of a causal explanation of Britain's relative industrial decline an 'illustration' *of critical realism*? The meaning and very possibility of such an illustration is called into question.

Let us return to the assessment of the specific causes of Britain's relative industrial decline. Lawson (1997, p. 256) makes the claim that:

> The most comprehensive attempt, that I am aware of, to *compare* the explanatory powers of the range of theories, has been carried out by Stafford (1983). This author deduces implications which would follow if the different theories considered were true, and checks each out empirically in the appropriate context. On the basis of a wealth of detailed evidence … this author concludes in favour of an explanation which attributes at least part of the responsibility for the experience of relatively slow growth in the UK to the … far more highly decentralized system of collective bargaining compared to that which emerged elsewhere, along with the associated relatively localised nature of worker organisation in the UK.

At first sight this seems an attempt to answer the problem of comparative causal assessment. Lawson cites Stafford, who does in fact give some explanatory precedence to the workplace organization thesis.[5]

---

[5] Lawson's over-dependence on the now outdated study by Stafford (1983) tempts him to exaggerate slightly. Stafford does not compare all major theories of the British decline. Stafford skips over the management failure thesis and is chronologically unable to deal with Ingham's (1984) sophisticated study of the role

Note Lawson's precise claim here. After comparing the explanatory powers of different theories, on the basis of an alleged 'wealth of detailed evidence' Stafford is said to conclude 'in favour of an explanation which attributes *at least part of the responsibility*' (emphasis added) to the relatively localized pattern of collective bargaining and worker organization in the UK.[6] However, saying that we have identified a cause that is partly responsible for a phenomenon is not saying that we have identified the most important cause of the phenomenon. We cannot yet exclude the possibility that other factors were more important in causing the relatively slow growth of the British economy. It is necessary to deal with the crucial problem of comparative causal assessment among competing and potentially compatible theories. This is especially the case if we wish to draw policy conclusions.

In principle, Lawson does not exclude other explanations from being part of the picture. Lawson (1997, p. 236) insists that there is 'a world of difference between leaving something (temporally) out of focus and treating it as though it does not exist'. But in his discussion of British industrial decline he leaves other possible mechanisms permanently out of the picture.

He attempts to exclude these alternatives on methodological grounds. Lawson (1997, p. 257) argues that the 'structure' of British work organization empowered worker resistance to technological change. 'In short, the explanation in question focuses on a set of structures that empowers workers (as well as others) to exercise a significant effect on all manner of outcomes'. Having emphasized structure, he writes that a 'social explanation which ignores the social reproduction of causally efficacious structures will often be too partial to constitute an adequate or sufficiently comprehensive understanding' (p. 268). However, while this persuasive methodological

---

of City in the British decline, or with the institutionalist approach of Elbaum and Lazonick (1986). Yet, fourteen pages later, Lawson (1997, p. 270) is again found overstating the case when he refers to Stafford 'as an example where competing hypothesis of Britain's relative productivity performance have already been assessed according to their relative empirical grounding'. On the contrary, Stafford's early and preliminary assessment of the empirical evidence hardly closes the issue. His single table of figures and his citation of a few historical studies is hardly 'a wealth of detailed evidence' as Lawson describes. Stafford (1983, p. 17) himself says that the 'evidence is certainly not abundant'. There are more detailed data in Caves (1980, p. 173) who found 'strong statistical evidence to support the negative influence on industrial productivity of both poor labor-management relations and deficiencies in British management'. For more recent evidence on managerial failure in the UK see Grinyer *et al.* (1998) and Sisson and Marginson (1996).

[6] Other than 'part of the responsibility', the only other possible meaning here of 'at least part of the responsibility' is 'all the responsibility'. Does Lawson wish to imply that there is just one cause of the relative decline of the UK? If not, then the phrase 'at least' is redundant here.

injunction would find some explanations inadequate, the workplace organization thesis is not the only explanation to conform to it. Several alternative theories would pass his methodological test.

Lawson admits the possibility of alternative or complementary explanations, but still does his best to raise the workplace organization thesis to the highest profile. The manner in which this is done is partly by exclusion. A host of alternative explanations, including Geoffrey Ingham's (1984) study of the financial role of the City of London, and my own focus on institutional rigidities (Hodgson, 1989) are simply omitted from Lawson's *Economics and Reality* (1997). Of course, it would be impossible to mention all possible rival theories. Nevertheless, any selectivity does give the impression that the preferred theory has some special status above the rest. Otherwise, why is it selected?

The second of Lawson's tactics is to belittle other competing or more inclusive explanations, by suggesting that they fail his methodological tests. This is how Lawson (1997, p. 270) addresses the management failure thesis:

> If ... British management is really somehow less capable or more complacent ... then presumably those brought in from overseas ... should be found to be associated with productivity performances that are frequently notably better.

But the conclusion does not follow from the premise. In the above passage, Lawson treats managers as if they are social atoms, who retain their individual competencies or inadequacies, as they are moved from one context to another. Even if some proponents have made this mistake, it is wrong to reduce the arguments and evidence of British management failure to matters of individual capability or complacency that derive from the individuals alone. On the contrary, a fairer treatment of the argument that British managers are less capable or more complacent would treat it on the same intellectual level as Lawson's own argument that British workers have been more militant and less accommodating to change.

To show this, let us treat workers as if they are social atoms, with unchanging capacities to resist in different contexts, and argue hypothetically that workers brought in from overseas are more accommodating, and British workers who emigrate retain their propensity to resist. If the above quoted passage by Lawson (1997, p. 270) is a valid objection to the management failure thesis, then the last sentence is a valid objection to the workplace organization thesis.

Neither argument is convincing. Both objections ignore the structural constraints and institutional determinations of managerial or worker behaviour. Lawson's rejection of the management failure thesis fails, because it ignores these in regard to managerial behaviour. He is inconsistent in his criteria of theory assessment and his comparative assessment of the two theories is inadequate. It may be that versions of the management failure thesis are equally 'illustrative' of critical realism. We have no reason to assume otherwise.

Importantly, underlying structural and institutional factors are included in some accounts of entrepreneurial or management failure in Britain. For example, in a sophisticated and multi-faceted institutional analysis, Bernard Elbaum and William Lazonick (1986, p. 2) write:

> We attribute the decline of the British economy in the twentieth century to rigidities in the economic and social institutions that developed during the nineteenth century … Britain's problem … was that economic decision-makers, lacking the individual or collective means to alter existing constraints, in effect took them as 'given'. In failing to confront institutional constraints innovatively, British businessmen can justifiably be accused of 'entrepreneurial failure'. But this failure cannot be adequately explained by reference to cultural conservatism, despite the frequency of such assertions. … Britain's failure derived less from the conservatism of its cultural values *per se* than from a matrix of rigid institutional structures that reinforced these values and obstructed individualistic as well as collective efforts at economic renovation.

It is abundantly clear from this quotation that managerial or entrepreneurial failure is seen as rooted in social and economic institutions, and contrary to Lawson's critical depiction, it is not merely a matter of the personal or psychological propensities of atomistic individuals.

In a brief and restrictive discussion of some of the alternative theories, Lawson (1997, p. 269) admits: 'To the extent that such claims can be supported empirically and are complementary to the sort of explanation identified here there is no problem'. But again he gives little guidance as to the way in which we may assess the relative importance of each causal mechanism involved. The nearest we get to an answer to this crucial question is right at the end of the relevant chapter, where he writes of 'relative empirical grounding' as a basis of comparative theory assessment. A theory would be supported if it 'is found to be the most empirically adequate' (Lawson, 1997, p. 270). But the precise test of empirical adequacy is unclear. These words are extremely inadequate, and do nothing to exclude a whole host of rival explanations of Britain's relative economic decline. Above all, Lawson's account of critical realism in economics does not show us how to engage in the crucial task of comparative causal assessment. As yet, critical realism is far from grounding and demonstrating the particular theoretical conclusions that it uses as exemplars, or to which it declares allegiance.

This argument does not resolve the debate over British relative economic decline but shows that critical realism does not especially countenance the particular explanation favoured by Lawson. In particular, Lawson's attempt to exclude the important 'management failure thesis', using critical realist tools, fails. Contrary to Lawson, there is nothing that is essential to the 'management failure thesis' that is inconsistent with critical realism.

Critical realism is useful in helping to exclude some explanations, particularly those with inadequate causal explanations. But as so far constructed it leaves us, not only with a substantial set of remaining and contrasting theories, but also without adequate means to discriminate between them, on explanatory or empirical terms. Lawson's attempt to use critical realism to discriminate between the 'management failure thesis' and his own preferred theory is a failure.

Critical realism is in danger of claiming too much by stressing and focusing upon one explanation. As Lawson (1997, p. 268) himself admits, he has been too 'partial' on this question. Lawson wavers between presenting the workplace organization thesis as one explanation among many, and presenting the thesis as a front runner by ignoring or attempting to reject other theories. In fact, critical realism gives us no reason to exclude or belittle alternative explanations. Critical realism has not shown that alternative theories – such as managerial failure, or institutional sclerosis – are less plausible or powerful. As yet, critical realism has not led us to any particular explanation of Britain's industrial decline. Furthermore, it has not shown us how to assess the relative causal weights of several plausible and possibly complementary theories. As Lawson (1997, pp. 270–1) himself admits, the task is not yet done.

6.4 CONCLUDING REMARKS

We have examined two case studies of critical realism and their claimed implications or illustrations for economics. Here are the results:

A1. Collier's claim that critical realism supports Marx's 'law of the tendency of the rate of profit to fall' is not based on an assessment of the appropriate critical literature and powerful key arguments against Marx's law are ignored.

A2. Using the same critical realist arguments and terminology, it is possible to formulate an (equally dubious) 'law of the tendency of the rate of profit to rise'. Consequently, critical realism is compatible with both Marx's law and its opposite.

B1. Lawson claims that critical realism is 'illustrated' by the workplace organization explanation of the relative decline of the British economy. His version of the workplace organization thesis passes a critical realist test, by pointing to underlying structures and causal mechanisms.

B2. The problem is that a substantial number of other theories would also seem to pass the test, and critical realism provides no good reason for excluding them. Above all, critical realism, as so far formulated, fails at the crucial point of comparative causal assessment of rival and potentially complementary theories.

B3. Lawson argues against the 'management failure thesis'. However, this alternative theory, when properly formulated, is also consistent with critical realism. Consequently, critical realism is compatible with at least two theories, including one that is rejected by Lawson.

C. Consequently, considering both case studies, critical realism has not yet developed adequate criteria to distinguish between rival alternative explanations, at least in two foremost areas of study chosen by its exponents.

It does not follow from the above propositions that critical realism is unfruitful or has to be rejected. The point of this chapter is not to challenge critical realism as such, but to criticize some claims that are allegedly based upon it. Consequently, leading and other critical realists (including Bhaskar, Collier and Lawson) should be more careful in making explanatory, normative or illustrative claims on behalf of their philosophy. Whether or not critical realism is a sound and useful approach, exaggerated claims on its behalf will not help its advancement in the scholarly community. Furthermore, if explanatory or other stronger claims are to be made for critical realism, then more attention has to be made to developing the criteria for comparative assessment of theories or policies. As a scholarly approach, critical realism would not be weakened if critical realists were much more cautious about their claims of theoretical or policy implications.

At the methodological level, critical realism succeeds in being able to criticize and exclude some theories, on the grounds that they do not point to viable causal mechanisms. However, in a number of respects, including the key question of relative causal importance, critical realism gives us no adequate means of discrimination between a number of different and plausible theories. Consequently, the claimed theoretical 'illustration' of critical realism is somewhat limited in its impact.

Critical realists make much of the concept of abstraction. But the two examples discussed here show that the question of abstraction is problematic. I am not arguing against the value of abstraction: it is a necessary feature of all science. The problem is that critical realism gives no clear and adequate guideline concerning what abstractions are appropriate. For example, it has been shown above that the criteria provided by Collier for abstracting the more powerful tendencies causing the rate of profit to rise, could equally well apply to those causing it to fall. Similarly, Lawson focuses on the workplace organization theory of the British economic decline, but gives no adequate reason for downplaying several other causal mechanisms and explanations. The upshot of the two case studies discussed above is that critical realism does not as yet provide enough guidance on the question of abstraction to overcome these more concrete difficulties.

I wish to raise another question here. Collier's adherence to Marxism as well as to critical realism is obvious from his writings. It is also perhaps no accident that the single theory that Lawson chose to 'illustrate' critical realism is one prominently described as a 'Marxist view' (Coates and Hillard, 1986). The workplace organization thesis found favour among many Marxists because it suggested two stark political alternatives: *either* to smash the organized resistance of the working class and restore capitalism to greater profitability, *or* to support a socialist worker's revolution. In their dislike of reformist compromises, Marxists have a preference for such stark choices. But the reasoning behind them does not always stand up to critical examination.

This failure to choose additional 'illustrations', outside the orbit of what is widely described as 'Marxist' is symptomatic of something else going on within critical realism. It is notable, that prominent theoretical claims and 'illustrations' of critical realism are generally of a Marxist character, even if not all critical realists are declared Marxists. To this we may add the statements of Bhaskar and Collier, cited in the previous chapter, which associate critical realism with some form of socialism and with a rejection 'of contemporary social democracy'. The socialist and Marxist overtones of much (but not all) critical realist writing are blatant.

Critical realism as a philosophy, at least as so far developed, does not support such stances. But also, given these symptoms, it is also appropriate to examine their causal origin. The 'sociology' of critical realism as a 'movement' is a suitable topic for study. For many, the apparent attraction of critical realism may be that it appears to combine a radical leftist policy stance with apparent philosophical sophistication.

7. The Problem of Formalism in Economics

> Modern economics is sick. Economics has increasingly become an intellectual game played for its own sake and not for its practical consequences for understanding the economic world. Economists have converted the subject into a sort of social mathematics in which analytical rigour is everything and practical relevance is nothing.
>
> Mark Blaug, 'Ugly Currents in Modern Economics' (1997b)

7.1 MODERN ECONOMICS IS SICK

In his *Reorienting Economics,* Tony Lawson (2003b) cites the magnificently appropriate above quotation by Mark Blaug (1997b, p. 3).[1] Lawson, Blaug and I are in full agreement that the supremacy of technique over substance is a chronic problem within modern economics. Although the victory of formalism can be dated to the 1950s (Blaug, 1999, 2003) – following the dramatic decline of American institutional economics after the Second World War (Hodgson, 2004a) – by the 1980s the problem had become much more serious. Today, because mathematics has swamped the curricula of leading universities and graduate schools, many student economists are neither encouraged nor equipped to analyze real world economies and institutions.

In 1988 the American Economic Association set up a commission on the state of US graduate education in economics. In a crushing indictment, the commission feared that 'graduate programs may be turning out a generation with too many *idiot savants* skilled in technique but innocent of real economic issues' (Krueger *et al*., 1991, pp. 1044–5). Commission member Alan Blinder (1990, p. 445) found economists to be 'obsessed with technique over substance' with only 14 per cent of the students reporting core courses with an emphasis on 'applying economic theory to real-world problems'.

David Colander (2005a) repeated a study of students in seven top US graduate programmes in economics, like one that had been performed about fifteen years earlier (Klamer and Colander, 1990). Students in the later survey gave slightly more emphasis to empirically grounded research and slightly less to mathematical technique for its own sake. But the figures are still

[1] A shorter version of this chapter was published in the *Post-Autistic Economics Review,* Issue 28, October 2004. A draft was presented at a Monday night seminar on critical realism in Cambridge in November 2005. I thank the participants for their comments.

alarming. Colander (2005a) found that only 9 per cent thought that having 'a thorough knowledge of the economy' was 'very important' for professional success. Only 24 per cent thought that it was 'moderately unimportant' and 51 per cent thought it was 'unimportant'. Also in the later study, 89 per cent thought that 'being smart … at problem solving' was 'very important' or 'important' and 82 per cent thought that 'excellence in mathematics' was 'very important' or 'important'. Colander observed that the teaching of techniques was still dominant, with little attempt in the graduate programmes to show how and why the techniques have been developed.

Alarm bells concerning technique displacing substance in economics have been sounding for many years (Ward, 1972). However, although mainstream economics has made some significant theoretical advances in the 1990s, including an increasing attention to institutional and evolutionary themes, the situation concerning formalism has not improved a great deal.

Perhaps the most serious emerging problem is that the graduate students of the 1980s and 1990s, who are skilled in technique but who have a limited understanding of economic principles and their evolution, are now beginning to achieve positions of seniority and influence within the university departments, associations and journals of the economics profession. Their growing power and influence will mean that formalism further consolidates its overwhelming hegemony, to the detriment of wider-ranging conceptual and methodological enquiry. This problem is particularly serious in Britain and America, where formalism has achieved its earliest and most complete victories. The process is delayed rather than absent elsewhere.

Blaug and Lawson identify the problem of formalism, but their evaluations differ. Blaug complains that formalism has been associated with a detachment of economics from substantial and practical issues. Lawson's (1997, 2003b) attack is more radical. He develops a methodological critique of what he calls 'deductivism' and sees this as the root of the formalist malady. Lawson (2003b, p. 21) expects that mathematical and econometric tools will be illegitimate except under 'seemingly rare' conditions. Here I examine prominent aspects of Lawson's critique of formalism. I argue that his stance is too restrictive and extreme. We require an analysis of formalism that is more sensitive to its potential, as well as its limitations.

7.2 TONY LAWSON'S CRITIQUE OF FORMALISM

Following Roy Bhaskar's (1975, p. 70) definition of a closed system 'as one in which a constant conjunction of events obtains', Lawson (1997, p. 19) describes closed systems in the terms of event regularities 'whenever event x then event y'. Both Bhaskar and Lawson insist that the systems addressed by the social sciences are generally open, in that they do not comply with this condition.[2] Openness makes the task of prediction difficult or impossible. For Lawson (1997, p. 288), 'event prediction is usually infeasible' and 'in any case not required for a successful science of economics'.

Lawson (1997, pp. 16–17) sees 'deductivism' as presuming 'event regularities' or 'constant conjunctions of events or states of affairs' with regularities of the form 'whenever event x then event y'. This is a philosophically atypical definition of deductivism, because it refers to empirical regularities concerning events rather than logical deductions concerning propositions.[3]

Lawson's critique of the use of formalism in economics readily follows. Social reality involves open systems, generally lacking in 'constant conjunctions of events'. By contrast, formal models generate regularities in the form: if x then y. Such event regularities are highly limited in the social realm. Accordingly, there is a general mismatch between formal models and reality. If economics is to progress, then formal modelling must be limited those cases where such regularities pertain, and these appear to be rather rare.

Note the implicit criterion of theory judgement here. Lawson suggests that logical or mathematical constructions, to be of relevance or use, must be some kind of map of reality. In one passage Lawson (2003b, p. 22) writes of the importance of a '"fit" with reality', suggesting that all theory has somehow to dovetail with the real world. According to him, formal models generally fail to 'fit' reality because they invoke event regularities, whereas these are 'rare' or absent in the real world.[4]

---

[2] This is a strange and challengeable definition of a closed system. Philosophers and systems theorists have long defined system openness and closure in different terms. Von Bertalanffy (1950, p. 23) wrote in a definitive essay: 'A system is closed if no material enters or leaves it; it is open if there is import and export and, therefore, change of the components'. The philosopher Bunge (1979, p. 9) put it tersely: 'A system that neither acts on nor is acted upon by any other thing is said to be closed'. These definitions are preferable because they rest on fundamental ontological characteristics, rather than descriptions at the level of events. For all its emphasis on ontology, it is rather odd that critical realism adopts an event-level definition of one of its central concepts. In an excellent discussion of the meanings of closure and openness, Chick and Dow (2005, p. 373) write: 'The difference between us and the critical realists lies in defining openness and closure in terms of the structure of the system versus its manifestation or outcome'.

[3] Hands (2001, p. 323 n.) points out that Lawson's use of the term deductivism 'is different from the way in which the term is generally used within the philosophical literature'. Hands (2001, p. 327) suggests and M. Wilson (2005) argues that in any case neoclassical economics does not fit Lawson's characterization of 'deductivism'.

[4] Note that Lawson (1997, p. 239) rejects the correspondence theory of truth, on the grounds that 'things in general exist and act independently of our knowledge of them' whereas all knowledge is dependent on 'particular, historically transient,

What does the theorist do in the absence of formal models? Lawson realizes that no theory (formal or discursive) can proceed without some degree of abstraction: it is impossible to consider all elements and interactions at once. He develops his methodological notion of abstraction at length. But he faces a difficulty: if abstraction is necessary, and it involves the limitation of the sphere of consideration and the exclusion of additional relations or disturbing forces, then doesn't this too imply the assumption of a closed system? Stephen Nash (2004) has argued in the affirmative, suggesting that Lawson too must assume conditions or forms of closure. However, Lawson (1997, p. 236) anticipates this objection. He proposes a distinction between 'abstraction' and 'isolation' in the following terms:

> When we focus upon varying productivity performances here, conditions of work there, rising or falling unemployment rates, and so on, we do not suppose that these features we choose to emphasise exist in isolation, even as a temporary, heuristic, measure. To do so is to assume a totally different world from the one in which we live, and one that has no bearing upon it. … In short, there is literally a world of difference between leaving something (temporarily) out of focus and treating it as though it does not exist. The achieving of an abstraction and treating something as though it existed in isolation are not the same thing at all.

He uses this distinction to protect his argument against the objection that his method of abstraction implicitly assumes closure: abstraction does not imply closure but isolation does. With some important qualifications, Lawson (1997, pp. 131–3) associates the notion of isolation with the work of Uskali Mäki (1992, 1994) and contrasts isolation with his own concept of abstraction. However, I shall argue later below that the distinction is, at least in prominent practical instances, very difficult to sustain.

Lawson takes a relatively extreme position in his attitude to formalism in economics, even among critics of mainstream economics, and even among critical realists. For example, critical realists such as Paul Downward (2000, 2003) defend a more extensive use of some econometric techniques. Unlike Lawson, Downward points to several concrete instances where econometrics has been appropriately deployed. Furthermore, while declaring support for critical realism, Erik Olin Wright (1994, pp. 183–9) strongly supports the use of 'explicit abstract models, sometimes highly formalized as in game theory' and other 'rational choice models'. An extreme position such as Lawson's is

---

descriptions'. However, this argument would not exclude the idea that as far as possible theory should attempt to map the world, accepting that a complete or incontestable map is unattainable. Significantly, he does seem to uphold that specific ontological commitments can be inferred directly and substantially from an item of theoretical knowledge, such as a formal model.

not necessarily inappropriate or wrong by virtue of its extremism, but it does invite repeated criticism, even from other critical realists.

7.3 LATER SHIFTS IN TONE AND EMPHASIS

Perhaps as a result of these contrary stances on his philosophical doorstep, in Lawson's later writing there has been a slight shift of tone and emphasis, if not substance. For example, Lawson (1999, pp. 7–8) proposes that from the fact that 'the world is open and structured, it does not follow' that economists 'ought thereby not to engage at all in formalistic methods such as econometrics'. He continues:

> The possibility of successes with the latter requires local closures. … Critical realism thus cannot and does not rule out *a priori* their limited occurrence. Rather, critical realism adopts an essentially *ex posteriori* orientation … the opponent is the advocate of any form of *a priori* dogma.

Lawson (2003b, pp. xix, 27, 178–9) repeats a similar argument in several places in his second monograph. He insists that he is not against the use of econometrics or models in principle, but that they are of highly limited use given the closure conditions upon which they depend. He writes that 'a blanket rejection of econometrics, or indeed of any other method, is not a stance that is, or could be, sponsored in critical realism'. What is opposed is not econometrics but 'the *reduction* of economics to formalistic analysis'. But he then goes on to say that the 'application of formalistic methods requires certain (closure) conditions constituting special configurations of social reality that (unsurprisingly from the perspective sustained) have turned out to be rather rare'. In another essay, Lawson (2004) again repeats his insistence that he is not 'anti-mathematics'. But his expectation remains that appropriate conditions for its use in economics would be rare.

In these later passages at least two features are emphasized. The first is a general claim of anti-dogmatism, including concerning whether or not mathematics can or should be used. He lays down criteria for its use, including the requirement of (approximated[5]) local closure. He explains that critical realism suggests that closed systems are 'limited' or even 'rather rare' in reality. These ontological arguments in critical realism lead him right away to expect that the possibilities for formalism are highly restricted. Although Lawson imposes no ban on the use of mathematics, his arguments limit its legitimate use to 'rare' circumstances only.

At first sight, general anti-dogmatism seems virtuous. It could mean an ongoing challenge to established authority and received wisdom, it being the

---

[5] I discuss Lawson's invocation of this qualification in parenthesis below.

duty of an academic to question established belief. However, contrary to what Lawson seems to be suggesting here, a universal anti-dogmatist stance is impossible. Some prior 'dogmatic' presuppositions are necessary for any engagement with the world. We assume that the sun will rise and our car will start in the morning. We assume that the face we recognize is of the same person with which it was associated yesterday. We assume that the meanings of words have not changed overnight. The removal of all dogma would end in a disabling nihilism. Scepticism would be so extreme that no observation could be completed, no theory could be established and no act could be accomplished. Human activity would be paralyzed if we ceased to believe in the essential dogma that most of the natural regularities and social institutions of today will survive until tomorrow. We often admire anti-dogmatism as a commendable personality trait, and regard scepticism as an engine of liberation and progress, but modern philosophy of science upholds that a considerable degree of dogmatism is unavoidable. As Charles Sanders Peirce (1934, p. 156) put it long ago, contrary to the extreme scepticism of René Descartes, we 'cannot begin from complete doubt. We must begin with all the prejudices which we actually have'.

In an earlier article, Lawson (1987) himself considers at some length the fact that certainty of belief is a ubiquitous feature of human agency, alongside substantial measures of ignorance and doubt. He further establishes that the pervasive existence of certainty does not stem from omniscience or perfect information. He implies that some certainties are unavoidable, if we are to act in the world. Lawson (1997, p. 211) elsewhere mentions 'prior beliefs' and associates his stance on this question with Peirce. Lawson's earlier emphasis on the pervasiveness and necessary role of certainty contradicts his later stand against any form of 'dogmatic' belief.

A second feature of Lawson's more recent 'anti-dogmatist' stance is the proclamation of 'an essentially *ex posteriori* orientation', although what precisely is meant by this is insufficiently clear. In philosophy, an *a posteriori* stance upholds the primacy of experience or empirical data, as classically expressed in definitive versions of empiricism and positivism. But this would seem to contradict the critical realist emphasis on the importance and priority of ontological commitments, which by their nature cannot be derived directly from experience. Ontological commitments are not *a posteriori*. They are *a priori* knowledge, and upon them depends the possibility of knowledge in general.

The *Concise Oxford Dictionary* describes dogmatic belief as 'based on a priori principles, not on induction'. In directly associating his anti-dogmatism with 'an essentially *ex posteriori* orientation' Lawson seems to be adopting this particular dictionary meaning. However, the *a posteriori* stance that experience or data are the foundation of all knowledge is untenable.

Consider fundamental ontological commitments such as 'ubiquity determinism' (Bhaskar, 1975, pp. 70–1), which means that every event has a cause. We have known at least since the days of David Hume that it is impossible to deduce causes *a posteriori* from our perceptions of events. It is in the very nature of such primary ontological commitments that they are neither based on nor deduced from experience. One of the crucial aspects of the philosophical assault on positivism in the middle of the twentieth century was the reaffirmation of the importance of such prior ontological commitments, which cannot be established by appeal to evidence or experience alone (Quine, 1951; Caldwell, 1982). So one is left wondering what 'an essentially *ex posteriori* orientation' means, and how it can be reconciled with an insistence on the primacy of ontology.[6]

Another shift of tone and emphasis is evident in his post-1997 writings. Lawson (2003b, pp. 20–1) openly discusses the possibility that econometrics might be of use in some instances:

> Clive Granger has argued convincingly that it is possible to use econometrics to provide relatively successful short-run forecasts of phenomena such as electricity loads and peaks in regions wherein one factor, temperature, or more specifically the extreme cold, dominates behaviour. ... The point remains, however, that the sorts of conditions in question appear *a posteriori* not to be typical of the social realm. Rather, as I say, social reality is found to be a quintessentially open, structured, dynamic and highly internally-related system, amongst other things, whilst the conditions for achieving a local closure are seemingly rare.

This is the only example I can find in Lawson's writings on critical realism where he has pointed to a specific piece of econometric analysis and acknowledged its legitimacy. Note, however, the strictness of the key condition involved. According to this passage, for econometrics to be applicable 'local closure' must be actually achieved, not merely approximated. However, it is clearly the case that real world electricity consumption (even in cold regions) is a feature of an open rather than a closed system. For instance, electricity consumption is generally affected by its price. Such prices are heavily influenced by global market conditions. Global markets themselves are not closed systems. Contrary to Lawson, Granger does not provide an example that establishes local closure. Granger's (2004) defence of econometrics applies to a broader class of phenomena. By the logic of his own (2003b) argument, Lawson should regard econometrics to be inapplicable to the situation described by Granger. Lawson's single

---

[6] There is significant evidence, particularly since the rise of experimental economics in the 1990s, that mainstream economics as a whole has become less *a prioristic* and more inductivist and evidence-based (Colander, 2005a, 2005b; Colander *et al.*, 2004a, 2004b; Davis 2006). Lawson's argument seems insensitive to these changes.

example of the legitimate use of econometrics turns out to be illicit according to his own key criterion.

If we require that formal models can only be applied in contexts where local closure is actually achieved, then this would mean that such models were inappropriate in other sciences and disciplines, such as biology, physics or engineering. Generally, in both the natural and social world, such closures are absent, as Bhaskar (1975) as well as Lawson have emphasized. If formal models require strict local closure, then formal models are *never* appropriate. But this would overlook the achievement of mathematical models in some sciences. It may be suggested that local closure is sometimes approximated in physics, and because of this some formal models can be of use. But it must be added that models generated through experiments in situations where local closure is approximated have often been demonstrated to be of considerable value in much wider applications. Furthermore, models and simulations have also been used with some success in biology and evolutionary anthropology, which face a high degree of complexity and openness (Murray, 1989; Boyd and Richerson, 1985; Gintis and Bowles, 2006).

At least in some seminars since 2004, Lawson has amended his position still further, by proposing that econometrics might apply when local closure is ‘approximated in reality’. This qualification would indeed be necessary in other contexts. Closed systems are rare in the physical world, so by Lawson’s argument this would prohibit all formal modelling in physics unless approximation was allowed. The ‘approximated in reality’ formulation contrasts with his two (1997, 2003b) books, which generally insist that local closure conditions must actually apply for formalism to be acceptable. From his amended standpoint, admitting a degree of approximation to closure, it would be possible to admit the Granger example as a case of the legitimate application of econometric techniques.

However, the general problem for Lawson in applying this modified criterion more widely is that the *degree* of acceptable approximation is left unspecified. In general, once the insistence on the actual achievement of local closure is removed, and approximations to closure are admitted, then the door to econometrics is opened. Lawson must specify what degree of approximation is admissible.

7.4 OMISSIONS FROM LAWSON’S CRITIQUE

Much of Lawson’s discussion of formalism concerns econometrics. His main focus is on the use of models as means of prediction. He gives insufficient attention to other applications of mathematical techniques, which serve primary purposes other than the prediction or explanation of measurable variables. Such additional applications of formalism include (a) heuristics and (b) internal critiques. I shall address each of these in turn.

The purpose of a heuristic is to identify possible causal mechanisms that form part of a more complex and inevitably open system. Heuristics can be useful without necessarily making adequate predictions or closely matching existing data. Their purpose is to establish a plausible segment of a whole causal story, without necessarily giving an adequate or complete explanation of the phenomena to which they relate.

A persuasive example of a formal heuristic in economics is the ethnic segregation paper of Thomas Schelling (1969).[7] Using a very simple model of housing location, Schelling shows that ethnic segregation can result even from very small feedback effects. Even if people only have a very slight preference for their own ethnic group, this can be enough to cause migration out of mixed ethnic areas, with the end result of segregated ethnic ghettos. He also shows that even if people prefer to live in mixed areas (within a specified range of mixes) then segregation can still result. The model is extremely simple, and far from realistic in its detailed assumptions.

Making the Schelling model more complicated and realistic would be beyond the point, partly because it becomes obvious that similar outcomes could result from more complicated models. Instead, the Schelling model points to a credible mechanism that shows that ethnic segregation does not necessarily depend upon the actions of bigoted racists. Such racists exist in the real world, so their inclusion in the model would make it more realistic. But this would defeat the object of the model, which is to show that segregation might result even without them. The model abstracts from the more forceful versions of racism that we find in the real world to establish this key point. It also abstracts from ethnic segregation that resulted not simply from the preferences of individuals but from institutions or organized racist groups. The persuasive power of this model is helped by its unrealisticness. The strength of the model lies in its capacity to abstract a plausible but hitherto neglected causal mechanism.

In a very useful discussion of such 'credible worlds', Robert Sugden (2000a) asks probing questions concerning the role and 'realisticness' of this and other heuristic models in economics. These heuristic models have the paradoxical claim that they are literally unrealistic yet they seem to illuminate important aspects of reality. Sugden also cites George Akerlof's (1970) famous article on 'The market for "lemons"', which again claims to establish meaningful propositions about the world on the basis on an admittedly

[7] Actually there is no algebra in Schelling's 1969 paper, but he depicts the segregation process with symbols and diagrams that portray closed systems. Schelling's paper has stimulated a substantial literature, involving mathematical models and agent-based simulations.

unrealistic model. Sugden (2000a, p. 28) describes these models as 'credible counterfactual worlds' that give 'some warrant for making inductive inferences from model to the real world'.

In no case can the construction of a heuristic or counterfactual model clinch the argument concerning the causal mechanisms that actually exist in the real world. However, what they sometimes do show – as in the case of the Schelling model – is that outcomes might not necessarily result from the causal factors that may be presumed at first sight. To complete the argument, further theoretical development and empirical enquiry are always required.

I suggest above that heuristics may be appropriate if they successfully abstract an important causal mechanism in reality. But Lawson suggests that heuristics are isolations rather than abstractions. So I must return to Lawson's (1997, p. 236) attempted distinction between isolation and abstraction, as quoted above. According to him, the key difference is 'between leaving something (temporarily) out of focus and treating it as though it does not exist'. Taking the Schelling model as an example, Schelling does not deny that bigoted racists exist, yet he leaves them out of his model. Its purpose is to neither excuse nor deny racism, but the more severe forms of racism are deliberately removed. Nevertheless, the model is highly persuasive and its results are more worrying *because* of this omission.

No-one to my knowledge, including Schelling, has suggested that such a model is an adequate causal representation of the processes underlying ethnic segregation in reality. The model is simply a heuristic step along the road towards that more complete end. More generally, no sensible mainstream economist would deny that the world is open, and no adequate presentation of a formal model would fail to mention that other (omitted) causal mechanisms exist. Are their models abstractions or isolations?

Lawson's attempted distinction between abstraction and isolation hinges on the precise meaning of notions such as treating that which is left out of the picture 'as though it does not exist' and the implied distinction between a 'temporary heuristic' and 'leaving something temporarily out of focus'. Again Lawson is insufficiently precise here. If I 'focus' on the workings of a national economy and ignore its trade with other nations, then in what sense might this qualify as a 'temporary' account, rather than a presumption that such exports and imports do not exist? Surely, some verbal statement would be required, acknowledging the existence of international trade, explaining its omission from the current discussion, and suggesting that further work must be done to incorporate it into the analysis. But this is also the kind of necessary qualification that we should expect from the best presentations of formal models. On the other hand, it would be impossible to mention all the things that we have left out of the account. In this sense all theory is 'temporary'. But do such unmentioned omissions amount to treating some causal linkages as though they do not exist? If this were the case, then every theory – including non-formal, discursive theory – would be a failure by Lawson's criteria. Once we attempt to apply Lawson's criteria, then their insufficiency and vagueness become apparent, and his attempted distinction between abstraction and isolation is revealed as highly problematic.

A crucial point here is that in economics we should not and cannot judge models in isolation. The meaning of any model depends upon an interpretive framework that is not contained in the formalities of the model itself. If heuristic models such as the Schelling model are suitably hedged and qualified, in the manner suggested above, then these qualifications form part of the interpretative apparatus for the model. If heuristic models are treated within an adequate interpretative context, then such heuristic packages can successfully defend themselves against the charge that they treat other aspects of reality as though they do not exist.

By contrast, Lawson treats any model as if it were an intrinsic claim to be a partial map of the world. He isolates formal models from their interpretative contexts and denies the validity of even 'temporary' heuristic models *per se*. The strictures of appropriate contextualization that Lawson rightly requires of discursive theory should also apply to his treatment of formal models.

Bringing the interpretative framework of a heuristic model into the picture is highly important in appraising the problem of excessive or misplaced formalism in economics. An alternative diagnosis emerges, in which the malady is not the use of formalism as such but the inadequacy and underdevelopment of the interpretative context in which they are placed. Technique takes priority over substance as a result of the relative neglect of interpretative context. An adequate interpretative framework would depend on the discussion of the genesis, meaning and methodological significance of key concepts that relate to the model. This is never a small task, and if done properly it will be at least as weighty as the formal content of any model. Yet in modern economics such interpretative and conceptual matters are often marginalized and underdeveloped. The profession often seems more concerned with mathematical prowess than interpretative sophistication. This is one of the main problems with formalism in economics today.

While Lawson implicitly treats formal models as if they were claims to map the world, his favourite metaphor is of the model as a tool. Lawson (2003b, p. 12) notes the ontological mismatch between formal models and reality and suggests that this is grounds to question their use: 'Few people … would attempt to use a comb to write a letter … or a drill to clean a window'. This argument is not as illuminating as it may seem at first sight. Of course, we use a pen to write a letter and a clean cloth to clean a window. Yet the ontology of pens is very different from that of letters, and likewise there is a big ontological difference between clean cloths and dirty windows. So there is nothing in this appropriateness-of-tools argument that rules out using closed models to help understand an open reality.

I now turn to the second use of formalism that Lawson neglects, that of an internal critique. Generally, the impact of an effective internal critique is negative rather than positive; it shows the limits of an existing theory rather than providing a new one. It is nevertheless important. For example, in their critique of mainstream capital theory, Piero Sraffa (1960) and others developed models with disaggregated physical capital and showed that aggregated measures of capital are generally dependent on profits, wages or prices. Consequently, any attempt to explain profits, wages or prices by means of an aggregated capital variable must assume that which it has to explain. The validity of this argument was later accepted by Paul Samuelson and others (Harcourt, 1972). It meant that several of the models and arguments used in the mainstream theory of capital and distribution were either invalid or dependent on highly restrictive assumptions.

Demonstrations that a widely adopted approach depends on restrictive or even implausible assumptions characterize many of the successful internal critiques in economics. For example, Rolf Mantel (1974) and several others showed that even with the assumption of individual utility-maximization there is no basis in standard general equilibrium theory for the assumption that excess demand functions are generally downward sloping. Their work proved influential in bringing the microfoundations project in general equilibrium theory to an end (Kirman, 1989; Rizvi, 1994). In another case, Robert Rowthorn (1999) showed that prominent models used by governments in macroeconomic policy-making are based on highly restrictive and unwarranted assumptions.

Such critiques do not themselves provide new theories, although they may establish some relevant pointers. By their nature, internal critiques are not claims to map the real world. Instead, they are attempts to show that that other theories are inadequate or overly restrictive in regard to the kind of world to which they relate. I have not come across an adequate discussion of the role of internal critiques in Lawson's work, despite his location in the same department of economics as where Joan Robinson (1953) and Sraffa (1960) began the Cambridge capital critique.

Significantly, neither heuristics nor internal critiques are attempts to map the world with a model. Accordingly, insofar as they are of some scientific use, severe doubt is cast on Lawson's central argument that the adoption of a particular model involves explicit or implicit assumptions about the ontology of the social world. For him, if an assumption does not occur (approximately) in reality, then it is illegitimate in theory – a proposition that would invalidate much theory in most disciplines. By contrast, some models remain valuable, despite significant misfits with reality. Lawson's main argument thus falls.

7.5 SHOULD ECONOMIC THEORY EMBRACE FALSE ASSUMPTIONS?

Economics deals with open systems. However, against Lawson's critique of formalism, I have argued that any (discursive or formal) theory must necessarily abstract or isolate. Given that theory cannot embrace and describe every facet and causal mechanism, much will always be excluded. Consequently some degree of closure is inevitable in any theory. As noted above, Lawson tries to get round this problem with his attempted distinction between isolation and abstraction. However, his idea of abstraction involving 'leaving something (temporarily) out of focus' would not exclude a formal model published with the caveat that it is a temporary simplification or heuristic, to which excluded features or mechanisms will be added later.

I claim that closed models can be of value in helping us to understand real causal mechanisms and processes in open systems. Does this mean the adoption of false assumptions? And is my stance untenable for this reason?

Lawson (2002, p. 76) warns against false assumptions, proposing that if they are allowed 'it is clearly possible to derive any conclusions whatsoever – true ones or false ones – simply by deductive logic'. This argument is wrong. If I make the (false) assumption that 'the economy consists of just two goods' then there is no way that anyone can deduce from this proposition alone that the economy consists instead of four, five or a million. The correct argument from classical logic (first-order predicate calculus) is that in principle we can derive by deduction any conclusion from a *logical contradiction*. Accordingly, with the two contradictory propositions 'X is true' and 'X is false' we can establish both that 'God exists' and 'God does not exist'.

A seminal discussion of 'false assumptions' is in Alan Musgrave's (1981) dissection and criticism of Milton Friedman's (1953) famous defence of 'unrealistic' propositions. Musgrave distinguishes between (a) *negligibility* assumptions upholding that some factor has a negligible effect on the phenomenon under investigation, (b) *domain* assumptions that specify the domain of applicability of a theory and (c) *heuristic* assumptions involving a simplifying focus on some aspects of the phenomenon as a first step towards developing a fuller theory or model. He shows that Friedman conflates and confuses these very different ramifications of what might be meant by an 'unrealistic' assumption.[8]

All three types of assumption have their place in science. However, both (a) and (c) are clearly 'false' or 'unrealistic'. Physicists sometimes usefully assume zero atmospheric friction to calculate the trajectory of an object: this is a negligibility assumption. But it is generally false. Isaac Newton started

[8] See Mäki (2000) for important clarifications and refinements of Musgrave's typology.

by assuming that there was only one planet circling the sun, and deduced with his laws of motion that the planet would follow an ellipse, with the sun at one of its foci. Yet the basic assumption of a singular planet is neither true nor an adequate descriptive approximation of our solar system. Furthermore, the prediction was itself false: no planet moves in a perfect ellipse.

Lawson's 'method of abstraction' involving 'leaving something (temporally) out of focus' does not distinguish between negligibility and heuristic assumptions. His verbal references to closed systems sometimes being 'approximated in reality' might warrant negligibility assumptions. But his (1997, pp. 235–6) favourite illustrative example of a temporary analytical focus on one football player among several others suggests a heuristic assumption. However, if we apply this to planets rather than football players, it is not clear whether Lawson would allow the heuristic device of deriving the (false) prediction of an elliptical orbit. His criteria are insufficiently sophisticated to deal with the problem.

In one passage where he does discuss Musgrave's (1981) article, Lawson (1997, pp. 127–9) attempts to distinguish between the one-planet argument, and the (once ubiquitous) assumption in mainstream economics of omniscient human agents. His argument is that the gravitational forces acting on a single planet are 'real causal factors' whereas there are no 'real structures, capacities or tendencies well expressed by such conceptions as omniscience or infallibility'. Consequently, the one-planet assumption is legitimate but the assumption of omniscience is not.

Let us dissect this. Lawson saves the Newtonian one-planet assumption by ignoring its false description of the totality and concentrating on Newton's presentation of the forces and tendencies that apply to individual planets. To be fair, similar dispensations must also apply to the (false) assumptions of human omniscience or infallibility. To balance the argument, we must here also focus on forces and tendencies at the individual human level. An equivalent claim could be that individual agents are disposed to act on the basis of the information that they possess. This parallel truth-claim points to causal powers or capacities. Today I am planning a journey, based on the assumption that the M25 (London orbital motorway) still exists and is relatively uncongested. This piece of information in my head is a 'real causal factor' affecting my decision concerning the most convenient route. Furthermore, even if this information were false, my (mistaken) knowledge would still be a 'real causal factor' affecting my decision.

Hence on closer inspection Lawson's argument is biased by its one-sided focus on total descriptions such as omniscience and infallibility in one case, but not in the other. No human is omniscient. The equivalent Newtonian falsehood to omniscience is the idea of a one-planet universe. But Newton was right to say that planets are moved by gravitational forces. To be fair, we must consider a proposition concerning 'real causal factors' at the individual level, such as humans acting on the basis of the information that they possess.

I am not here defending the assumption of omniscient agents. Instead, my argument suggests that our primary critical focus should be on the fundamental truth-claim that humans have the will and capability to act on the basis of the information that they hold. If this is unwarranted, then the (temporary) heuristic assumption of omniscience can be challenged. In fact, I have elsewhere elaborated my reservations concerning this fundamental truth-claim concerning individuals (Hodgson, 1988). I have no challenge to the idea that individual planets are moved by gravitational forces.

Should economic theory embrace false assumptions? In response we must first distinguish the different meanings of 'false' or 'unrealistic'. Second, in heuristic or negligibility senses of these terms, some 'false' or 'unrealistic' assumptions are *unavoidable in science*. The real question is *what particular* 'false' or 'unrealistic' assumptions are to be accepted in each particular context. Lawson himself offers no alternative methodological strategy. His method of involving 'leaving something (temporally) out of focus' is itself a heuristic device that produces false descriptions in the sense that they are incomplete. His proposal that closed systems are sometimes (but rarely) 'approximated in reality' amounts to a negligibility assumption, permitting models or descriptions that are not exactly true.

7.6 CONCLUDING REMARKS ON FORMALISM

Many economists take the extreme view that formalism is the only means by which economics becomes rigorous and scientific, and the dominance of formalism is a positive sign of success. Lawson takes a position near the opposite extreme. He argues that formalism is justified in 'rare' circumstances only, where local closure exists (or is approximated). I propose that both attitudes to formalism are flawed, partly because they both downplay its necessary interface with interpretative structures.

While Lawson and mainstream economists are at odds, they share some presuppositions. Many mainstream economists assume that their models are sufficient to represent the world, neglecting the interpretative discourses required to make such a claim meaningful. Lawson too believes that a formal model intrinsically upholds substantial claims concerning the nature of reality. I believe that both positions are false.

Both positions confuse the model with the reality. In one case the elaboration of formal models is regarded as sufficient for scientific enquiry. In Lawson's case the assumptions within a model are necessarily assumptions about reality. He largely ignores the philosophy of mathematics, where the ontology of mathematical categories and the representativeness of mathematical constructions are hotly debated (Benacerraf and Putnam, 1984).

An alternative stance would be, for example, that models are instruments for obtaining truth along with other conceptual tools. A refined version of this outlook is found in pragmatist philosophy, which sees true theories as scientifically warranted tools for engaging practically and effectively with the real world. Pragmatism reflects the influence of Darwinism, which treats knowledge as essentially an evolved adaptation to ongoing problems (Plotkin, 1994). Such a stance would not evaluate models in terms of their 'fit with reality'. Accordingly, failure of any part of reality to approximate a closed system would not itself provide grounds for rejecting any (unavoidably closed) formal model.

If modern economics is sick, then what is the nature of the sickness? A good answer to this question is needed to identify an appropriate remedy. Lawson's medicine is to restrict the application of formalism only to cases when local closure is achieved (or perhaps approximated). This remedy is an inversion of the disease itself, and it is based on a faulty diagnosis.

Lawson has insisted that he is not against formalism as such: he has no dogmatic prescription concerning its use. However, I am aware of only one example of a piece of econometrics which Lawson has deemed as legitimate, and even here he has to fudge the criterion of strict closure declared in his *Reorienting Economics* (2003b). Subsequently (at least in some verbal statements) he has relaxed this criterion to allow econometrics to be used when closure is 'approximated', rather than actually achieved.

The challenge for Lawson is to be more specific about the degree of approximation and to point to still further examples of the legitimate use of mathematical models in economics. Until this is done, he remains in the extreme position of admitting as legitimate only one specific case, among hundreds of thousands of examples that are available to us.

Middle ground solutions on the question of formalism are not intrinsically warranted simply because they are middle ground. But part of the tragedy of modern economics is that they have so far received limited attention and consideration, with notable exceptions such as recent articles by Victoria Chick and Sheila Dow (2001, 2005). As Chick (1998) puts it elsewhere, for formalism it is a question of 'knowing one's place'.

The problem with formalism is not an intrinsic inappropriateness for open systems. Instead it is the problem identified by Blaug in the quotation at the beginning of this chapter. He sees formalism in modern economics as 'an intellectual game played for its own sake' rather than a tool for explaining and engaging with the real economic world. Blaug complains that in modern economics 'analytical rigour is everything and practical relevance is nothing'. Again the solution here is not necessarily to confine formalism to the very rare conditions of actual or approximated closure, but to bring concerns for practical relevance to the fore. Formal techniques should become the servants rather than the masters of scientific enquiry.

It is impossible here to develop criteria and contexts for the appropriate use of formalism in economics. Nevertheless, some important issues may be briefly identified. My stress on the interpretative context of formal models is consistent with the view that a model should not be valued primarily on the impressiveness or novelty of its mathematical techniques. Some good economic models use simple or familiar mathematics. The conceptual context is crucial, and its development involves particular skills, including the ability to reflect on definitions and meanings, which is usually derived from a wider knowledge of the social sciences, including their history and philosophy. Technical competences and specialist skills have to be compensated by honed capacities of judgement derived from a broader education. Modern economics is sick, largely as a consequence of over-specialization and an obsession with technique, and the under-training of economists in broader contextual skills of conceptual interpretation and judgement.

Lawson suggests that the health of an academic discipline that addresses open systems is likely to be inversely related to its use of mathematics. Look at sociology. Apart from its use of statistics, formal models have therein been put to relatively little use. Should economists treat sociology as a superior mentor? No. Sociology is widely acknowledged to be in a state of severe disorder concerning its core presuppositions, its self-identity, its boundaries, and its relations with other disciplines, particularly economics and biology (Mouzelis, 1995; Lopreato and Crippen, 1999). The persistence of its acute scientific maladies, with a relatively infrequent use of formalism, indicates that additional problems exist within the social sciences today. Defects include the postmodernist affirmation that one theory is as good as another, the frequent choice of a theory on ideological rather than scientific grounds, and an occasional self-inflicted blindness concerning the biological aspects of human nature and their significance for the study of human society.

Despite our differences, I wish to emphasize that Lawson, myself and others including Blaug, Chick, Dow and Mäki, adopt a realist philosophical perspective. Realism acknowledges that a world exists beyond our perceptions. Realists uphold that, to be adequate, sciences including economics should not be self-contained logical games but attempts to address and understand aspects of the real world. Accordingly, there is no room for a philosophy of science in which ‘anything goes’. Instead there is a shared realist imperative: to understand the real world.

Nevertheless, I argue here that there is a place for mathematics in economics, even when conditions of closure are absent or fail to be approximated. I have emphasized the importance of the interpretative structure within which the theory is placed. We need to investigate the inadequately explored middle ground between unacceptable extreme stances that either treat mathematics as the *sine qua non* of theory, or practically exclude it in all but 'rare' cases. I advocate this middle ground position, not because central areas are intrinsically or universally superior to extremes, but because the extremes in this case jointly downplay the necessary interpretative structure of any formal theory.

7.7 EPILOGUE ON CRITICAL REALISM

Having touched on several issues in Chapters 5–7, we are in a position to attempt a more general appraisal. What is the overall contribution of critical realism? In fact, many of its attributed philosophical strengths are unoriginal. Its core idea of an ontological hierarchy is traceable to philosophical emergentists and social theorists of the early–twentieth century (Blitz, 1992; Ward, 1903) and is commonplace in the philosophy of science today. Its emphasis on underlying propensities and dispositions is found in the work of Karl Popper (1990) and many others. Critical realists replicate with inadequate acknowledgement much that is already well established within philosophy, albeit often ignored outside that discipline. In social theory, the emphasis in critical realism on social structures is found not only in Marxism but also in sociology over a hundred years ago (Durkheim, 1895; Ross, 1901; Ward, 1903).

Although ideas of causality and emergent properties are central to its discourse, critical realism so far has generally neglected much of the recent criticisms and refinements of these concepts within philosophy itself.[9] To some extent these defects may be remedied, as critical realists become more aware of this literature. But this would be the incorporation of existing insights from outside, and not necessarily evidence of the originality and philosophical integrity of critical realism itself. Critical realists have engaged inadequately with developments within modern philosophy of science.

When faced with specific problems of theory evaluation and construction, critical realism has crucial weaknesses, partly due to the unrefined use of key concepts. As Wade Hands (2001, p. 327) puts it: 'Critical realists want to identify – and believe science can identify – the enduring and intransitive causal structures that lie behind the surface phenomena of social life, and yet

---

[9] Critical realist Elder-Vass (2005, p. 315) candidly observes: 'The concept of emergence is routinely invoked in critical realist theory, but rarely examined … few critical realists have examined the nature of emergence itself, while those few have been far from consistent in their approach'. Key works on emergence include Beckerman *et al.* (1992), Kim (1993), Emmeche *et al.* (1997), Humphreys (1997), and Cunningham (2000). See also Sosa and Tooley (1993), Salmon (1998), Pearl (2000) and Woodward (2003) on causality.

they offer *no unique method*, no particular approach, or technique, that gives us privileged access those enduring structures'.

As critical realism reproduces many of the strengths of longstanding discourses in philosophy and social theory, it also replicates some of their weaknesses. Consider its explanation of human agency. It typically relies on a prominent but defective 'folk psychology' in which all actions are simplistically explained by beliefs. Yet this 'mind first' concept of action is open to sustained criticism, particularly concerning its neglect of emotions, habits, instincts and other culturally or biologically inherited dispositions.[10]

In part, critical realism has prospered because of the widespread unawareness among social scientists of key material in the modern philosophy of science. Critical realists have acted as ambassadors for key philosophical ideas, but often presented them as their own. To this it has added the peculiar marketing strategy of repeatedly associating its strong philosophical message with imprecise radical leftist politics.

Overall, the contribution of critical realism, at least in its engagement with economics, is somewhat chequered. Critical realism is burdened by a thematic but unsubstantiated leftist political rhetoric, which may attract some adherents but is so casually presented that it undermines academic credibility. Critical realism has inadequately demonstrated its capacity to guide, illustrate or evaluate particular theories in economics. Moreover, in Lawson's (1997, 2003b) version it effectively writes off all or most theories that involve formal modelling or econometrics. Critical realism contains some important philosophical insights, but only time will tell if these can be rescued from the challengeable political and theoretical trappings that have been identified in the above chapters.

---

[10] See Bunge (1980), P. M. Churchland (1984, 1989), P. S. Churchland (1986), Damasio (1994), Faulkner (2002), Hodgson (2004a), Joas (1993, 1996), Kilpinen (2000), Rosenberg (1995, 1998), Stich (1983).

Part 3:

Habits and Individuals; Routines and Institutions

8. What Are Institutions?

The proper subject-matter of economic theory is institutions.

Walton Hamilton, 'The Institutional Approach to Economic Theory' (1919)

8.1 INTRODUCTION

The word 'institution' has a long history in the social sciences, dating back at least to Giambattista Vico in his *Scienza Nuova* of 1725.[1] Today, in economics, sociology, politics and geography, there has been a revived interest in institutions and in various institutionalist theoretical approaches. A prominent sociological journal has noted 'the current institutional turn across the social sciences' (Clemens and Cook, 1999, pp. 443–4) and similar references to an 'institutional turn' are found in economic geography (Amin, 1999), political science (Jupille and Caporaso, 1999) and elsewhere. Accordingly, the term 'institution' has become widespread in recent years. However, even today, there is no unanimity in the definition of this concept.

Furthermore, endless disputes over the definitions of key terms such as 'institution' and 'organization' have led some writers to give up matters of definition, and to propose getting down to practical matters instead. But it is not possible to carry out any empirical or theoretical analysis of how institutions or organizations work without having an adequate conception of what an institution or an organization is. All empirical inquiry requires a prior and appropriate conceptual framework.

I propose that those that give up are too hasty; potentially consensual definitions of these terms are possible, once we overcome a few obstacles and difficulties in the way. It is also important to avoid some biases in the study of institutions, where institutions and characteristics of a particular type are over-generalized to the set of institutions as a whole. This chapter outlines some dangers, with regard to an excessive relative stress on self-organization and agent insensitive institutions.

This chapter is organized in seven sections. The following three sections are devoted to the definition and understanding of institutions in general terms. Section 8.2 explores the meaning of key terms such as institution, convention, and rule. Section 8.3 discusses some general issues concerning how institutions function, and how they interact with individual agents, their

[1] This chapter is based on Hodgson (2006), which in turn makes use of material from Hodgson (2001b, 2002c, 2004a).

habits and their beliefs. Section 8.4 examines the difference between organizations and institutions, and what may be meant by the term 'formal' when applied to institutions or rules, by focusing on some of Douglass North's statements in on these themes. Section 8.5 identifies an excessive bias in the discussion of institutions towards those of the self-organizing type, showing theoretically that these are a special case. Section 8.6 argues that institutions also differ with regard to their degree of sensitivity to changes in the personalities of the agents involved. Section 8.7 concludes the chapter.

8.2 ON INSTITUTIONS, CONVENTIONS AND RULES

Institutions are the kind of structures that matter most in the social realm: they make up the stuff of social life. The increasing acknowledgement of the role of institutions in social life brings a recognition that much human interaction and activity is structured by overt or implicit rules. Without doing much violence to the relevant literature, we may define institutions as systems of established and prevalent social rules that structure social interactions.[2] Language, money, law, systems of weights and measures, table manners, firms (and other organizations) are thus all institutions.

Following Robert Sugden (1986), John Searle (1995) and others, we may usefully define a convention as a particular instance of an institutional rule. For example, all countries have traffic rules, but it is a matter of (arbitrary) convention whether the rule is to drive on the left or on the right. So in regard to the (say) British institutional system of traffic rules, the specific convention is to drive on the left.[3]

---

[2] Knight (1992, p. 2), for example, similarly defines an institution as '*a set of rules that structure social interactions in particular ways*'. However, there is a debate within the new institutional economics whether institutions should be regarded essentially as equilibria, norms or rules (Aoki, 2001; Crawford and Ostrom, 1995). But this interpretative conflict arises essentially within an intellectual tradition that takes individual preferences or purposes as given. Being relatively stable, institutions have equilibrium-like qualities, even if their equilibria can be disturbed. These equilibria are reinforced as preferences or purposes become moulded by the outcomes. Turning to norms and rules, they are not simply the 'environment' in which the (rational) actor must decide and act; they are also internalized in the preferences, and replicated through the behaviour, of the individual. Repeated, conditional, rule-like behaviour acquires normative weight as people accept the customary as morally virtuous, and thus help stabilize the institutional equilibrium. Once we see the effects of institutions on individuals, as well as the effects of individuals upon institutions, the three aspects of institutions become entwined.

[3] Note that the French *economie des conventions* school adopts a broad definition of convention that is closer to the notion of a rule adopted here (Thévenot, 1986; Orléan, 1994; Favereau and Lazega, 2002),

At some stage we need to consider how institutions structure social interactions, and in what senses they are established and embedded. In part, the durability of institutions stems from the fact that they can usefully create stable expectations of the behaviour of others. Generally, institutions enable ordered thought, expectation and action, by imposing form and consistency on human activities. They depend upon the thoughts and activities of individuals but are not reducible to them.

Institutions both constrain and enable behaviour. The existence of rules implies constraints. However, such a constraint can open up possibilities: it may enable choices and actions that otherwise would not exist. For example: the rules of language allow us to communicate; traffic rules help traffic to flow more easily and safely; the rule of law can increase personal safety. Regulation is not always the antithesis of freedom; it can be its ally.

As Alan Wells (1970, p. 3) puts it: 'Social institutions form an element in a more general concept, known as social structure'. The original institutional economists, in the tradition of Thorstein Veblen and John R. Commons, understood institutions as a special type of social structure with the potential to change agents, including changes to their purposes or preferences.

However, some institutionalists such as John Fagg Foster (1981, p. 908) have misleadingly defined institutions as 'prescribed patterns of correlated behavior'.[4] Defining institutions as behaviour would mislead us into presuming that institutions no longer existed if their associated behaviours were interrupted. Does the British monarchy cease to exist when the members of the royal family are all asleep and no royal ceremony is taking place? Of course not: royal prerogatives and powers remain, even when they are not enacted. It is these powers, not the behaviours themselves, which mean that the institution exists. Nevertheless, such powers may lapse, and institutional dispositions may fade, if they are not exercised with sufficient frequency. Furthermore, the only way in which we can observe institutions is through manifest behaviour.[5]

Not all social structures are institutions. Social structures include sets of relations that may not be codified in discourse, such as demographic

---

[4] Lawson (2003a, pp. 189–94) lists several behavioural definitions in the institutionalist literature and rightly criticizes them. Hamilton's (1932, p. 84) famous definition of an institution as 'a way of thought or action of some prevalence and permanence, which is embedded in the habits of a group or the customs of a people' is preferable to some of the later institutionalist definitions, as long as habits and customs are interpreted as dispositions rather than merely behaviours.

[5] While flawed, definitions of institutions in terms of behaviours were understandable during the positivist era in psychology and the social sciences – from about the 1920s until well after the Second World War – when it was widely and mistakenly upheld that discussions of unobservables had no place in science (Hodgson, 2004a).

structures in animal species or in human societies before any understanding of demography. Demographic structures may limit social potentialities, in terms of the number of infants or elderly requiring care, and the number of able-bodied adults available to care, produce and procreate. But they do not necessarily do this through the operation of rules.[6]

The term 'rule' is broadly understood as a socially transmitted and customary normative injunction or immanently normative disposition, that in circumstances *X* do *Y*.[7] A prohibition rule would involve a large class of actions *Y*, from which the prohibited outcomes are excluded. Other rules may involve requirements to perform a smaller class of actions in *Y*. A rule may be considered, acknowledged or followed without much thought. The phrase 'immanently normative' requires that if the rule is scrutinized or contested, then normative issues will emerge.

The term 'socially transmitted' means that the replication of such rules depends upon a developed social culture and some use of language. Such dispositions do not appear simply as a result of inherited genes or instincts; they depend upon contingent social structures, and may have no direct or obvious representation in our genetic make-up.

Rules include norms of behaviour and social conventions, as well as legal rules. Such rules are potentially codifiable. Members of the relevant community share tacit or explicit knowledge of these rules. This criterion of codifiability is important because it means that breaches of the rule can be identified explicitly. It also helps to define the community that shares and understands the rules involved.

The normative aspect of a rule would not be so relevant, and would have no compelling reason to be passed on from generation to generation, if physical and natural circumstances allowed only one option *Y** in circumstances *X*. If we were compelled by the laws of nature to do *Y** in circumstances *X*, then there would be no need for normative compulsions or sanctions. In contrast, multiple options can typically be imagined for the form of a rule. One culture may uphold in circumstances *X* do *Y*; another may require in circumstances *X* do *Z*. Nevertheless, the laws of nature constrain the set of possible rules that may be formulated. A feasible rule cannot ask us to defy the laws of gravity or to become Julius Caesar. The set of possible rules can be enlarged by technological and other institutional developments.

---

[6] Archer's (1995) useful discussion of demographic structure nevertheless fails to identify the distinction between structures in general and institutional, rule-based structures.

[7] See Ostrom (1986) and Crawford and Ostrom (1995) for detailed analyses of the nature of institutional rules.

For example, the technology of writing makes feasible the rule that a valid contract on paper must be signed.[8]

As Searle (1995, 2005) has argued, the mental representations of an institution or its rules are partly constitutive of that institution, since an institution can only exist if people have particular and related beliefs and mental attitudes. Hence an institution is a special type of social structure that involves potentially codifiable and (evidently or immanently) normative rules of interpretation and behaviour. Some of these rules concern commonly accepted tokens or meanings, as is obviously the case with money or language. However, as Max Weber (1978, p. 105) pointed out in 1907, some rules are followed 'without any subjective formulation in thought of the "rule"'. For example, few of us could specify fully the grammatical rules of the language that we use regularly, or completely specify in detail some practical skills. Nevertheless, institutional rules are in principle codifiable, so that breaches of these rules can become subjects of discourse.

Even with this criterion of potential codifiability, a problem arises as to how far we can stretch the meaning of the term 'rule' in the definition of an institution. Friedrich Hayek (1973, p. 11), for example, emphasized that: 'Man is as much a rule-following animal as a purpose-seeking one'. However, his notion of a rule was extremely broad. For Hayek (1967, p. 67) the term 'rule' is 'used for a statement by which a regularity of the conduct of individuals can be described, irrespective of whether such a rule is "known" to the individuals in any other sense than they normally act in accordance with it'. Hayek (1979, p. 159) entertains rules that emanate from the 'little changing foundation of genetically inherited, "instinctive" drives' as well as from reason and human interaction. For Hayek, therefore, a rule is any behavioural disposition, including instincts and habits, which can lead to 'a regularity of the conduct of individuals'.

This excessively broad definition would include such behavioural regularities as breathing or the pulsation of the heart. This stretches the notion of rule-following to unacceptable extremes (Kley, 1994). Despite Hayek's general emphasis on purposeful behaviour and his rejection of behaviourist psychology, Hayek ends up with a definition of rule that hinges solely on behavioural regularities, neglecting the ontology of rules and the mechanisms involved in their creation and replication.

Social rules are replicated through mechanisms other than the genes. However, while rules are not in the DNA, it would be a mistake to regard rule-following as something entirely deliberative. Michael Polanyi (1967) argued convincingly that there is always and unavoidably a tacit substratum of knowledge that can never be fully articulated, even with the most

[8] The definition of technology is itself problematic, and is not attempted here. See Nelson and Sampat (2001) among many others.

deliberative of acts. Rules, to be effective in the social context, can never be purely or fully matters of conscious deliberation.

The tacit dimension of knowledge creates a problem when we attempt to draw the line between instinctive or autonomic behavioural regularities, on the one hand, and genuine rule-following on the other. Some authors refer to the latter but not the former category of behaviour as 'intentional'. A problem here is that the concept of intentionality is sometimes stretched to cover cases of behaviour that are not deliberative (e.g. Bhaskar, 1989a; Searle, 1995; Lawson, 1997). Arguing that such an unconscious 'intentional' state 'has to be in principle accessible to consciousness' (Searle, 1995, p. 5) creates boundaries for this enlarged concept of intentionality, but extends its territory to some autonomic or instinctive behaviours, such a breathing and blinking (but not heartbeats), which to some degree on some occasions can be placed under conscious control. Searle's criterion would thus suggest that breathing and blinking were *always* intentional.[9]

An alternative strategy, preferred by the present author, consists of two elements. First, the concept of intentionality is reserved for conscious prefiguration and self-reflexive reasoning, with regard to future events or outcomes. As Hans Joas (1996, p. 158) puts it, intentionality 'consists in a self-reflective control which we exercise over our current behavior'. Unintended acts lack any such conscious deliberation and prefiguration. Second, rules are regarded as socially or culturally transmitted dispositions, with actual or potential normative content. An often serviceable test of socio-cultural rather than genetic transmission is the potential or actual existence of very different rule systems, even in similar natural environments.

Raimo Tuomela (1995) distinguishes between rules and norms, according to the manner of their enforcement. He also develops a notion of collective intentionality, similar to that of Searle (1995).[10] Collective intentionality arises when an individual attributes an intention to the group to which she belongs, while holding that intention, and believing that other group members hold it too. We act thus because we believe that others have a similar aim. Many behavioural regularities develop because of such reciprocating intentions and expectations. Tuomela describes such regularities as norms. They involve a network of mutual beliefs rather than actual agreements

---

9 Bhaskar (1989a, pp. 80, 85, 112) writes: 'intentional human behaviour is ... always caused by reasons' and 'the reason for the behaviour is itself a belief'. But, it is then admitted: 'Beliefs may be unconscious, implicit or tacit'. Consequently, the concept of intentionality is stretched to cover unconscious behaviour, and we have no criterion by which we can decide whether a form of behaviour is 'action' or 'mere movement'.

10 For a critical discussion of Searle's treatment of collective intentionality see Vromen (2003).

between individuals. Norms involve approval or disapproval. In contrast, for Tuomela, rules are the product of explicit agreement brought about by some authority, and they imply sanctions. Rules and norms thus differ by virtue of the different ways they enforce tasks on individuals.

However, such a hard and fast distinction is difficult to maintain. Reciprocating mutual beliefs become explicit agreements with the addition of single and shared signs or words of assent. Some behavioural regularities may emerge originally without external enforcement, but later some external authority may impose sanctions. The difference between such enforced sanctions and the perceived threat of disapproval by others is eroded when one considers that both involve some discomfort for the individual concerned. Robert Sugden (2000b) goes further down this road, arguing that both are explicable in terms of preferences alone. But even if we reject the utilitarian conflation of values and preferences, neither external sanctions nor social disapproval are devoid of questions of value. External sanctions and laws have a capacity to promote their own moral authority, and their transgression may also involve social disapproval. People thus obey laws not simply because of the sanctions involved, but also because legal systems can acquire the force of moral legitimacy and the moral support of others.

8.3 ON HOW INSTITUTIONS WORK

Generally, how do people understand rules and choose to follow them? We have to explain not only the incentives and disincentives involved, but how people interpret and value them. This appreciation and valuation of rules is unavoidably a process of social interaction. As Ludwig Wittgenstein (1958, p. 80) pointed out: 'a person goes by a sign-post only in so far as there exists a regular use of sign-posts, a custom'.

Such considerations are important when we address the special case of legal rules. For laws to become rules in the sense discussed here, they have to become customary. As discussed later below, there are examples of laws that are widely ignored, and have not acquired the customary or dispositional status of a rule. Ignored laws are not rules. For new laws to become rules, they have to be enforced to the point that the avoidance or performance of the behaviour in question becomes customary, and acquires a normative status.

Pragmatist philosophers and institutional economists in the Veblenian tradition argue that institutions work only because the rules involved are embedded in prevalent habits of thought and behaviour (James, 1892; Veblen, 1899; Dewey, 1922; Joas, 1993, 1996; Kilpinen, 2000). However, there has been some ambiguity in the definition of habit. Veblen and the pragmatist philosophers regarded habit as an acquired proclivity or capacity, which may or may not be actually expressed in current behaviour. Repeated behaviour is important in establishing a habit. But habit and behaviour are not the same. If we acquire a habit we do not necessarily use it all the time. A habit is a disposition to engage in previously adopted or acquired behaviour or thoughts, triggered by an appropriate stimulus or context.[11]

Accordingly, the pragmatist sociologists William Thomas and Florian Znaniecki (1920, p. 1851) criticized 'the indistinct use of the term "habit" to indicate any uniformities of behavior. … A habit … is the tendency to repeat the same act in similar material conditions'. Also treating habit as a propensity, William McDougall (1908, p. 37) wrote of 'acquired habits of thought and action' as 'springs of action' and saw 'habit as a source of impulse or motive power'. As John Dewey (1922, p. 42) put it: 'The essence of habit is an acquired predisposition to *ways* or modes of response'. Many habits are unconscious. Habits are submerged repertoires of potential thought or behaviour, to be triggered by an appropriate stimulus or context.[12]

Brain imaging studies on human subjects (Poldrack *et al.*, 2001) show that the formation of habits involves a shift away from parts of the brain associated with conscious, declarative memory and goal-setting (the medial temporal lobe and pre-frontal cortex) towards areas associated with procedural memory and context-triggered responses (the basal ganglia).

Habit is the psychological mechanism that forms the basis of much rule-following behaviour. For a habit to acquire the status of a rule, it has to acquire some inherent normative content, to be potentially codifiable, and to be prevalent among a group. Persistent and shared habits are the bases of customs. James (1892, p. 143) proclaimed: 'Habit is thus the enormous fly-wheel of society, its most precious conservative agent'.

The prevailing rule structure provides incentives and constraints for individual actions. Channelling behaviour in this way, accordant habits are further developed and reinforced among the population. Hence the rule structure helps to create habits and preferences that are consistent with its reproduction. Habits are the constitutive material of institutions, providing them with enhanced durability, power and normative authority. In turn, by reproducing shared habits of thought, institutions create strong mechanisms

[11] Lawson (2003b, p. 333) interprets Veblen differently, without textual evidence, 'as using the term habit to indicate certain (repeated) forms of action'. On the contrary, there are several passages in Veblen's works that suggest a view of habits as propensities or dispositions (see Hodgson, 2004a, p. 169).

[12] The works of James (1890) and Dewey (1922) remain two of the best accounts of the nature of habit as understood here. The misconception of habit as behaviour led Dewey (1922) to emphasize repeatedly that habit is an acquired disposition or propensity. The conception of a habit as a propensity or disposition is also found in modern works such as Camic (1986), Margolis (1987), Murphy (1994), Ouellette and Wood (1998), Kilpinen (2000), Wood *et al.* (2002) and others.

of conformism and normative agreement. As Charles Sanders Peirce (1878, p. 294) declared, the 'essence of belief is the establishment of habit'. Accordingly, habit is not the negation of deliberation, but its necessary foundation. Reasons and beliefs are often the rationalizations of deep-seated feelings and emotions that spring from habits laid down by repeated behaviours (Kilpinen, 2000; Wood *et al.,* 2002). This interplay of behaviour, habit, emotion and rationalization helps to explain the normative power of custom in human society. Hence 'custom reconciles us to everything' – as Edmund Burke (1757) wrote – and customary rules can acquire the force of moral authority. In turn, these moral norms help to further reinforce the institution in question.

Habits are acquired in a social context and not genetically transmitted. By accepting the foundational role of habit in sustaining rule-following behaviour, we can begin to build an alternative ontology of institutions, in which we avoid the conceptual problems of an account based primarily on intentionality. This is not to deny the importance of intentionality, but to regard it as a consequence as much as a cause, and to place it in the broader and ubiquitous context of other, non-deliberative behaviours.[13]

By structuring, constraining and enabling individual behaviours, institutions have the power to mould the capacities and behaviour of agents in fundamental ways; they have a capacity to change aspirations, instead of merely enabling or constraining them. Habit is the key mechanism in this transformation. Institutions are social structures that can involve *reconstitutive downward causation*, acting to some degree upon individual habits of thought and action. The existence of reconstitutive downward causation does not mean that institutions directly, entirely or uniformly determine individual aspirations, merely that there can be significant downward effects. Insofar as institutions lead to regularities of behaviour, concordant habits are laid down among the population, leading to congruent purposes and beliefs. In this way the institutional structure is further sustained.[14]

Because institutions simultaneously depend upon the activities of individuals and constrain and mould them, through this positive feedback they have strong self-reinforcing and self-perpetuating characteristics. Institutions are perpetuated not simply through the convenient coordination rules that they offer. They are perpetuated because they confine and mould

[13] The dispositional treatment of habit here is broadly consistent with Vanberg's (2002) concept of 'program-based' activity, which he insists must be rendered consistent with our knowledge of human evolution.

[14] Reconstitutive downward causation is discussed further in Hodgson (2002d, 2004a) and in the following two chapters.

individual aspirations, and create a foundation for their existence upon the many individual minds that they taint with their conventions.

This does not mean, however, that institutions stand separately from the group of individuals involved; institutions depend for their existence on individuals, their interactions and particular shared patterns of thought. Nevertheless, any single individual is born into a pre-existing institutional world, which confronts him or her with its rules and norms.[15] The institutions that we face reside in the dispositions of other individuals, but also depend on the structured interactions between them, often also involving material artefacts or instruments. History provides the resources and constraints, in each case both material and cognitive, in which we think, act and create.

Accordingly, institutions are simultaneously both objective structures 'out there', and subjective springs of human agency 'in the human head'. Institutions are in this respect like Klein bottles: the subjective 'inside' is simultaneously the objective 'outside'. The institution thus offers a link between the ideal and the real. The twin concepts of habit and institution may thus help to overcome the philosophical dilemma between realism and subjectivism in social science. Actor and institutional structure, although distinct, are thus connected in a circle of mutual interaction and interdependence.

Commons (1934, p. 69) noted that: 'Sometimes an institution seems analogous to a building, a sort of framework of laws and regulations, within which individuals act like inmates. Sometimes it seems to mean the "behavior" of the inmates themselves'. This dilemma of viewpoint persists today. For example, North's (1990, p. 3) definition of institutions as 'rules of the game ... or ... humanly devised constraints' stresses the restraints of the metaphorical prison in which the 'inmates' act. In contrast, Veblen's (1909, p. 626) description of institutions as 'settled habits of thought common to the generality of men' seems to start not from the objective constraints but from 'the inmates themselves'. However, as Commons hinted and Veblen (1909, pp. 628–30) argued in more depth, behavioural habit and institutional structure are mutually entwined and mutually reinforcing: both aspects are relevant to the full picture. A dual stress on both agency and institutional structure is required, in which it is understood that institutions themselves are the outcomes of human interactions and aspirations, without being consciously designed in every detail by any individual or group, while historically given institutions precede any one individual.

---

[15] See Hodgson (2004a) for a discussion of historical accounts of this insight, from Comte, through Marx, Lewes, Durkheim, Veblen and others to Archer (1995).

8.4 SOME PROBLEMS WITH DOUGLASS NORTH'S EXPOSITION

Starting with a definition of institutions as socially embedded systems of rules, it is evident that organizations are a special kind of institution, with additional features. Organizations are special institutions that involve (a) criteria to establish their boundaries and to distinguish their members from non-members, (b) principles of sovereignty concerning who is in charge and (c) chains of command delineating responsibilities within the organization.

However, in several influential statements, by Douglass North, he has characterized institutions and organizations in a different way. The purpose of this section is to expose some difficulties in his account and to maintain my alternative definitions. These difficulties concern North's apparent distinctions (i) between institutions and organizations, and (ii) between 'formal rules' and 'informal constraints'. North has been insufficiently clear. This has led to many people misinterpreting him as suggesting that organizations are not a type of institution. He is also misinterpreted as making a distinction between formal and informal institutions. Strictly, North upholds neither of these distinctions. I also argue that North has insufficiently elaborated the nature and functioning of social rules that he rightly identifies as the essence of institutions. His emphasis on the rule-like character of institutions is consistent with my definition, but I believe that something else needs to be added. Concerning institutions in general, North (1990, pp. 3–5) wrote:

> Institutions are the rules of the game in society or, more formally, are the humanly devised constraints that shape human interaction. In consequence they structure incentives in human exchange, whether political, social, or economic. … Conceptually, what must be clearly differentiated are the rules from the players. The purpose of the rules is to define the way the game is played. But the objective of the team within that set of rules is to win the game … Modeling the strategies and skills of the team as it develops is a separate process from modeling the creation, evolution, and consequences of the rules.

North rightly insists that rules must be 'clearly differentiated … from the players'. The distinction between players and rules is similar to the distinction between agents and structures, as discussed elsewhere (Archer, 1995; Lawson, 1997; Hodgson, 2004a). Structures depend upon agents, but the two are different and distinct. North (1994, p. 361) also wrote:

> It is the interaction between institutions and organizations that shapes the institutional evolution of an economy. If institutions are the rules of the game, organizations and their entrepreneurs are the players. Organizations are made up

> of groups of individuals bound together by some common purpose to achieve certain objectives.

North reasonably sees organizations as including political parties, firms, trade unions, schools, universities and so on. People have interpreted North as saying that organizations are not institutions. But North does not actually write this. He simply establishes his own primary interest in economic systems rather than the internal functioning of individual organizations. He is not so interested in the social rules that are internal to organizations, because he wants to treat them as unitary players and focus on interactions at the national or other higher levels.

There is nothing in principle wrong with the idea that under some conditions organizations can be treated as single actors, such as when there are procedures for members of an organization to express a common or majority decision. As Barry Hindess (1989, p. 89) argues, organizations can be treated as social actors as long as 'they have means of reaching decisions and of acting on some of them'. James Coleman (1982) comes to a similar conclusion. Interestingly, the criteria that sometimes allow us to treat organizations as actors require an understanding of organizations as social systems with boundaries and rules.

However, a problem arises if we *define* organizations as actors. This would amount to an unwarranted conflation of individual agency and organization. Organizations – such as firms and trade unions – are structures made up of individual actors, often with conflicting objectives. Even if mechanisms for 'reaching decisions and of acting on some of them' are ubiquitous, the treatment of an organization as a social actor should not ignore the potential conflict within the organization. The treatment of the organization as a social actor abstracts from such internal conflicts, but an abstraction should not become a fixed principle or definition that would block all considerations of internal conflict or structure.

Abstraction and definition are entirely different analytical procedures. When mathematicians calculate the trajectory of a vehicle or satellite through space they often treat it as a singular particle. In other words, they ignore the internal structure and rotation of the vehicle or satellite. But this does not mean that the vehicle or satellite is *defined* as a particle.

North does not make it sufficiently clear whether he is *defining* organizations as players or regarding organizations as players as an *analytical abstraction*. This has created much confusion, with other authors insisting that organizations should be *defined* as players. However, North (2002a, 2002b) has made it clear that he treats organizations as players simply for the purpose of analysis of the socio-economic system as a whole, and that he does not regard organizations as essentially the same thing as players in all circumstances. In saying that 'organizations are players' North is making an abstraction, rather than defining organizations in this way.

When North writes that organizations 'are made up of groups of individuals bound together by some common purpose' he simply ignores instances when this may not be the case. He is less interested in the internal mechanisms by which organizations coerce or persuade members to act together to some degree. Crucially, these mechanisms always involve systems of embedded rules. Organizations involve structures or networks, and these cannot function without rules of communication, membership or sovereignty. The unavoidable existence of rules within organizations means that, even by North's own definition, organizations must be regarded as a type of institution. Indeed, North (2002b) essentially accepted that organizations themselves have internal players and systems of rules, and hence by implication organizations are a special type of institution.[16]

As North acknowledged, it is possible for organizations to be treated as actors in some circumstances *and* generally to be regarded as institutions. Individual agents act within the organizational rule-system. In turn, under some conditions, organizations may be treated as actors within other, encompassing institutional rule-systems. There are multiple levels, in which organizations provide institutional rules for individuals, and possibly in turn these organizations can also be treated as actors within broader institutional frameworks. For example, the individual acts within the nation, but in turn the nation can sometimes be treated as an actor within an international framework of rules and institutions.

Further ambiguities arise with North's distinction between formal 'rules' and informal 'constraints'. Some distinction between the formal and the informal is important, but this distinction is attempted in different and confusing ways by various authors. Some identify the formal with the legal, and see informal rules as non-legal, even if they may be written down. In turn, if 'formal' means 'legal', then it is not clear whether 'informal' should mean illegal or non-legal (i.e. not expressed in law). Another possibility is to make the formal/informal distinction one of explicit versus tacit rules. Still another variant in the literature is to identify the formal with designed, and the informal with spontaneous institutions, along the lines of Carl Menger's famous distinction between pragmatic and organic institutions. We have at least three important distinctions, not one. North, like many other writers, does not make his intended distinction between 'formal' and 'informal' sufficiently clear.

The picture is further complicated by North's use of the different terms 'rule' and 'constraint'. North (1990, 1991, 1994) wrote most often of formal and informal constraints, rather than formal and informal rules, but he did not

---

[16] See the Appendix to this chapter for the correspondence with North.

indicate why he dropped the word 'rule' and whether or not constraints are also rules. North wrote frequently of 'formal rules' but not of 'informal rules'. But some writers interpret North as making a distinction between formal and informal rules (e.g. Schout, 1991). North's (1994, p. 360) examples of 'formal constraints' are 'rules, laws, constitutions'; and of 'informal constraints' are 'norms of behavior, conventions, self-imposed codes of conduct'. This suggests that rules are a special kind of formal constraint.

This creates a further problem for North. *If all rules are formal, and institutions are essentially rules, then all institutions are formal.* However, North (1995, p. 15) subsequently redefined institutions in the following terms: 'Institutions are the constraints that human beings impose on human interactions'. By redefining institutions essentially as constraints, rather than rules, this raised the question of a possible distinction between formal and informal constraints. This 1995 definition of an institution neglects the enabling aspect of institutions by emphasizing constraints alone. North (1997, p. 6) then shifted back to a conception of institutions as 'the rules of the game of a society'.

In correspondence with the present author, North (2002b) identified 'formal rules' with legal rules 'enforced by courts'. In contrast: 'Informal norms are enforced usually by your peers or others who impose costs on you if you do not live up to them'. Despite the persistent analytical emphasis in North's work on the power of informal and customary relations, his definitions dispose him to identify both rules and institutions with 'formal' (i.e. legal) regulations.[17]

This confinement of the concept of an institution to legal rule systems excludes social orders that are not legally expressed from the category of an institution. An emphasis on legal rules can downplay the existence of other rules and institutions that can also constrain and mould human behaviour in significant ways. Important examples include language and powerful social customs, such those pertaining to class in Britain, caste in India, gender in numerous countries and many other phenomena. Some rules and institutions – such as language and some traffic conventions – can emerge largely spontaneously as coordination equilibria, which are reproduced principally because it is convenient for agents to conform to them. To some degree, moral beliefs, sanctions and constraints operate in all these cases. Not all powerful rules or institutions are decreed in law.

North rightly emphasizes 'informal constraints' but does not admit the category of informal rules. But all contingent constraints that derive from

[17] Commons (1934) also advanced a predominantly legal conception of an institution, criticized elsewhere (Hodgson, 2004a, Ch. 13). See Fiori (2002) for a discussion of the distinction between formal rules and informal constraints in North's work.

human action (rather than the laws of nature) are essentially rules. Accordingly, there is not a clear line between rules and constraints, as North suggests, and instead social constraints are essentially rules.

Furthermore, an overemphasis on the formal and legal aspects can overlook the reliance of legal systems themselves on informal rules and norms. As Émile Durkheim (1984, p. 158) argued in 1893: 'in a contract not everything is contractual'. Whenever a contract exists there are rules and norms that are not necessarily codified in law. The parties to the agreement are forced to rely on institutional rules and standard patterns of behaviour, which cannot for reasons of practicality and complexity be fully established as laws. Legal systems are invariably incomplete, and give scope for custom and culture to do their work (Hodgson, 2001b).

North fully accepts the importance of the informal sphere, and frequently discusses the informal aspects of formal (i.e. legal) institutions. He emphasizes, for example, the roles of ideology and custom. But he insufficiently acknowledges informal *institutions* that are not decreed in law, including those that arise spontaneously, such as coordination equilibria. North (1990, p. 138) rightly and additionally emphasizes 'informal constraints' and the 'cultural transmission of values' but unnecessarily confines his definition of institutions to rules codified in law.

Whether we are dealing with formal or informal rules, we need to consider the ways in which rules are enacted. While it does not necessarily have to enter into the *definition* of an institution or rule, there has to be some account of how rule-systems affect individual behaviour. Pointing to the incentives and sanctions associated with rules is insufficient because it would not explain how individuals evaluate the sanctions or incentives involved. We also have to explain why they might, or might not, take incentives or sanctions seriously.

Clearly, the mere codification, legislation or proclamation of a rule is insufficient to make that rule effect social behaviour. It might simply be ignored, just as many drivers break speed limits on roads, and many Continental Europeans ignore legal restrictions on smoking in restaurants. In this respect, the unqualified term 'rule' may mislead us.

North acknowledges that mere rule proclamation is not enough. But in trying to understand how behaviour is fixed or changed, his attention sometimes shifts to the 'informal constraints' of everyday life. Of course, the informal sphere is vital, but ironically, according to North's own definitions, 'informal constraints' are not institutions at all. Instead I prefer a broader conception of institutions that accommodates the informal basis of all structured and durable behaviour. That is why I define institutions as *durable systems of established and embedded social rules* that structure social interactions, rather than rules as such. In short, institutions are *social rule-systems*, not simply rules.

The ambiguity of the terms 'formal' and 'informal' with regard to institutions and rules suggests that these words should either be abandoned or used with extreme care. It may be best to use more precise terms such as 'legal', 'non-legal' and 'explicit' instead.

While broadly subscribing to North's definitions, Pavel Pelikan (1988, p. 372; 1992, p. 45) compared North's 'rules' to the 'genotype' within the 'phenotype' of the organizational structure.[18] If rules are like genes, then this underlines the importance of considering their mechanisms of survival and replication, and they way in which they can affect individuals or organizations. Rules do not have the capacity to copy themselves directly; they replicate through other psychological mechanisms. From a pragmatist perspective, the gene-like entities behind rules are individual habits, because these habits are the conditional, rule-like dispositions that marshal behaviour. Rules generally work only because they are embedded in prevalent habits of thought and behaviour. Hence it is best to treat habits rather than rules as social genotypes.

8.5 SELF-ENFORCEMENT VERSUS EXTERNAL ENFORCEMENT

With one possible exception, all institutions depend on other institutions. As Searle (1995, p. 60) points out, 'language is the basic social institution in the sense that all others presuppose language, but language does not presuppose the others'. Language is basic because all institutions involve social interaction and interpretation of some kind. Accordingly, all institutions involve at least rudimentary interpretative rules.

This literature on self-organization and spontaneous orders provides the essential insight that institutions and other social phenomena can arise in an undesigned way through structured interactions between agents. The focus on self-organizing aspects of the social system can be traced back to David Hume and Adam Smith, and it is a major theme in the Austrian school of economics from Carl Menger to Friedrich Hayek. This literature shows that social order can emerge that is not itself an intention or property of any single individual or group of individuals.

However, even self-organizing institutions require a (rudimentary) language so, with the exception of language itself, the concept of *self*-organization must be qualified by the acknowledgement of the prior and extrinsic organization of communicative or interpretative rules.

---

[18] Pelikan's (1988, 1992) definitions are similar to those of North. He treats institutions as 'rules' but also explicitly considers internal 'institutions' (rules) of organizations.

Furthermore, the concepts of self-organization or spontaneous order are insufficient for an understanding of all institutions. Menger (1871) himself recognized a distinction between 'organic' (self-organizing) and 'pragmatic' (designed) institutions. But many subsequent authors ignore the latter to concentrate on the former. Indeed, much of the existing literature on institutions exhibits an excessive emphasis on the (albeit essential) idea of self-organization, to the detriment of other vital mechanisms of institutional emergence and sustenance.

With institutions that are not self-organizing, there is a stronger dependence on other institutions that are required to enforce the internal rules. We first examine some typical mechanisms of self-organization, and then move on to cite some cases where such external dependence pertains.

An archetypical self-organizing configuration is a coordination game. Coordination rules typically provide incentives for everyone to conform to the convention. Consequently, a coordination equilibrium can be self-policing and highly stable. Language is an example. In communication we have strong incentives and inclinations to use words and sounds in a way that conforms as closely as possible to the perceived norm. Norms of language and pronunciation are thus largely self-policing (Quine, 1960).

Similarly, some (but not all) legal rules have a strong self-policing element. For example, there are obvious incentives (apart from avoiding legal sanctions) to stop at red traffic lights and to drive on the same side of the road as others. Although infringements will occur, these particular laws can be partly enforced by motorists themselves, because infringements can increase perceived personal risks.

A coordination equilibrium can be self-enforcing; not only does each player lack any incentive to change strategy, but also each player wishes that other players keep to their strategy as well (Schotter, 1981, pp. 22–3). If agents have compatible preferences and strategies in this sense, then coordination rules can often emerge spontaneously and be self-reinforcing. Even if I prefer to drive on the left, when I find myself in a country where driving on the right is the convention, then I will drive on the right, and others will prefer that I do this. A coordination equilibrium has characteristics of stability and self-enforcement, even when the equilibrium is not ideal for everyone involved.

However, coordination games are a special case. Contrasting configurations include the famous Prisoners' Dilemma game, which allegedly represents several types of social situation, including the socially suboptimal but individually advantageous use of private cars rather than public transport (Best, 1982), the famous 'tragedy of the commons' (Hardin, 1968), and aspects of the employment contract (Leibenstein, 1982).

At least in a one-shot play of the Prisoners' Dilemma game, each player has an incentive to defect. The situation of mutual cooperation is not a Nash equilibrium because each player can gain an advantage by shifting from cooperation to defection. The Nash equilibrium is where both players defect, but each player gets less than she would if both players cooperated. A 'spontaneous order' may emerge but it is clearly suboptimal, by any reasonable criterion.[19]

Coordination rules are followed primarily because of convenience. By contrast, suboptimal outcomes in the Prisoners' Dilemma game raise normative questions in a more acute manner. Although all rules involve costs and benefits, there is a big difference between following a rule simply because it is convenient to do so, and following a rule because of a normative belief. Viktor Vanberg (1994, p. 65) rightly points out that writers in the spontaneous order tradition – from Hume and Smith through Menger to Hayek – acknowledge inadequately the additional moral and legal mechanisms that are required for enforcement in non-coordination games. Walter Schultz (2001, pp. 64–6) stresses a similar distinction in his powerful discussion of the problem of enforcement of social rules.

Until recently, the problem of enforcement has been relatively neglected in the literature. As noted above, some rules are largely self-enforcing. In contrast, laws that restrict behaviour, where there are substantial, perceived net advantages to transgression, are the ones that require the most policing. Hence people frequently evade tax payments or break speed limits. Without some policing activity the law itself is likely to be infringed, debased and 'brought into disrepute'.

For example, there are incentives to debase money. If they can evade detection, individual agents have an obvious incentive to use less costly, poor quality or faked versions of the medium of exchange. If such forgeries or debasements are allowed to endure, then bad money will drive out the good. Money is not self-policing in the same way as language, and may require some external authority to enforce its rules, as Menger himself acknowledged (Latzer and Schmitz, 2002).

Self-policing mechanisms can be undermined if there is the possibility of undetected variation from the norm and there is sufficient incentive to exert such variations. Language and money differ in this respect. The argument for enforcement by a third party such as the state is thus stronger in the case of money and some laws, than in the case of language.

Attempts to explain the evolution of contract and private property in entirely spontaneous terms have failed. Some authors try to explain the enforcement of property rights by means of trading coalitions (Greif, 1993). Itai Sened (1997) shows that property rights are not entirely self-reinforcing,

---

[19] Although mutual cooperation can emerge in repeated Prisoners' Dilemma games, Axelrod's (1984) 'tit-for-tat' strategy can be out-competed by alternative strategies (Kitcher, 1987; Lindgren, 1992; Binmore, 1998b).

and some external institution such as the state is required to enforce them. With a larger number of actors it is more difficult for individuals to establish mutual and reciprocal arrangements that ensure contract compliance (Mantzavinos, 2001, Ch. 8). If trading coalitions do emerge, then these themselves take upon state-like qualities to enforce agreements and protect property. In a world of incomplete and imperfect information, high transaction costs, asymmetrically powerful relations and agents with limited insight, powerful institutions are necessary to enforce rights.

It is an open question as to whether another strong institution, apart from the state, could fulfil this necessary role. We simply note that an important class of institutions exists in which such institutions depend on other institutions in order to enforce effectively their rules. In the real world there are many examples where some institutions are sustained and supported by others. The role of the state in enforcing law and protecting property rights is but one example. A major agenda for enquiry is to explore the extent of such complementarities and understand their mechanisms in depth.

8.6 AGENT SENSITIVE AND AGENT INSENSITIVE INSTITUTIONS

Here I introduce a different distinction, with the terms 'agent sensitive' and 'agent insensitive' institutions. *An agent sensitive institution is one in which the reigning equilibria or conventions can be significantly altered if the preferences or dispositions of some agents are changed, within a feasible set of personality types.* This issue is best approached by considering some examples of agent insensitive institutions.

In an early paper Gary Becker (1962) demonstrates that behaviour ruled by habit or inertia is just as capable as rational optimization of predicting the standard downward-sloping demand curve and the profit-seeking activity of firms. He shows how the negatively inclined market demand curve could result from habitual behaviour, up against a moving budget constraint. A constraint means that agents, whether super-rational or habit-driven, have to stay one side of the line. With agents of each type, rotations in the budget constraint can bring about downward-sloping demand curves, irrespective of whether agents in his terms are 'habitual' or 'rational'.[20]

Much later, Dhananjay Gode and Shyam Sunder (1993) show that experiments with agents of 'zero intelligence' produce behaviours that differ

[20] G. Becker (1962) first saw a dichotomy between 'habitual' and 'rational' behaviour, which he later abandoned in his attempt to explain habitual behaviour in rational terms (Becker and Murphy, 1988). Both positions contrast with pragmatism, where habit is the grounding rather than the antithesis or outcome of rational deliberation.

little from those with human traders. Gode and Sunder suggest that structural constraints can produce similar outcomes, whatever the objectives or behaviour of the individual agents. As in Becker's (1962) model, systemic constraints prevail over micro-variations. Ordered market behaviour can result from the existence of resource and institutional constraints, and may be largely independent of the 'rationality', or otherwise, of the agents. Structural constraints, not individuals, do much of the explanatory work. We thus face the possibility of a study of markets that focuses largely on institutions and structures, to a degree independent of the assumptions made about agents.[21]

These models suggest that ordered and sometimes predictable behaviour can sometimes result largely from institutional constraints. The explanatory burden is carried by system structures rather than the preferences or psychology of individuals. I describe such cases as 'agent insensitive' institutions, because outcomes are relatively insensitive to individual psychology or personality.

Partly on the basis of the Gode and Sunder (1993) results, Philip Mirowski (2002) argues that to understand markets we do not have to pay much attention to the psychologies, cognitive processes or computational capacities of the agents involved. Instead he treats the market itself as a computational entity. His arguments may apply to some institutional structures, including some markets, and to that extent they are important and worthwhile. But they do not constitute a general theoretical strategy, unless agent insensitivity is itself general among institutions.

What is common to the Becker (1962) and Gode and Sunder (1993) models is the existence of hard and insurmountable (budget) constraints. They push the agents into position and offer them few alternatives, whatever their inclinations. Hence these models are agent insensitive and the constraints do much of the explanatory work. Such hard constraints do exist in reality, but they are a rather special case. Other institutional constraints operate through disincentives or legal penalties. But in such cases it may be possible to cross the line or break the law. The propensity to break rules or transgress constraints will in part depend on the preferences and dispositions of each individual agent. If the constraints were softer, then the agents would have more discretion, and it would be likely that the personalities of the agents will have to be taken into account. By wrongly suggesting that agent

---

[21] For useful discussions of these results see Denzau and North (1994), Mirowski (2002) and Mirowski and Somefun (1998). Grandmont (1992) has similarly demonstrated that aggregate demand can be well behaved under certain distributional restrictions, merely by assuming that individual behaviour satisfies budget constraints, without any reference to utility maximization. See also Hildenbrand (1994).

insensitivity is generally the case, Mirowski's research strategy carries the danger of a general conflation of agency into the institutional structure.

Consider the alternative possibility of relatively high incentives to conform to a convention. A coordination game is ostensibly agent insensitive, because the players have an incentive to conform to the reigning convention, even if it is not their most favoured option. British drivers will drive on the right in America and Continental Europe, even if they find it easier to drive on the left. To a degree, such traffic conventions are agent insensitive. However, a convention can be overturned if a sufficient number of people defy it. As long as the benefits of coordination are finite, the possibility exists of a relatively extreme personality type that may be inclined to overturn the prevalent convention. In the different case of hard constraints, all agents are required to comply, whatever their inclinations.

In contrast to a system with hard constraints, a number of configurations are agent sensitive. Consider, for example, a reigning pattern of cooperation in a repeated Prisoners' Dilemma game resulting from a population dominated by units playing the tit-for-tat strategy. However, they can be invaded by an influx of others who always cooperate. If this occurs, then the consequent population of cooperators would clearly be vulnerable to an invasion by a species that consistently defects. In turn, if this invasion was incomplete, or subject to a slight amount of error, then a new invasion of tit-for-tat players could take advantage of the fact that consistent defection was not absolute. Each of these outcomes is unstable (Kitcher, 1987; Lindgren, 1992). The prevailing conventions are sometimes sensitive to the types of player that are involved. Another possibility of agent sensitivity results from the existence of multiple (Nash) equilibria. Slight differences between the personalities of agents may matter if there is a choice between two or more (near) optimal positions.

If we introduce greater variance in personality and observe the stability of reigning conventions, then we can gauge the agent sensitivity of the institutional set-up involved. Institutions exhibit different degrees of agent sensitivity and insensitivity, and investigations should not be confined to extreme or particular types.

8.7 CONCLUDING REMARKS

This chapter has proposed some key definitions, as follows:

- *Social structures* include all sets of social relations, including the episodic and those without rules, as well as social institutions.
- *Institutions* are systems of established and embedded social rules that structure social interactions.

- *Rules* in this context are understood as socially transmitted and customary normative injunctions or immanently normative dispositions, that in circumstances *X* do *Y*.
- *Conventions* are particular instances of institutional rules.
- *Organizations* are special institutions that involve (a) criteria to establish their boundaries and to distinguish their members from non-members, (b) principles of sovereignty concerning who is in charge and (c) chains of command delineating responsibilities within the organization.
- *Habituation* is the psychological mechanism by which individuals acquire dispositions to engage in previously adopted or acquired (rule-like) behaviour.

Some of the discussion in this chapter has involved putting some flesh on these bare-boned definitions, particularly in the case of institutions and rules. This involves the key concept of habit, which is regarded as a key element in the understanding of how rules are embedded in social life and how institutional structures are sustained.

Many writers attempt distinctions between 'formal' or 'informal' institutions or rules. However, these terms have been used misleadingly and in different ways. Does the term 'formal' mean legal, written, explicit, codifiable or something else? The ambiguities surrounding these terms mean that they cannot be taken for granted. One is required to specify more clearly what is meant in each case, or use more precise terms such as 'legal', 'non-legal' and 'explicit' instead.

Generally, the idea that there is a dividing line between institutions that are entirely 'formal' on the one hand and entirely 'informal' institutions on the other is false, because 'formal' institutions (in any of the above senses) *always* depend on non-legal rules and inexplicit norms in order to operate. If laws or declarations are neither customary nor embodied in individual dispositions, then – 'formal' or not – they have insignificant affects. They are mere declarations or proclamations, rather than effective social rules. Some declarations simply codify existing customs. Other proclamations may eventually become effective rules, but only through additional powers, such as persuasion, legitimation or enforcement.

An attempt has also been made here to avoid some over-generalizations concerning the nature of institutions. In particular, while self-organization is an extremely important phenomenon in both nature and society, it would be a mistake to suggest that all institutions are of this type. It has been shown here that some institutional rules require other institutions for their enforcement.

Second, while there are cases where institutional rules or constraints do much of the explanatory work, and therefore the institutional outcomes are relatively insensitive to the personalities or psychologies of the agents involved, these instances are not universal. To regard all institutions as agent insensitive is to lead to the further error of conflating individuals into the institutional structure, where the interplay of both is required to understand how institutions are formed and sustained.

APPENDIX: EXTRACTS FROM CORRESPONDENCE BETWEEN DOUGLASS C. NORTH AND GEOFFREY M. HODGSON

NORTH, 10 September 2002

'First of all … organizations, you say, are special institutions. I think that for certain purposes we can consider organizations as institutions, but for my purposes organizations are to be separated out from institutions. That is, I am interested in the macro aspect of organization, not in the internal structure of organization. If I was interested in the latter … I would be interested in internal structure, governance and indeed all the kind of internal problems of structure, organization and conflicts of interest … I am not interested in that. What I am interested in is … the actors in the process of overall societal, political economic change, and … I can forget about the internal structure, even how decisions are made internal to the organization and simply look on the entrepreneurs of organizations as the key players in the process of institutional change. … For certain purposes one can consider organizations as institutions but for the purposes that I am dealing with – looking at the macro aspects of institutional change – I do not have to; indeed, I do not want to. … As I said at the beginning, I think that we are really not in too much disagreement. I think the issue really is the kinds of questions that I am asking which make me focus in a particular way.'

HODGSON, 19 September 2002

'I understand fully that you are interested primarily in overall, socio-economic change, rather than the internal structure of organizations. I believe that such a special focus is entirely legitimate. And I am one of very many who warmly appreciate your major contribution in this area.

I would presume that you also believe it to be legitimate to study the internal structure of organizations. … What concerns me is the need for conversation and common understanding between those … who concentrate on the internal structure or organizations and those (like yourself) who concentrate on overall socio-economic change. For a conversation to take place there must be shared meanings of terms.

In this respect I find a statement like "organizations are players" to be potentially problematic. If "organizations are players" means "I will treat organizations as players for the purposes of my kind of analysis" then, given certain conditions, that would be OK in my view. However, if "organizations are players" means "organizations are defined as players" or "organizations are essentially the same as individuals or players" then I would find these formulations to be misleading. … When you say "organizations are the players" do you mean to say:

(a) "for the purposes of analysis of the socio-economic system as a whole it is legitimate to treat organizations as if they are players"? or
(b) "organizations are essentially the same thing as players", i.e. in all circumstances?

If you follow (a) – and your letter of September 10th seems to lean in this direction – then a definition of organization is still outstanding. So in this case, I would ask a further question:

(a*) Would you accept a definition of organization that accepted that organizations themselves had internal players and systems of rules, and hence organizations were a special type of institution?

I would very grateful for your help and clarification on these points. If your answers to (a) and (a*) were in the affirmative then I would be in complete agreement with you.

I would like also to turn to a second issue where I am still unclear. This concerns the distinction between the formal and the informal. I also think that this issue is important but I think that there is much confusion in the broad literature on this topic. …

(c) Does the formal/informal dichotomy refer to a distinction between legal and non-legal, or a distinction between explicit and tacit rules/constraints?
(d) Given the answer to (c), are there such things as informal rules?
(e) Is a social/organizational/behavioural constraint also a rule? …

I know that I am pressing you a bit but I think that it is important to achieve maximum clarity, and then hopefully consensus, in this area. … My hope is that we can increase our agreement and then move on.'

NORTH, 7 October 2002

'In reply to your letter, I am in complete agreement with you on the first part of your question. That is, I agree that (a) and (a*) are exactly what I have in mind, so we are in complete agreement. On the other issue, I regard informal norms not as rules but as norms of behavior which have different kinds of enforcement characteristics than formal rules. Formal rules are enforced by courts and things like that. Informal norms are enforced usually by your peers or others who will impose costs on you if you do not live up to them. In that sense, because they have different enforcement characteristics, I do not consider them to be a rule in the same sense that formal rules are.'

9. The Hidden Persuaders

> Institutions systematically direct individual memory and channel our perceptions into forms compatible with the relations they authorize. They fix processes that are essentially dynamic, they hide their influence, and they rouse our emotions to a standardized pitch on standardized issues. Add to all this they endow themselves with rightness and send their mutual corroboration cascading through all the levels of our information system. … For us, the hope of intellectual independence is to resist, and the necessary first step in resistance is to discover how the institutional grip is laid upon our mind.
>
> Mary Douglas, *How Institutions Think* (1987)

9.1 INTRODUCTION

In his bestseller *The Hidden Persuaders* (1957), Vance Packard painted a grim picture.[1] The post-war vision of a prosperous world, in which genuine human needs were to be met by a strong, efficient and growing economy, was shattered. Instead of serving human needs, the big corporations were manipulating our very wants and desires, using everything from subliminal messages to the exploitation of sexual images. Arguably, however, the social influences on our aspirations are more general, and often more subtle. In the manner discussed below, many forces that mould our personalities are undesigned. The more deeply hidden persuaders are not the products of any corporate marketing department, or government office, but are those that emanate in some way from our social institutions and our history.

This chapter is about these more deeply 'hidden persuaders'. An aim is to examine how such persuasion is possible, and the possible causal mechanisms that are involved. In their research, mainstream economists often ignore the possibility that our purposes and preferences are reconstituted by our circumstances. Some problems with this mainstream perspective are outlined. The chapter moves on to consider how 'hidden persuaders' can change our preferences in fundamental ways. Some possible objections to this argument are considered. The chapter concludes by reviewing the argument as a whole and suggesting a direction for future research.

---

[1] This chapter is based on the author's inaugural lecture, as Research Professor at the University of Hertfordshire on 16 March 2000. It was originally published as Hodgson (2003b) and has been significantly revised here.

9.2 THERE'S NO DISPUTING TASTES

Whatever the limitations of Packard's analysis, most theoretical models within economics admit no real persuaders at all. There are merely transmitters of information. Admittedly, a minority of economists, such as Nicolas Kaldor (1950), and especially John Kenneth Galbraith, take a different view. For them, advertising is both manipulative and wasteful. For example, in *The Affluent Society,* Galbraith (1969, pp. 150–152) writes:

> the institutions of modern advertising and salesmanship … cannot be reconciled with the notion of independently determined desires, for their central function is to create desires – to bring into being wants that previously did not exist … wants can be synthesized by advertising, catalysed by salesmanship, and shaped by the discreet manipulations of the persuaders.

In contrast, the Chicago economists George Stigler and Gary Becker (1977) declare that advertising could be treated simply as 'information'. In their classic article, they allege that 'tastes neither change capriciously nor differ importantly between people' (p. 76) they argue that 'it is neither necessary nor useful to attribute to advertising the function of changing tastes' (p. 84). Treating advertising as information, consumers seek the 'knowledge … produced by the advertising of products'.

Becker extends this model in his book *Accounting for Tastes* (1996). Alongside 'human capital' he adds 'social capital' and other 'cultural' variables. Against any objection that individuals in former models were insensitive to their cultural and social circumstances, Becker now brings such variables into the model. This later model does not simply encapsulate behavioural changes in response to advertising; it also includes behavioural responses to changes in social culture as well.

But Becker does not fulfil his promise to 'account for tastes'. We have no account of the origins or derivation of the key functional forms in his theory. They are simply assumed, as in previous models, or 'immaculately conceived'. There is no accounting for the origin or nature of the functions that generate tastes.

9.3 CAN THESE ISSUES BE PUT TO THE TEST?

We are faced with two irreconcilable positions. Galbraith and others argue that tastes and preference functions are altered by circumstances. Becker and Stigler argue, on the contrary, that the underlying functions are unaltered – they only have to be specified properly. Can the issues in dispute be put to empirical test? The answer to this question is negative. The reason is that the standard core of utility theory is *non-falsifiable*.

In a neglected article, Lawrence Boland (1981) asks if any conceivable evidence would refute the standard assumptions of maximizing behaviour. He then shows that such an attempt at falsification could never work. Any claim that a person is not maximizing anything can always be countered by the response that the person is in fact maximizing something else. Given that we can never in principle demonstrate that 'something else' (perhaps unknown to us) is not being maximized, then the theory is invulnerable to any empirical attack. To show empirically that nothing is being maximized we would have to measure every possible variable that could impinge upon humanity, from the changing of the weather to the twinkling of the stars. The maximization assumption could be false – but it is impossible to prove that it is. While the maximization assumption is non-falsifiable, Boland also rightly pointed out that it is not a tautology. This is because it is *conceivably false*. It might be the case that nothing is being maximized. But we can never know.

The problems with the maximization argument are doubly severe when it is assumed that utility is being maximized. There is no experimental or other phenomenon that cannot in principle be 'explained' within a utility-maximizing framework. Even the so-called anomalies revealed by experiments with human subjects can be explained away. If experiments show that some consumers appear to prefer a monetary reward that is less than the expected outcome, or appear to have intransitive preference orderings, then we can always get round these problems by introducing other variables. For example, evidence of apparent preference intransitivity can be explained away by taking account of the fact that the different choices take place under different conditions and at different points in time.

Preference reversals also fail to falsify utility theory, once we accept that utility is not necessarily measured in terms of the monetary payoffs in the experiment. If we assume an added disutility associated with involvement in a risky and low probability choice, then the theory that people are maximizing their utility is not overturned by these experiments. In general, a risk-averse actor may not maximize expected monetary value but still be maximizing expected utility.[2]

No evidence can, in principle, falsify the assumption that behaviour results from individuals or households maximizing their utility. This has implications for both neoclassical and institutionalist views. Galbraith (1969) is wrong to presume that 'the institutions of modern advertising and

---

[2] Experimental economists such as V. Smith (1982) and others have addressed the problem of the possible absence of a linear correlation between utility and monetary payoff. Smith proposes a number of 'precepts' of experimental assumption and design constituting an 'induced value procedure'. But Smith (p. 929) himself is the first to admit that these precepts cannot guarantee any correspondence between observable monetary rewards and preferences that are 'not directly observable'.

salesmanship ... cannot be reconciled with the notion of independently determined desires'. If a theory is 'reconciled' with a phenomenon when it is empirically consistent with it, then the Stigler–Becker theory, involving 'independently determined' functions of desire, shows that such a reconciliation is possible. The only problem with such a reconciliation, merely hinted at by Galbraith, is the difficulty in the Stigler–Becker scheme of dealing with entirely new products.

However, is this capacity for infinite empirical reconciliation a sign of weakness or of strength? By encompassing all possible arrangements and interconnections, the important relationships and connections in particular circumstances are lost in the sea of universal possibilities. Accordingly, the universality of a theory does not necessarily mean that it is useful or informative (Hodgson, 2001b).

The non-falsifiability of any theory does not necessarily mean that it is invalid or unscientific, as Karl Popper himself was later to recognize (Ackerman, 1976). What it does indicate is that the dispute between the institutionalist and the neoclassical approaches cannot be resolved simply by looking at facts. Matters of methodology and interpretation are also involved.

Of course, many proponents of utility theory would be unwilling to push the argument to extremes. They may hold to some limited version of utility theory, perhaps also in the belief that there is no adequate theoretical alternative. This more nuanced position would require a more extensive evaluation, beyond the scope of the present chapter. The arguments in this section are directed, instead, against those, on the one hand, who would wrongly claim that utility maximization cannot explain some behaviour, and those, on the other hand, who are overly triumphalist about valid but largely barren claims that it can be applied to every possible phenomenon.

9.4 CRITICIZING GIVEN PREFERENCE FUNCTIONS

The assumption of given, utility-maximizing individuals (or households) has been widely criticized on theoretical grounds. One of the most famous theoretical criticisms is the argument that global, rational decision-making is impossible, given the complexity of real-world decisions and the computational limits of the human brain (Simon, 1957). Modern game theory has exposed other logical problems. In certain types of game the very definition of rationality becomes problematic (Sugden, 1991). However, all these criticisms are of maximizing behaviour, rather than of the assumption of the given preference function. The following arguments address the latter issue.

We start from the contention that socio-economic systems do not simply create new products and perceptions. *They also create and re-create individuals.* The individual not only changes her purposes and preferences, but also revises her skills and her perceptions of her needs. Both in terms of capacities and beliefs, the individual is changed in the process.

Much follows from this important point. In particular, learning in the fullest sense is more than the discovery or reception of information; it is the reconstitution of individual capacities and preferences, tantamount to a change in individual personality. Today, we may not like a particular work of art, but after exposure to it we may acquire a taste for it. Learning can *reconstitute* the individual (Hodgson, 1999a). In short, learning can change preferences, goals, capacities, skills and values.

Strictly, the very act of learning means that not all information is possessed and global rationality is ruled out. As Douglas Vickers (1995, p. 115) and others have acknowledged, to place learning in with the framework of the utility-maximizing, rational actor, the scope of the concept has to be overly restricted. Crucially, learning is the development of the modes and means of cognition, calculation and assessment. If the methods and criteria of 'optimization' are themselves being learned how can learning itself be optimal?

Remarkably, in the Stigler–Becker version, the preference function is already 'there', ready to deal with unpredictable and unknowable circumstances. Miraculously, the function already 'knows' its preferences for inventions yet to come; its parameter space includes variables representing the ideas and the characteristics of the commodities of the future. Mysteriously, it has already learned how to recognize and desire them. What does learning mean in such circumstances, when we already know much of what is to be learned? Such a conception of learning must be sorely inadequate.

Another group of criticisms emanates from recent developments in psychology. A group of psychologists emphasize that human reason is always situated in a context, and it typically relies on external objects and structures as scaffolding for ideas (A. Clark, 1997a, 1997b). It is suggested that much work in economics and other social sciences is based on an unsatisfactory conception of rationality (Cosmides and Tooby, 1994; Plotkin, 1994). In response, the temporal and the situated aspects of human reason are emphasized. In reality, reason is an iterated process of adaptive response, cued by a variety of external structures and circumstances, including social institutions.

This argument is consistent with that of David Lane *et al.* (1996). They argue that social interaction involves 'generative relationships' that induce changes of perception and consequent action, giving rise to new institutions and new capabilities. Whereas the given, utility-maximizer has given ends, generative relationships are about reconstitutive processes of learning within social institutions.

What I have termed the 'Principle of Evolutionary Explanation' (Hodgson, 1998a, 2004a) demands that any behavioural assumption in the social sciences must be consistent with our understanding of how human beings have evolved. Although economics is irreducible to biology, propositions in economics must be consistent with those in biology. However, the empirical and theoretical work of modern evolutionary psychologists such as Leda Cosmides and John Tooby (1994) suggests that minds essentially based on global, all-purpose, context-independent, deliberative rationality are very unlikely to emerge through evolution. In other words, global, all-purpose rationality fails to satisfy the Principle of Evolutionary Explanation.[3]

Strikingly, Veblen (1934, p. 79) made a closely related assertion in 1898. A scientist cannot reasonably argue that rational economic man is immanently and asocially conceived. A Veblenian evolutionary perspective requires that the exclusive focus on the given agent should be abandoned.

9.5 RECONSTITUTIVE DOWNWARD CAUSATION

I argue here that a strong process of 'downward causation' is associated with institutions in human societies. It is not confined to the conscious designs of the advertisers or propagandists. It emanates more widely from the ordinary customs and routines of everyday life. In this section the notion of downward causation is introduced and discussed in general terms. It is later applied to the topic of 'hidden persuaders' under consideration here.

The idea of 'upward causation' is already widely accepted in the social and natural sciences. Elements at a lower ontological level affect those at a higher one. For example, influenza epidemics reduce economic productivity and voting can change governments. Upward causation can be reconstitutive, because lower-level changes may alter fundamentally a higher-level structure. However, reductionists are obliged to deny the possibility of reconstitutive downward causation that is being proposed here. With reconstitutive downward causation it is impossible to take the parts as given and then explain the whole. Furthermore, for reasons examined below, the notion of reconstitutive downward causation does not fall foul of critiques of 'holism' or methodological collectivism.

---

[3] Note that this claim concerns deliberative capacities rather the conformity (or otherwise) of behaviour with the axioms of utility maximization. A number of writers claim that evolutionary selection leads to human agents that conform to expected utility theory (Binmore, 1994, 1998a; Robson, 2001a, 2001b, 2002). However, these arguments do not carry so much force as might appear at first sight. As noted above, the axioms are formally consistent with *any* behavioural outcome (Hodgson, 2001b).

In its literature, the notion of 'downward causation' has weaker and stronger forms.[4] In a weaker formulation, Donald Campbell (1974) sees it in terms of evolutionary laws acting on populations. He argued that all processes at the lower levels of an ontological hierarchy are restrained by and act in conformity to the laws of the higher levels. In other words, if there are systemic properties and tendencies then individual components of the system act in conformity with them. For example, a population of individual organisms is constrained by processes of natural selection.

By contrast, Roger Sperry (1991, pp. 230–231) suggests a stronger interpretation of downward causation. He recognizes, for example, that 'higher cultural and other acquired values have power to downwardly control the more immediate, inherent humanitarian traits.'

At first sight this may seem to go against the stricture of Mario Bunge (1979, p. 39) that: 'There is no action of the whole on its parts; rather, there are actions of some components upon others'. However, if structures can enable or constrain individual behaviours, then interactions with other individuals will partly reflect structural properties. Hence, through individual interactions, structures have causal powers at the individual level. With this formulation, Bunge's stricture is not overturned.

Claus Emmeche *et al.* (2000) identify three versions of downward causation: strong, medium and weak. By 'strong' downward causation they mean some mechanism by which entities or processes at a higher level bring about 'a direct change in the laws of the lower level (or at least a change in lawful regularities at this level) effected from above' (p. 19). They rightfully reject this possibility: although higher level entities can constrain processes at a lower level, the laws of nature at the lower level cannot be overturned. Chemistry, for example, cannot defy the laws of physics, and biology has to be consistent with both physics and chemistry. For Emmeche *et al.* the only viable cases of downward causation are 'medium' and 'weak'. Medium downward causation means that '*higher level entities are constraining conditions for the emergent activity of lower levels*' (p. 25).

I propose a 'reconstitutive' version of downward causation that is consistent with the 'medium' conditions of viability advanced by Emmeche *et al.* (2000). It is not suggested that reconstitutive downward causation means that social laws or forces can overturn the principles governing the operation of human mental and physical activity at the level of the individual. Sperry (1991, p. 230) himself insists on a similar condition: 'the higher-level phenomena in exerting downward control do *not disrupt* or *intervene* in the causal relations of the downward-level component activity'. This could

[4] The term 'downward causation' originates in psychology in the work of the Nobel psychobiologist Sperry (1964, 1969). It was elaborated further by Sperry (1976, 1991), Popper and Eccles (1977), Murphy (1994), Andersen *et al.* (2000) and others.

usefully be termed 'Sperry's Rule'. It ensures that emergence, although it is associated with emergent causal powers at a higher level, does not generate multiple types or forms of causality at any single level. Any emergent causes at higher levels exist by virtue of lower-level causal processes.

Adherence to Sperry's Rule excludes any version of methodological collectivism or holism where an attempt is made to explain individual dispositions or behaviour entirely in terms of institutions or other system-level characteristics. Instead, Sperry's Rule obliges us to explain particular human behaviour in terms of causal processes operating at the individual level, such as individual aspirations, dispositions or constraints. Where higher-level factors enter, it is in the more general explanation of the system-wide processes giving rise to those aspirations, dispositions or constraints.

Accordingly, at the level of the human agent, there are no magical 'cultural' or 'economic' forces controlling individuals, other than those affecting the dispositions, thoughts and actions of individual human actors. People do not develop new preferences, wants or purposes because mysterious 'social forces' control them. What have to be examined are the social and psychological mechanisms and constraints leading to such changes of preference, disposition or mentality. The argument here is that the pragmatist and institutionalist concept of habit provides part of a plausible and reconstitutive mechanism.

9.6 HABITS AS HIDDEN PERSUADERS

A hidden and most pervasive feature of institutions is their capacity to mould and change aspirations. This aspect of institutions is neglected in the 'new institutional economics'. Because institutions not only depend upon the activities of individuals but also constrain and mould them, this positive feedback gives institutions even stronger self-reinforcing and self-perpetuating characteristics.

Pragmatist philosophers and 'old' institutional economists argue that institutions work only because the rules involved are embedded in prevalent habits of thought and behaviour. From this perspective, institutions are conditioned by and dependent upon individuals and their habits, but they are not reducible to them. Habits are the constitutive substrate of institutions, providing them with enhanced durability, power and normative authority.

A habit is a *propensity* to behave in particular ways in a particular class of situations. Crucially, we may have habits that lie unused for a long time. A habit may exist even if it is not manifest in behaviour. Habits are submerged repertoires of potential behaviour; they can be triggered by an appropriate stimulus or context. The dependence of institutions upon habits partly roots institutions in the dispositions of individuals.

From the pragmatist and institutionalist perspective, habits are foundational to all thought and behaviour. As argued elsewhere, all deliberations, including rational optimization, themselves rely on habits and rules (Hodgson, 1997). Even rational optimization must involve rules. In turn, as suggested above, rules have to become ingrained in habits in order to be deployed by agents. Hence rationality always depends on prior habits and rules as props (Hodgson, 1988). This primary reliance on habits and rules limits the explanatory scope of rational optimization. Hence rational optimization can never supply the complete explanation of human behaviour and institutions, for which some theorists seem to be striving. At the centre of a more adequate explanation of human agency would be the reconstitutive processes through which habits are formed and changed.

Our habits help to make up our preferences and dispositions. When new habits are acquired or existing habits change, then our preferences alter. Dewey (1922, p. 40) thus wrote of 'the cumulative effect of insensible modifications worked by a particular habit in the body of preferences'. Alternatively, we could presume, following Gary Becker and Kevin Murphy (1988) and others, that habitual modifications are consistent with some unchanging 'meta-preference' function. As argued above, empirical consistency with such a utility function might obtain. However, meta-preference explanations of habit overlook the fact that meta-preferences themselves must be grounded on learned habits and dispositions. Otherwise we have no plausible story of their origin.

Consider an example of the role of habit. For reasons of cost, and a desire to minimize pollution and road congestion, a commuter may use the bus to travel to work. As a result of this repeated behaviour, specific habits of thought and behaviour will be reinforced. If the bus service is withdrawn, then the individual will be obliged to use another means of travel. It may be that there is no alternative to the car. The individual will then begin to drive to work and develop another set of habits. Even if a preference for public transport is maintained for a while, it could eventually be undermined by repeated personal car use. The change in the provision of public transport can alter preferences for that mode.

Institutional changes and constraints can also lead to alterations habits of thought and behaviour. Institutions constrain our behaviour and develop our habits in specific ways. The framing, shifting and constraining capacities of social institutions give rise to new perceptions and dispositions within individuals. Upon new habits of thought and behaviour, new preferences and intentions emerge. Alfred Marshall (1949, p. 76) observed 'the development of new activities giving rise to new wants'. But we need to know how this happens. Veblen (1899, p. 190, emphasis added) was more specific about the psychological mechanisms involved: 'The situation of today shapes the institutions of tomorrow through a selective, coercive process, *by acting upon men's habitual view of things*'.

We are typically constrained in our actions. Accordingly, we acquire habits consistent with the operation of these constraints. Even when these constraints are removed, habits dispose us to act or think in the same old way. As the institutional economist John R. Commons (1934, p. 701) remarked 'when customs change ... then it is realized that the compulsion of custom has been there all along, but unquestioned and undisturbed'.

The crucial point in the argument here is to recognize the significance of reconstitutive downward causation on *habits*, rather than merely on behaviour, intentions or beliefs. Clearly, the definitional distinction between habit (as a propensity or disposition) and behaviour (or action) is essential to make sense of this statement. Once habits become established they become a potential basis for new intentions or beliefs.

But a second point is also of vital significance. It is a central tenet of the pragmatist philosophical and psychological perspective to regard habit and instinct as foundational to the human personality. Reason, deliberation and calculation emerge only after specific habits have been laid down; their operation depends upon such habits. In turn, the development of habits depends upon prior instincts. Instincts, as typically defined, are inherited. Accordingly, *reconstitutive* downward causation upon instincts is not possible.[5]

The ongoing acquisition and modification of habits is central to individual human existence. For example, much deliberative thought is dependent on, as well as being coloured by, acquired habits of language. In addition, to make sense of the world we have to acquire habits of classification and habitually associated meanings. The crucial point is that all action and deliberation depend on prior habits that we acquire during our individual development. Hence habits have temporal and ontological primacy over intention and reason. As we have seen, reconstitutive downward causation works by creating and moulding habits. Habit is the crucial and hidden link in the causal chain.

Accordingly, as long as we can explain how institutional structures give rise to new or changed habits, then we have an acceptable mechanism of reconstitutive downward causation. In contrast, we cannot identify any causal mechanism where institutions lead *directly* to the reconstitution of purposes or beliefs. Institutional factors may lead directly to changes in some intentions, by acting as non-reconstitutive influences or constraints. For example, we decide to drive within the speed limit because we see a police

[5] However, 'downward causation' upon instincts, in the weaker sense of Campbell (1974), is possible, simply because instincts, like other human features, exist and evolve in consistency with higher level principles, such as the laws of evolution.

car on the motorway. The particular intention is explained in terms of the *existing* preference to avoid punishment. This explanation does not itself involve a reconstitutive process. Clearly, any attempt to explain changes in intentions through intentions alone must assume a *fixed* subset of (meta-) preferences behind the expedient changes of intention and action. In contrast, to provide a reconstitutive causal mechanism, we have to point to factors that are foundational to purposes, preferences and deliberation as a whole. This is where habits come in.

As a result, institutions are social structures with the capacity for reconstitutive downward causation, acting upon ingrained habits of thought and action. Powers and constraints associated with institutional structures can encourage changes in thought and behaviour. In turn, upon these repeated acts, new habits of thought and behaviour emerge. It is not simply the individual behaviour that has been changed: there are also changes in habitual dispositions. In turn, these are associated with changed individual understandings, purposes and preferences. We now consider some further examples of the processes involved.

9.7 HIDDEN MECHANISMS OF PERSUASION

A number of explanations are consistent with this general principle of habitual reconstitution. For example, in the fable of 'sour grapes' new preferences are announced because of ambition frustrated by circumstances (Elster, 1983). These circumstances could include structures or institutions. New habits would then arise, in accord with the changed preferences. Similarly, the theory of cognitive dissonance (Festinger, 1957) explains that when people are faced with a difficult choice between alternative courses of action their perception of the alternatives is adjusted to render one of them more acceptable. This is often done by imitating and acquiring the norms and perceptions of others (Hodgson, 1988). This can result in the transmission of habits of thought and behaviour from one person to another.

There is an established post-war literature in social psychology on mechanisms of power, social influence, individual compliance and opinion change (Kelman, 1958, 1961; Tedeschi, 1972, 1974). Much of this literature considers mechanisms that are broadly similar to the idea of reconstitutive downward causation. Another body of literature from psychology that is relevant here is the empirical and theoretical work on obedience to authority (Milgram, 1974; Kelman and Hamilton, 1989). Obedience to authority can result from the direct effect of rewards for compliance or of punishments for non-compliance. Alternatively, it may result from a deeper identification with the values of those in authority. In the former case, reconstitutive downward causation will occur only if compliance eventually gives rise to habits of thought or behaviour consistent with obedience. In the latter case, to minimize unease and self-doubt, an original habit of deference to authority might be expanded into a reconstitutive acceptance of the norms and values of those in power.

It is often underestimated that people have a need for meanings and explanations in their everyday lives. In all cultures known to anthropology there is evidence of the universal human hunger for meaning. It is fed by religion, by ritual, through playful curiosity or by modern science. In meeting our desire for meaning we acquire the habits of thought and behaviour of our culture. As Mary Douglas and Baron Isherwood (1980) have argued, much of consumer behaviour acquires its meaning through social interaction. In establishing such meanings we interpret, imitate and compare with the behaviour of others. We acquire habits of thought and behaviour that dovetail with those of the culture as a whole. These are the social mechanisms by which the habits that are associated with social institutions are transmitted and reinforced to the individuals involved.[6]

If we take the arguments discussed above from modern psychology on situated cognition seriously, then we must recognize that our aspirations and choices are cast in institutional moulds (A. Clark, 1997a, 1997b; Lane *et al.*, 1996). Much of our deliberation takes place within and through social institutions. We use institutions and their routines as templates in the construction of our habits, intentions and choices.

Consequently, reconstitutive downward causation is an indelible feature of social life. Yet it has been absent from mainstream economics.[7] Becker (1996, p. 225) is typical of many economists when he describes situations where individual purposes and choices are moulded as 'brainwashing'. This neglects undesigned institutional processes of persuasion. The mechanisms of reconstitutive downward causation are far more widespread and subtle than the overt 'brainwashing' of individuals. Typical of many economists, Becker recognizes nothing in between 'brainwashing' on the one hand, and 'free choice' based on given preference functions, on the other. The truth is that most of social behaviour lies between these two extremes.

On the other hand, Galbraith and other critics of mainstream economics have often focused too much on advertising, to the neglect of the subtler and typically undesigned institutional mechanisms of persuasion. It is important

---

[6] This account of habit formation is admittedly sketchy and needs much more refinement. It has to be shown how behaviours are identified, interpreted, understood and replicated, before habits themselves are 'transmitted' from one agent to another. This aspect of the analysis awaits further elaboration.

[7] But the tide may be beginning to turn. Both Bowles (1998, 2004) and Akerlof and Kranton (2005) consider endogenous and context dependent preference formation.

to theorize the middle grounds between brainwashing or advertising, and 'free choice'.

9.8 POSSIBLE THEORETICAL AVENUES

It has been argued here that the causal processes of reconstitution discussed here are not mysterious 'social forces' but plausible psychological mechanisms of imitation, conformism, conditioning and cognition. These mechanisms are subtle and pervasive. Let us briefly consider some further implications, in terms of the type of economic theory that can be sustained by this approach.

In the 1970s, the name of James Duesenberry could still be found in some recommended economics textbooks. Duesenberry (1949) developed a model of consumer behaviour, inspired by the work of Veblen and based on habits and learning effects. In his model, as incomes rose, people acquired new habits of consumption that persisted, even if incomes later fell. Their tastes and preferences altered as they acquired new lifestyles. This model of aggregate consumer behaviour performed well in several econometric tests. Nevertheless, Duesenberry's model fell out of favour, not because it performed badly in statistical tests, but because it was not based on the mainstream idea of the rational, utility-maximizing consumer (Green, 1979). Today, few students of macroeconomics will learn of Duesenberry's theory.

Yet this type of approach remains as vital as ever. Notably, in a review of the relationship between economics and psychology, Matthew Rabin (1998, p. 13) argues that because consumers are often more sensitive to changes than to absolute levels of income means that factors as habitual levels of consumption should be incorporated into analysis.

Another possible theoretical illustration of the general approach noted here is Walter Runciman's (1972) theory of relative deprivation. It is quite similar to Duesenberry's theory. According to Runciman, the capacity to accept and endure deprivation is positively correlated to the incidence of that same deprivation in that person's peer group. As a result, workers will often begin to demand higher wages when they see the wages of a related group of workers rising significantly above theirs. This theory is also consistent with the idea that preferences and expectations are formed in a social context.

Another implication concerns the explanation of the existence of firms. Oliver Williamson (1975) has followed Ronald Coase (1937) in putting the burden of the argument for the existence of the firm on the proposition that transaction costs in viable firms are lower than they would be if production were coordinated through the market. In this argument the individual is taken as given: social institutions bear upon individuals simply via the costs they impose. However, once we abandon the idea of the given individual, then we can give much greater prominence to the possibility that, in becoming a part of a firm, workers develop capacities and allegiances that result from their new institutional environment. Crucial to this institutional explanation would be the concept of corporate culture and its role in reconstituting the goals and capabilities of the workforce. The firm would have a reconstitutive effect upon individuals (Hodgson, 1998b).

A predictable objection to all these theoretical initiatives is that they can all be fitted into more sophisticated models of the individual utility-maximizer, perhaps along the lines of Becker (1996). After all, Becker (1992) and others claim that they can deal with culture, habit, relative deprivation and all the other issues raised here. It is evident that their models can embrace every possibility. However, the dispute between neoclassical and institutionalist views is not primarily a question of whether the data can be accommodated into the theory. The debate is on the question of theoretical coherence and adequate explanation. In the following chapter it is argued that a complex, Becker-type preference function would involve the processing of a huge amount of historic data, beyond the memory capacities of the human mind.

9.9 THE RETURN OF HABIT

The mechanisms of reconstitutive downward causation proposed here depend on a rehabilitated concept of habit. However, although the concept of habit was once central to social and political philosophy, it has been eliminated from large parts of contemporary social science. Habit and custom were dropped from sociology during the transition from Max Weber to Talcott Parsons (Camic, 1986; Hodgson, 2001b, 2004a). The concept of habit was long marginalized in psychology, but after the decline of behaviourism it has now re-emerged (Wood *et al.*, 2002; Ouellette and Wood, 1998). This provides an explicit psychological basis for reconstitutive downward causation.

While many behaviourist psychologists rejected habit because it was a concealed disposition rather than overt behaviour, sociologists were sceptical because they believed that habit involves a mechanical conception of human behaviour. Parsons (1935) saw no essential distinction between the pragmatist stress on habit and the behaviourist emphasis on behavioural conditioning. He was mistaken. Behavioural psychologists stress the conditioning of overt behaviour, while the pragmatists and instinct psychologists saw habits as bundles of potentialities and dispositions. Upon this repertoire of habits there is scope for decision and will (Dewey, 1922).

Furthermore, habits exist at different levels of consciousness and deliberation. There can be context-dependent cascades of triggered habits, with possible high sensitivity to small changes of circumstance. Habit does not deny choice. Different sets of habits may give rise to competing preferences. A choice is then made, and this choice may itself involve a further cluster of habitual interpretations or predispositions.

It is beyond the scope of this work to enquire into the difficult philosophical question of the freedom of the will. We may simply point out that the act of deliberation within a tangled complex of interlayered habits is at least as free as the utility-maximizing robot of mainstream economics. Choice is a largely unpredictable outcome of the complex human nervous system, situated in a complex, open and changing environment. On the other hand, our inheritance, upbringing and circumstances affect our choices. Human agency is neither uncaused nor generally predictable.

The pragmatist philosophers who influenced Veblen and the institutionalists broke from the overly rationalistic and deliberative conception of action that had dominated Western thought since the Enlightenment. In the deliberative conception of action, beliefs are the drivers of deliberation and action, perhaps later to be modified in the light of experience. However, the causal origins of beliefs themselves are inadequately explained. By contrast, in the pragmatist tradition, beliefs are seen as erections upon acquired habits.

A hallmark of the habit-based conception of action is that the individual's preferences are no longer taken as given. Furthermore, beliefs may change, not simply as a result of receiving information, but also because habitual mechanisms of interpretation may alter. In contrast to the pervasive idea of the given individual, the individual is formed and reconstituted in an ongoing process. Institutions matter in both cases. But in the habit-based conception they can also lead eventually to new habits and new preferences or beliefs.

In order to give a more complete, habit-based picture, some account of the development of the original habits of the individual is required. Acquired habits are themselves founded upon inherited instincts, which trigger behaviours and give rise to habits. Nevertheless, instinctive propensities are heavily diverted or overlaid by habits and beliefs acquired through interaction with others in a social culture. Accordingly, habit is a bridging element between the biological, psychological and social domains.

While natural selection operates upon inherited instincts, other evolutionary processes of selection operate at the cultural or social level. This is the 'natural selection of institutions' (Veblen, 1899, p. 188). In the social sphere, habits have genotypical qualities, although they are not nearly as durable as the biotic genes. However, unlike the replication of DNA, habits do not directly make copies of themselves. Instead they replicate indirectly (Hodgson, 2001a). They impel behaviour that is, in turn, consciously or unconsciously imitated by others. Eventually, this copied behaviour becomes rooted in the habits of the imitator, thus transmitting from individual to individual an imperfect copy of each habit by an indirect route. Like natural selection, cultural selection works at the level of the population, not simply of the individual. It exerts 'downward causation' by exploiting mechanisms of imitation, conformism and constraint.

9.10 SOME CONCLUSIONS AND IMPLICATIONS

The standard mainstream view of the utility-maximizing human agent has come under much criticism. The concern of the present chapter is both to highlight some less familiar criticisms and to move towards the construction of an alternative approach. It has been argued that models of the utility-maximizing agent might fit every possible circumstance, and this is a weakness rather than a strength. The non-falsifiability of the model requires us to focus on matters of theoretical rather than empirical adequacy.

If individuals are taken as given, then we overlook explanations of their origin, either in terms of evolution or of individual human development. The Principle of Evolutionary Explanation requires that all assumptions concerning human behaviour should be consistent with our knowledge and understanding of human evolution. This leads us to a conception of human decision-making involving instincts and habits as grounding for conscious deliberation, rather than a supreme, all-purpose, deliberative rationality.

The line of theoretical research suggested here is to develop an enhanced picture of the role of habit in economic life. Mainstream economists have often discussed habit, but by making it an outcome of rational choice.[8] On the contrary, it has been argued here that habits are developmentally and practically prior to any form of conscious reasoning. Even rational choices require habits as a substratum. Remarkably, despite the uncountable number of mathematical models of human behaviour in economics, very few examples are *based* on habit. There are two notable exceptions: Arrow (1986) and G. Becker (1962).[9] Apart from this, little else has been tried. However, these earlier precedents suggest some fruitful possibilities for habit-based analysis, if it were pursued.

---

[8] For example, Pollak (1970), Lluch (1974), Winston (1980), Blanciforti and Green (1983), Phlips and Spinnewyn (1984), G. Becker and Murphy (1988), Alessie and Kapteyn (1991), G. Becker (1992).

[9] When Becker published his 1962 paper he was at the Columbia University. This was the institution where Mitchell had taught for many years and where institutional economics had a lingering influence. Becker moved to Chicago in 1969. From then on, his work was populated with utility-maximizers rather than creatures founded upon habit. In this choice of theoretical approach, perhaps Becker too was moulded by institutional circumstances.

With the theoretical framework proposed here, it may be possible to overcome the dilemma between methodological individualism and methodological collectivism. By acting not directly on individual decisions, but on habitual dispositions, institutions exert downward causation without reducing individual agency to their effects. Furthermore, upward causation, from individuals to institutions, is still possible, without assuming that the individual is given or immanently conceived. Explanations are reduced neither to individuals nor to institutions alone.

One possible objection to this line of research would be to suggest that the assumption of agents with such institutional influences on their preference functions would be hopelessly complicated and intractable. Accordingly, it could be argued, it is necessarily to simplify matters and assume agents with preference functions that are given. Any assumption of 'endogenous' preferences must take *some* factors as given, so why not assume that preferences have this status?

To respond to this argument it is necessary to show what is possible within the framework discussed above. This is largely a matter for future research, involving the hypothesis that the assumption of malleable preferences may sometimes simplify matters rather than complicate them. The process of reconstitutive downward causation may provide a degree of durability and stability in institutional structure that is not explained adequately in standard models. The circular, positive feedback from institution to individuals and from individuals to institutions can help to enhance the durability of the institutional unit. What would then be theorized is the self-reinforcing institutional structure. Accordingly, malleable preferences may lead to stable emergent properties. This not a proven result but a plausible conjecture that remains to be explored. A step in this direction is made in the following chapter, with a heuristic model of agent-structure interactions.

10. The Complex Evolution of a Simple Traffic Convention

An institution is of the nature of a usage which has become axiomatic and indispensable by habituation and general acceptance.

Thorstein Veblen, *Absentee Ownership and Business Enterprise in Recent Times* (1923)

10.1 INTRODUCTION

This chapter presents an agent-based simulation of the emergence of a traffic convention – concerning whether to drive on the left or the right of the road. The interaction between agents and structures involve causal influences in two directions, showing how agents constitute institutions and how institutions can have reconstitutive causal effects on individuals.[1]

The evolution of conventions and institutions has become the subject of much analysis, modelling and discussion.[2] We raise here some further analytical and conceptual issues on the basis of a heuristic, agent-based simulation with heterogeneous agents. The general *outcome* of the simulation is relatively uncomplicated because we choose one of the most straightforward of decisions and conventions: whether to drive on the right or on the left of the road.[3] In our model, artificially intelligent 'drivers' in 'cars' are programmed to negotiate a circular road configuration along with a number of other, similar vehicles. We show that the emergence of a convention is possible but by no means guaranteed. Furthermore, some manipulation of the decision processes through which these 'drivers' decide to move to the left or the right provides a basis to consider some of the deeper conceptual issues that are involved in the evolution of conventions, such as the nature of rational decision-making and its possible reliance upon habit.

---

[1] This chapter is a shortened version of Hodgson and Knudsen (2004a), excluding some of its data and regressions. I am very grateful for permission from Thorbjørn Knudsen to reproduce this joint work. After an invitation from Tony Lawson in 2001, I presented an earlier version of this chapter at one of his Monday night seminars on critical realism in Cambridge, earning the dubious distinction of the first person to present a formal model or simulation at these seminars.

[2] See, for example, Marimon *et al.* (1990), Wärneryd (1990b), H. P. Young (1993) and Howitt and Clower (2000).

[3] H. P. Young (1996) provides an interesting historical account of the evolution of traffic conventions.

Each driver is boundedly rational. To negotiate the track and avoid collision, it would seem to be rational for each driver at least to consider *conformity* with the perceived distribution of traffic to the left and right and *avoidance* of cars that are immediately ahead. To these factors, our model adds *habit*.

Any left/right convergence outcome in this model is likely to depend on initial conditions and circumstances. Strong path dependence is likely, but we are more interested in the degree and resilience of any emergent convention than whether it is on the left or the right.

We show that in following or avoiding other traffic in some circumstances, strength of habit and processes of habituation can play a vital role alongside rational deliberation and selection pressure. This outcome not only raises important questions concerning the role of habit in decision-making, but also it challenges the frequent assumption that preference functions should always be taken entirely as exogenously given.

This chapter is structured in seven parts. As well as defining some key terms, the second part considers the theoretical background and points to some important differences of view concerning the manner in which institutions and conventions evolve. The heuristic model is presented in the third part. In the fourth part the basic results of the simulations are reported. The implications of the simulations concerning the concept of habit and regarding the concept of 'downward causation' are discussed in the fifth and sixth parts, respectively. The seventh part concludes the chapter.

10.2 THE EVOLUTION OF CONVENTIONS AND INSTITUTIONS

Institutions are durable systems of established and embedded social rules that structure social interactions. A convention is a particular instance of an institutional rule (Sugden, 1986; Searle, 1995). For example, all countries have traffic rules, but it is a matter of (arbitrary) convention whether the rule is to drive on the right or on the left.

Carl Menger (1871) pioneered a basic analysis of how institutions evolve. His chosen example was money. Menger saw the institution of money as emanating in an undesigned manner from the communications and interactions of individual agents. Traders look for a convenient and frequently exchanged commodity to use in their exchanges with others. Once such regularities become prominent, a circular process of institutional self-reinforcement takes place. Emerging to overcome the difficulties of barter, money is chosen because it is convenient, and it is convenient because it is chosen.[4]

In this Mengerian approach, individual preference functions are taken as given. Menger thus inspired a central, unifying project in the 'new institutional economics': to explain the existence of political, legal, or social institutions by reference to a model of given, individual behaviour, tracing out its consequences in terms of human interactions.[5]

However, theoretical analyses or simulation of the evolution of institutions have proved to be remarkably problematic. For example, in the work of Ramon Marimon *et al.* (1990) an attempt is made to model the emergence of money with artificially intelligent agents. Their results are qualified and partially inconclusive. A single monetary unit does not always readily emerge. Menger's discursive analysis of an emergent convention has proven to be difficult to replicate in a computer simulation. Our simulations also show the difficulties in reaching convergence even with a very simple convention.

The central hypothesis behind the present chapter is that there is often more to the emergence of real world institutions than mere matters of convenience and calculation by individual agents. Additional psychological factors intervene, including emotions, instincts and other dispositions. This basic idea can be found in the writings of the neglected tradition of 'old' institutionalism. For instance, arguing that the evolution of money cannot be understood simply in terms of cost reduction and individual convenience, Wesley Mitchell maintained that money 'stamps its pattern upon wayward human nature, makes us all react in standard ways to the standard stimuli it offers, and affects our very ideals of what is good, beautiful and true' (Mitchell, 1937, p. 371). Accordingly, the evolution of money changed the mentality, preferences and thinking patterns of individuals themselves. This does not necessarily mean that Menger's account is wrong, but that it is inadequate. It has to be supplemented by an analysis of how institutions can change individual perceptions and preferences.

The idea of the malleability of individual preferences pervades the 'old' institutional economics, from Thorstein Veblen to John Kenneth Galbraith.

---

[4] Despite the apparent simplicity of this argument, analyses, experiments and simulations based upon it are extraordinarily complex (R. A. Jones, 1976; Kiyotaki and Wright, 1989; Oh, 1989; Wärneryd, 1989, 1990a; Marimon *et al.*, 1990; Duffy and Ochs, 1999). Realizing this, we chose a simpler institution as the object of the present study in which each agent has a choice between only two behavioural options at any stage. Our intention was to illustrate the hypothesized results in the simplest possible institutional set up.

[5] For discussions of the limits of this approach see Field (1979, 1984), Knight (1992), Sened (1997), Hodgson (1998a) and Aoki (2001).

However, it has not yet been shown why some preference malleability may be necessary for the emergence and sustainability of institutions. In this chapter we begin to fill this gap by showing how a limited form of preference malleability can improve the possibility and stability of an equilibrium convention.

What is at issue here is the adequacy of the standard account of the emergence of institutions. Just as individuals constitute institutions, individuals may also be partially reconstituted by institutions. Once we raise this possibility, however, we encounter some conceptual problems concerning the specification of such preference endogeneity. It is not our intention to replicate a widely criticized picture of individuals as puppets of institutions, roles or cultural values. To avoid such pitfalls, we have to specify adequately the limits, nature and mechanisms of this reconstitution.

It is here that we come to the concept of habit. The simulation outlined in the next section shows how habit can be significant for institutional evolution, especially in circumstances of limited information. Circumstances help to form the predispositions of individuals by forming and changing their habits. As noted in the preceding chapter, several attempts have been made to accommodate a notion of habit within relatively sophisticated rational choice models. In these models, any habit is seen as ultimately an outcome of a rational choice. In contrast, in the pragmatist tradition of Charles Sanders Peirce, William James, George Herbert Mead and John Dewey, any rational deliberation is always seen as grounded on habit. The question then is whether rational choice is the foundation of habit, or whether the reverse is true (G. Becker, 1992; Hodgson, 1998a, 2003b, 2004a). It is shown below that the concept of habit developed in the cited rational choice models is not the same as the concept in our model and in pragmatist thought.

Our intention is not to treat habit as some kind of psychological panacea, but to investigate its significance in the 'experimental' context of a simulation. The model shows that in some circumstances habit can assist convergence to a left/right convention but it also depends upon, and interacts with, other variables and processes. We do not argue that habit is the only factor involved in convergence, but under frequent conditions it is important when allied with other factors. We also find that in some circumstances habit can be disruptive.

10.3 THE SIMULATION MODEL

10.3.1 The decision problem and the environment of choice

In our model,[6] 40 agents drive around a 100×2 grid, arranged in a ring, with two lanes and 100 zones. We use the terms 'agent', 'driver' and 'car' synonymously. The drivers are unique individuals, born to drive either clockwise or counter-clockwise around the ring, referred to as lengthways movement. Half of the agents drive clockwise and the other half counter-clockwise. For each car, the direction of its lengthways movement cannot be changed.

At time t=0, the drivers are randomly assigned a zone and a position on one of the two sides of the ring. The cars then move in turn. During each move, each driver must decide whether to drive on the left or the right side of the ring when making their next lengthways movement. This left/right movement is the driver's only choice variable. Each driver performs an incremental lengthways movement, placing itself in the next zone ahead, on either its left or its right lane.

The left/right decision is partly based on information about the traffic in front of the driver. The driver looks 10 increments ahead and counts in that region the number of cars in each lane and the number of cars going in each direction. Based on this information and given its behavioural and cognitive dispositions (defined below), the driver will decide on which side of the ring to drive in its next move. Each car drives around the ring until it is involved in a collision. A collision occurs when a car moves into a zone occupied by another car that is also in the same lane, irrespective of the direction of movement of the cars. Then both drivers die and new cars and drivers replace them. As a result, the number of cars on the grid is always 40. The replacement routine also ensures that the number of cars moving clockwise and counter-clockwise is always 20.

10.3.2 Behavioural and cognitive dispositions

Initially our objective was to make the drivers as 'intelligent' as possible, subject to the constraint of a limited number of cognitive and behavioural variables. After numerous runs with additional cognitive parameters, we found that a highly parsimonious model was very effective.[7] Additional

---

6 The simulations described here were performed using Matlab software. All random numbers are generated from a multiseed generator with the theoretical lower limit of 2^{1492} before the number will repeat itself.

7 Given the relative simplicity of the decision environment, and the effectiveness of our 'parsimonious' decision algorithm, it seemed neither necessary, appropriate nor fruitful in this model to incorporate more complex learning procedures such as the 'elaboration likelihood model' of Petty and Cacioppo (1986) and the non-linear

decision parameters had little effect in enhancing the survival of individual cars or the convergence characteristics of the model.[8]

When first placed on the ring, each driver receives a unique set $\{SSensitivity_n, OSensitivity_n, Avoidance_n, Habitgene_n, Habituation_{n,t}\}$ of five cognitive and behavioural dispositions. The first four of these dispositions are randomly assigned and cannot be changed. These variables are randomly chosen according to normal distribution with mean 1 and standard deviation δ (referred to as the mutation variable). Negative numbers are truncated to zero, but there is no upper bound.[9] The only disposition that can be changed during the life of the car is the car's acquired habits ($Habituation_{n,t}$). Furthermore, for all original or newborn drivers, the initial level of the habituation variable is zero ($Habituation_{n,0} = 0$).

Note that the terms 'left' and 'right' are relative to the driver involved. A car driving clockwise on the right will not collide with a car driving counter-clockwise on the right. The same applies to two cars both on the left, likewise moving in opposite directions. The terms 'ahead' and 'behind' are also relative to the car and its movement. A car may collide with another car moving in the same direction, but only if that other car is one zone ahead and does not move first, or if that other car is one zone behind and does move first.

(i) *Same-direction sensitivity*. Each driver *n* looks forward and observes the number of cars going in the same direction as itself up to and including 10 zones ahead, and calculates the proportion of this number driving on the left (or right) hand side of the road. (If no car is going in the same direction as itself, up to and including 10 zones ahead, then the proportion is taken as 0.5.) The variable $SSensitivity_n$ indicates the degree to which

---

models of attitude change by Eiser *et al.* (2001). However, more complex learning algorithms would clearly be appropriate in decision environments involving more learning parameters and behavioural choices than are present in our model.

[8] Earlier versions of this simulation included three 'inertia' parameters and an additional 'avoidance' variable applied to the area *two* zones ahead of the driver. The inertia parameters gave each driver a disposition to continue stubbornly with an inclination it has assumed in the recent past. We found that the effects of inertia are generally weaker than those of habit. The effect of the second 'avoidance' variable was at most marginal. Accordingly, the more parsimonious model was chosen, with the omission of these parameters.

[9] The probability that a negative number will be drawn is extremely small ($7.43*10^{-6}$). An alternative method of selecting the first four parameters would be to draw them randomly from a uniform distribution in a specified interval. Instead, a normal distribution was selected because it was found that it reduced the death rates in the simulation. Selection along an interval will typically create a larger number of drivers with less fit parameters.

driver n takes account of this ratio in determining its next move. If this variable is high then the car will tend to conform to the pattern of behaviour of the cars ahead of itself and moving in its own direction.

(ii) *Opposite-direction sensitivity.* Each driver n looks forward and observes the number of cars going in the opposite direction to itself, up to and including 10 zones ahead, and calculates the proportion of this number driving on *their* left (or right) hand side of the road. (Again, if no car is going in the opposite direction as itself, up to and including 10 zones ahead, then the proportion is taken as 0.5.) The coefficient $OSensitivity_n$ indicates the degree to which car n takes account of this ratio in determining its next move. As well as a rationale to conform to the convention established by others, there is an incentive to avoid this traffic coming in the opposite direction.

(iii) *Avoidance.* This coefficient captures a tendency for each driver n to avoid collision with close, oncoming traffic. Each driver looks forward and observes the number of cars going in both directions, *one* zone ahead, and calculates the number on the left and right hand side of the road, relative to the driver. Because each car moves in turn, another car that is positioned one zone ahead of driver n poses a collision danger, regardless of its direction of movement: cars moving in both directions threaten driver n with immediate collision. Driver n's avoidance is captured by the coefficient $Avoidance_n$, referring to the situation one zone ahead.

(iv) *Habit Gene.* A driver's habit gene must be distinguished from its habituation. The habit gene is the instinctive tendency that a driver has to take account of its acquired habituation. The habit gene cannot change but habituation can. The role of the habit gene is explained in the discussion of habituation below. Driver n's habit gene is captured by the coefficient $Habitgene_n$.

Every driver receives a unique personal profile in which the values of the above four behavioural and cognitive variables are randomly assigned. However, the following variable can change through the course of a driver's life.

(v) *Habituation.* Every driver starts with a habituation variable set initially at zero. As time goes on, this variable will be revised according to the car's movements. For instance, if a car has a history of moving on the left hand side of the road then the habituation variable is likely to be positive, and if a car has generally moved on the right hand side of the road then the habituation variable is likely to be negative. A more precise account of the habituation process is given below. The habit gene coefficient expresses the degree to which driver n takes its habituation into account. Driver n's habituation at time t is captured by the coefficient $Habituation_{n,t}$.

10.3.3 Calculation, habituation, decision and movement

Each car is addressed and moves sequentially. With no simultaneous moves, some associated problems of interpretation of the intentions of others are thus avoided. In each period, all drivers in turn make a (subjective) decision based on the (objective) information about the traffic ahead. Again the purpose was to make the drivers as 'intelligent' as possible, making use of the most important information for their survival, subject to reasonable computational constraints. As each car can only move one zone ahead, there is no reason to take account of traffic to its rear. As noted above, at time t, each driver calculates the following variables:

$S_{L,n}$ = the proportion of all cars, going in the *same* direction as driver n, up to and including 10 zones ahead, that are driving on the left hand side of the road, where $0 \leq S_{L,n} \leq 1$. If no car is going in the same direction as driver n, up to and including 10 zones ahead, then $S_{L,n} = 0.5$.

$O_{L,n}$ = the proportion of all cars, going in the direction *opposite* to driver n and up to and including 10 zones ahead, that are driving on *their* left hand side of the road, where $0 \leq O_{L,n} \leq 1$. If no car is going in the opposite direction as driver n, up to and including 10 zones ahead, then $O_{L,n} = 0.5$.

$C_{L,n}$ = the number of very close cars, going in any direction, exactly one zone ahead of driver n, that are driving on the left hand side of the road relative to driver n, where $C_{L,n} = 0$ or 1.

$C_{R,n}$ = the number of very close cars, going in any direction, exactly one zone ahead of driver n, that are driving on the right hand side of the road relative to driver n, where $C_{R,n} = 0$ or 1.

After having gathered this information and calculated the above ratios, the driver then updates its habit function according to the following formula:

$$Habituation_{n,t} = Habituation_{n,t-1} + LR_{n,t} / (K + Moves_{n,t}),$$

where $LR_{n,t}$ is the situation of car n at time t, whether it is on the left ($LR_{n,t} = 1$) or on the right ($LR_{n,t} = -1$) hand side of the road. K is an arbitrary positive constant and $Moves_{n,t}$ is the total number of moves the driver has undertaken, up to and including the present move at time t. In addition, $Habituation_{n,t}$ is bounded between –1 and 1. Clearly the tendency to change habit decreases with the number of moves; the habit function is cumulative with a decreasing increment. The driver uses the above equation to update its habituation variable.[10]

---

[10] Experiments were performed using different habit functions, with similar but slightly weaker results. Perhaps the main rival alternative habit function would be

To make a decision to go left or right, the value of the following expression is calculated:

$$
\begin{aligned}
LREvaluation_n = {} & w_{Sdirection} \times SSensitivity_n \times (2S_{L,n,t} - 1) + \\
& w_{Odirection} \times OSensitivity_n \times (2O_{L,n,t} - 1) + \\
& w_{Avoidance} \times Avoidance_n \times (C_{R,n,t} - C_{L,n,t}) + \\
& w_{Habit} \times Habitgene_n \times Habituation_{n,t} .
\end{aligned}
$$

The w_X coefficients ($w_{Sdirection}$, $w_{Odirection}$, $w_{Avoidance}$ and w_{Habit}) are fixed, non-negative weights common to all 40 drivers. The weights determine how much the components of every driver's unique set of cognitive and behavioural dispositions will influence the driver's subjective evaluation and thus its choice to go left or right at time t. The coefficient w_{Habit} is referred to as the 'habit weighting'. The term $w_{Habit} \times Habitgene_n \times Habituation_{n,t}$ is referred to as 'the strength of habit' of a car.

Note that each term on the right hand side of the equation above includes two positive elements plus one element with expected values equally distributed around zero, all multiplied together. Hence each term on the right hand side has expected values equally distributed around zero. As a result, there is no bias to the right or the left in the model.

The subjective evaluation of each car is given by the variable $LREvaluation_n$. If $LREvaluation_n$ is greater than zero then the car intends to move to the left. Otherwise it intends to move to the right. The final element to be taken into consideration is the possibility of error. An error probability variable ε is pre-set at the beginning of the simulation. A random number generator is used to determine whether each car, with probability ε, makes the move opposite to its subjective evaluation. At this final stage, the left or right inclination of the car in the upcoming move is determined.

The car then moves one increment forward onto the next zone, on the left or right as determined. If there is no other car on the same side of the road and in the same zone, then there is no collision. In each period, all drivers in turn go through these steps.

Taking account of the most important local information, each car responds and manoeuvres in order to survive. The decision algorithm combines

---

similarly cumulative, but with geometrically decreasing increments, as in the classic work of Clark Hull (1943). However, in the present context, a Hull function has the disadvantage that the sum of a suitable geometric series of increments (with a geometric coefficient between zero and unity) is always finite. As a result, the indefinite reversibility of an acquired habit from one extreme to the other and back again would not be possible. In contrast, the chosen increments in the habit function in the present work decline at a rate that permits in principle the indefinite reversal of habituation from one extreme value to the other: no sign nor degree of habituation is ever irreversible.

decision elements that vary according to the cognitive personality of the driver and the global parameter weights. The population of varied decision algorithms itself evolves due to selection pressure, leading to surviving decision algorithms of some fitness value.

10.3.4 Replacement of colliding drivers

If there is neither birth nor death, then the pool of fixed characteristics among the population cannot change. At least a small amount of death and replacement is necessary to select the combinations of fixed cognitive and behavioural dispositions that are conducive to survival. However, this means that a replacement routine is necessary for new cars and its form can influence the outcomes in the model. It should be emphasized, however, that the overwhelming majority of deaths generally occur in the early, transition phase of the simulations.

If there is a collision, then – regardless of blame or circumstances – the two drivers die and are replaced by two new cars and drivers. The weights w_X are common to all agents and also used by the newborn drivers. However, the two newborn drivers require a new set of four fixed cognitive and behavioural dispositions $\{SSensitivity_n, OSensitivity_n, Avoidance_n, Habitgene_n\}$. These are chosen randomly in the same manner as the cars in the population at the beginning of the simulation, with the habituation level $\{Habituation_{n,t}\}$ always set initially to zero.

Their cognitive and behavioural characteristics being determined, each new car is allocated to a random position on the track. However, to reduce the frequency of immediate collisions, no new car is allocated to a zone occupied by another car.

10.3.5 Design adjustments and parametric searches

Experiments were performed with different values of the mutation variable δ. Although a convention emerged with many runs with a higher value, a relatively low value of 0.2 was chosen in order to achieve a lower and more plausible degree of mutation. Different values of K in the function above for $Habituation_{n,t}$ were also tried. Clearly, as K decreases to zero, the left/right choice by the car in its first move will increasingly dominate its strength of habit. The outcomes were relatively insensitive to variations in this coefficient, but habit had a slightly improved positive effect on convergence with values of K in the region of 10. This value ensured that habituation adjusted at a significant but modest rate.

The decision horizon is the number of zones ahead that a driver scans to estimate the traffic pattern. This data affects the driver's 'conformist' calculations concerning same-direction and opposite-direction sensitivity. As summarized in an appendix in the original article (Hodgson and Knudsen,

2004a), a number of simulations were performed with various decision horizons greater than 10 zones ahead, including the possibility that drivers see all 100 zones of the entire ring. It was found that habit significantly improves convergence for values of the horizon from zero up to and including 25 zones. The maximum habit effect appears with a horizon of 10, which is the value used in the standard runs reported in the main text below.

After all the design adjustments were complete, the values of the first three non-negative weights $\{w_{Sdirection}, w_{Odirection},$ and $w_{Avoidance}\}$ were considered by searching through their multidimensional parametric space, with progressively decreasing increments of search, with w_{Habit} always set at zero. The three positive weights were always normalized according to the rule that their average was unity. The convergence performance, death rates and other aspects of the model were monitored during these searches. At each search point, a sample of at least 100 repeated simulations were made to obtain mean values. Also at each point, error was increased uniformly from zero to 0.02, across the set of 100 or more samples. This search of parameter space identified the point of maximum convergence $\{w_{Sdirection} = 1.4$, $w_{Odirection} = 0.9$, and $w_{Avoidance} = 0.7\}$ with $w_{Habit} = 0$.[11]

10.4 SIMULATION RESULTS FOR THE STANDARD MODEL

10.4.1 Preliminary remarks

The principal aim of the simulations is to gauge the degree of left/right convergence in multiple runs of the model, exploring different points of parameter space and assessing the impact of different levels of habit and error.

Generally, when an equilibrium outcome emerges, the resulting convention, whether drive-to-the-right or drive-to-the-left, can be highly sensitive to initial conditions. Once the system begins to swing decisively and permanently one way or the other and a convention begins to emerge, then it can become locked into a process that is the cumulative result of tiny initial movements (Arthur, 1994).

However, two factors can disturb this process of convergence to a left/right convention. The first, and more ubiquitous, is error. The effects of error can be particularly disruptive in the early phases of this process. However, even in later phases, errors can trigger deaths that lead to replacements that are ill-adapted for the road conditions, leading to further

[11] Searches in parameter space confirmed that this was a global rather than a local maximum. However, the convergence optimization zone is almost flat, making accuracy to more than one decimal place superfluous.

collisions and so on. It is possible for such processes of positive feedback to destroy an established convention.

The second disturbing factor emerges under specific conditions only. It is prevalent in a relatively small neighbourhood of parameter space. In some circumstances agile drivers can evolve, typically with a low but positive level of the habit gene. These drivers are sufficiently agile to avoid the traffic ahead, by moving repeatedly from one side of the road to the other if required. A 'cycling' pattern can occur, when cohorts of agile drivers repeatedly move safely and laterally to avoid other oncoming groups. There may be a degree of local convergence in each group, but the conventions in different groups may be different. If there are no further collisions then replacement and mutation through death cannot occur. Consequently, a unanimous convention will not emerge among the population as a whole.

Figure 10.1 Two Illustrative Runs

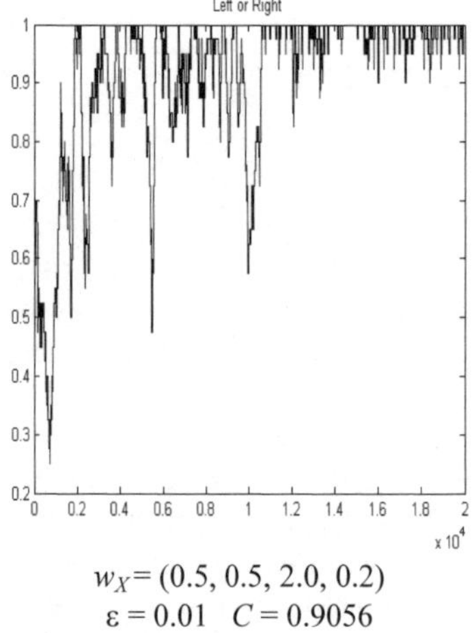

w_X= (0.5, 0.5, 2.0, 0.2)
$\varepsilon = 0.01 \quad C = 0.9056$

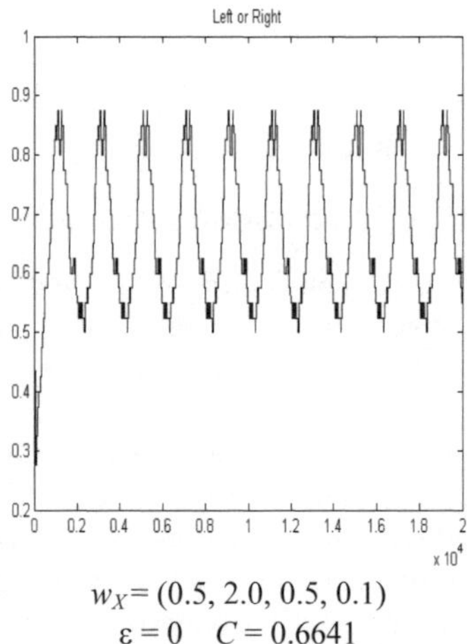

w_X= (0.5, 2.0, 0.5, 0.1)
$\varepsilon = 0 \quad C = 0.6641$

10.4.2 Some illustrative simulations

Illustrative results from two different runs are displayed in Figure 10.1. The vertical scale measures the average inclination of the cars to the left or right. The horizontal scale measures the number of car moves enacted through time. In Figures 10.1 and 10.2, a value of unity on the vertical scale would correspond to the unanimous use of either the right or the left hand side of the road by all cars. A value of 0.5 on the vertical scale would indicate that the cars were equally distributed on the right or the left. The expected value at the start of the run is 0.5. With a run of 20,000 car moves, the mean of the 20,000 vertical values is computed.

In order to compare results whether the drivers happened to converge on the left or the right, we used the following standardization procedure. If this average is less than 0.5, then it is subtracted from 1, ensuring that the overall convergence outcome (C) is always greater than or equal to 0.5 and less than or equal to 1. With this measure of convergence success, higher values indicate a greater degree of convergence. A figure of 0.95 would indicate that on average, for one entire run, 95 per cent of the cars were on one particular side of the road.

Hence the degree of convergence (C) for m moves with c cars is the total number of moves in which a car is on the left/right, divided by $c \times m$. In this calculation all cars are considered for each individual move of every car through the entire run. The choice of left or right in this definition is made to ensure that $C \geq 0.5$. Hence $0.5 \leq C < 1$.

In the run displayed on the left of Figure 10.1 there is imperfect and incomplete convergence to one side of the track. The small amount of error slightly disturbs the emergent convention and prevents complete convergence. The death rate (not illustrated) is fairly steady and does not greatly subside. In the run displayed on the right of Figure 10.1, complete convergence to a left/right convention is prevented by a minority cohort of 18 cars that defy convention and have a disposition to drive on the other side. When they meet oncoming cars they are able to manoeuvre to avoid collision. Partly because the error coefficient is zero in this case, no collisions or deaths occur after the first few moves. Consequently, no further evolution of the model in this run is possible and the 'cycling' pattern becomes permanent.

Many thousands of distinct runs were tried. In some simulations, the habit weighting (w_{Habit}) took the values of 0, 0.5, 1.0, 1.5 and 2.0 in turn. The purpose was to show the effects of increasing weightings to the habit term in the decision function for every car. For each level of $w_{Habit,}$ the error probability ε took the values of 0.000, 0.005, 0.010, 0.015 and 0.020. This meant that 25 combinations of different levels of w_{Habit} and ε were explored. We tried 200 runs, each with 20,000 car moves, for each of the 25 different combinations of the values for w_{Habit} and ε. This meant a total of 5,000 runs and 100 million car moves.[12]

---

[12] Convergence to the left or right was monitored in all runs, confirming that the model had no bias towards one side of the road rather than the other.

We found that the degrees of convergence, the death rates, the effects of error, and the impact of habit can vary substantially, depending on the values of the three parameters $\{w_{Sdirection}, w_{Odirection},$ and $w_{Avoidance}\}$. In some regions of parameter space, with a given level of error, increases in the overall strength of habit in the population as a whole (formed by the terms $w_{Habit} \times Habitgene \times Habituation$) can often help to improve the speed of convergence to a left/right convention. In addition, w_{Habit} can sometimes help the system cope with error and subvert 'cycling' behaviour. In other parts of parameter space, the impact of habit on convergence is small or negative.

However, it is important to emphasize that convergence is never achieved by the force of habit alone. Furthermore, convergence can sometimes occur with low or zero levels of habit. Crucially, habit helps convergence only when it is combined with selection pressure on the fixed 'instincts' in the population of cars.

Figure 10.2 Degrees of Convergence with 200 Runs for Each Level of Habit and Error

$w_X = (1.4, 0.9, 0.7, w_{Habit})$

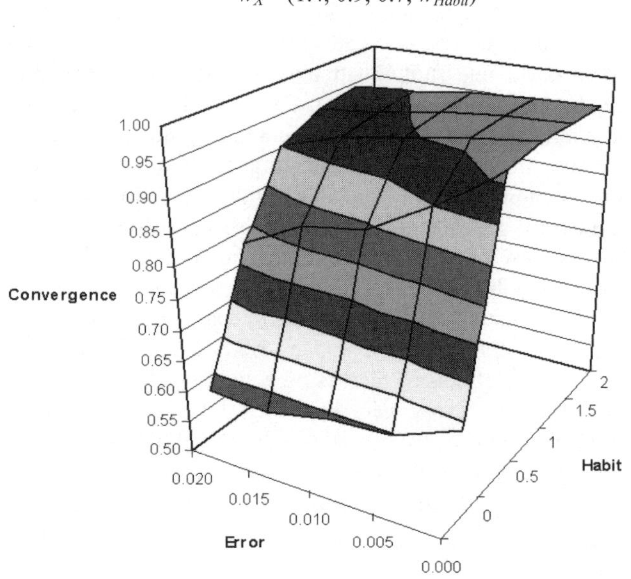

The results of a multiple simulation with different levels of w_{Habit} and ε are reported in Figure 10.2 above. The three weights in this model are from the point in parameter space where convergence is maximized with zero habit. The vertical axis on Figure 10.2 shows the degree of convergence to a left/right convention. The higher the value the greater the degree of convergence.

A striking outcome displayed in Figure 10.2 is the sensitivity of convergence to the habit weighting (w_{Habit}) and strength of habit. As w_{Habit} increases, at least from zero to unity, mean convergence levels improve for all levels of error (ε). Habit generally improves convergence.[13]

10.4.3 Multiple simulations in parameter space

The simulation reported in the previous section is from a point in parameter space where the convergence is maximized with zero habit. The question is raised whether other parts of parameter space exhibit the same positive habit effect, and if so, to what degree?

In Hodgson and Knudsen (2004a) we developed techniques for the systematic search through the entire parameter space. Based on the data from hundreds of observations in this parameter space, habit emerged as the most significant factor determining the degree of convergence.

No other variable emerged in general to improve convergence in our simulations. For instance, while the avoidance coefficient can help the drivers to survive, it does not significantly assist convergence.

We conclude that in this boundedly rational situation, where drivers cannot see the whole of the ring, habit emerged as the single most significant factor improving convergence. If drivers can see further ahead (Hodgson and Knudsen, 2004a, Appendix 2), habit still has a positive effect. In addition, when the decision horizon is greater than 10, and hence there is more information concerning the traffic ahead, 'conformist' factors related to the $w_{Sdirection}$ and $w_{Odirection}$, coefficients become significant and more important in aiding convergence. The relative importance of habit is inversely related to omniscience.[14]

---

[13] More data from this set of simulation results are presented in Hodgson and Knudsen (2004a).

[14] Our article was published before we came across Epstein (2001), which also involves artificial agents driving around a circular ring. Epstein adopts a simpler decision-making algorithm without habit, where a driver's horizon is reduced if there is no change in left/right decisions. He derives the important result that the necessary horizon and degree of rational deliberation is inversely related to the strength of the reigning traffic convention. Epstein's work complements ours. Both studies emphasize that conventions are not only convenient outcomes for agents, but also they help to reduce their computational and deliberational requirements.

10.5 DISCUSSION – THE NATURE OF HABIT

The most important result of the simulations described in section 10.4 concerns the effect of introducing processes of habituation into the modelling of agent behaviour. In a substantial region of parameter space, strength of habit can increase the systemic rate of convergence towards a left/right convention. In some circumstances it can also enhance systemic resistance to error.

In the above model, each car is programmed by three parameters ($SSensitivity_n$, $OSensitivity_n$, $Avoidance_n$) governing its sensitivity to traffic patterns ahead and its propensity to make an avoidance manoeuvre. A fourth parameter ($Habitgene_n$) governs the tendency that a driver has to take account of its acquired habituation. The values of these four exogenously given parameters are akin to instincts: they are fixed for the lifetime of each car. By contrast, a fifth parameter ($Habituation_{n,t}$) governing the particular habitual disposition to go left or right is an outcome of the actual behaviour of the car. The value of this parameter is not given and is literally path dependent.

The conception and role of habit in this model contrasts greatly with a definition of habit elsewhere. Gary Becker (1992, p. 328) writes: 'I define *habitual* behaviour as displaying a positive relation between past and current consumption'. Becker here defines habit not as a behavioural propensity but as sequentially correlated behaviour. A car may manoeuvre to the left to avoid oncoming traffic, but its propensity may still be to drive to the right. If there is an observed succession of left-driving behaviour, this is not necessarily the underlying disposition of the agent. Becker's definition conflates propensity with actuality. However, if past behaviour were taken to mean a potentially infinite sequence of past events, then a propensity acquired through habituation could approximate to mean past behaviour. In this extreme case, propensity with actuality could coincide, but in general, and in contrast to Becker, we distinguish between habit and behaviour by defining habit as a disposition or propensity, rather than correlated behaviour.

Becker (1992, p. 331) is on stronger ground when he writes: 'Habit helps economize on the cost of searching for information, and of applying the information to a new situation'. It is true that habit removes some actions from conscious deliberation and helps the agent to focus on other, more strategic or immediate decisions. However, the model here suggests that there is something more to habit than economizing on decision-making. After all, each car in the model makes only one simple binary decision at each point of time. Habit is doing much more in our model than simply economizing on the time taken to search for and process information.

The model suggests that a crucial role played by habit is to build up and reinforce an enduring disposition in each agent concerning the appropriate side of the road on which to drive, especially in a situation where information concerning the traffic ahead is limited. A sequence of similar and repeated behaviours creates in each agent a habitual predilection, which can stimulate a 'belief' or 'conviction' that a particular behaviour is appropriate.

Again this is reminiscent of the arguments of pragmatists such as Peirce and James, who saw acquired habits as the basis of firmly held beliefs. Habit is more than a means of economizing on decision-making for individuals; it is a means by which social conventions and institutions are formed and preserved.

Our model raises questions concerning the distinction between preference exogeneity and endogeneity. By introducing the concept of meta-preferences, Becker and others have argued habit-formation is not an example of meta-preference endogeneity. Becker's (1992, p. 340) argument is that habits and addictions can be placed within a meta-preference function in which data concerning 'different variables and experiences', pertaining to different time periods, enter as arguments. These

> *meta* preferences are stable. … The message is not that preferences at time *t* for different people depend in the same way on their consumption at time *t*. Rather, it is that common rules determine the way different variables and experiences enter the meta preferences that motivate most people at most times.

It is instructive to consider the scale of the mental operation that is implied here. Note that as the number of time periods increases, the number of arguments in Becker's meta-preference function must increase proportionately. Essentially, Becker argues that utility is a function of the following type:

$$U = f(\mathbf{x}_1, \mathbf{x}_2 \dots \mathbf{x}_i \dots \mathbf{x}_t)$$

where U is utility and each $\mathbf{x}_i$ is a vector of 'variables and experiences' at time i. In each complete standard run of our model, each surviving agent moves 500 times, meaning that its preference function would have to have 500 arguments for each of the five variables involved. However, ours is an extremely simple model, running overall for only 500 iterations per surviving agent. Assume that a nearer-to-human individual lives for 30,000 days, and makes 10^4 decisions each day, governing 10^4 variables. If so, the Beckerian meta-preference function must have 3×10^{12} arguments. It is likely that the demands of the Beckerian meta-preference function significantly exceed the computational capacities of the human brain. To use the words of Roy Radner (1970, p. 457), the unboundedly rational agent requires 'capabilities of imagination and calculation that exceed reality by many orders of magnitude'.

Habit, in the sense that we are using the term, makes computation manageable by vastly reducing the computational and memory requirements of the agent. Habit works not simply or principally by reducing the 'cost of searching for information' but also by reducing the memory and computational capacity required to make any decision to act. In formal terms,

$$U = f(\boldsymbol{h}, \boldsymbol{m}_{t-s}, \boldsymbol{m}_{t-s+1} \ldots \boldsymbol{m}_{t-1}, \boldsymbol{x}_t)$$

where $\boldsymbol{h}$ is the vector of habits and $\boldsymbol{m}_{t-s} \ldots \boldsymbol{m}_{t-1}$ constitute the selective memories of past events, where s is less than t. The number of elements in the vector $\boldsymbol{h}$ and in any vector $\boldsymbol{m}_i$ are each less than the number of 'variables and experiences' in $\boldsymbol{x}_t$.

The attribution of a Beckerian preference function to each driver in our model would mean that each driver would have to remember simultaneously, and *for every one of its moves*, at least three computed variables ($S_{L,n,t}$, $O_{L,n,t}$, $C_{R,n,t} - C_{L,n,tt}$) plus all of its past left/right positions. If the maximum number of moves were 500, then each agent would require a mental storage for at least 2,000 scalar variables. With a greater number of moves the memory requirement increases in proportion. Instead, in our model, only *two* scalar variables (current habituation, plus the number of past moves) have to be stored in the memory of each car at any point in time, *for any length of run*.

Another aspect of Becker's (1992, p. 340) treatment of individual preferences is also questionable. Becker continues, in the same passage as above,

> forward-looking rational actors maximize the utility from their meta preferences, not from current preferences alone, because they recognize that choices today affect their utilities in the future.

In contrast, it could be argued that many actions of agents in the real world, in this respect like the actions of drivers in our model, are not forward-looking in the sense that they consider the full consequences of present actions in the future. Habit is a disposition, sometimes even reinforced by ethical conviction; it does not typically involve a detailed or extensive consideration of future outcomes. No agent in the model considers whether the future emergent convention will be to the left or to the right. It just acts, in part to survive the traffic maelstrom and in part according to its acquired propensity or 'belief' that one type of behaviour is more appropriate. Of course, things are much more complicated in the real world. People do make decisions based on forward-looking considerations. However, the suggestion here is that forward-looking decisions cannot account for all of behaviour, including behaviour that is habit-driven. Habit is a past-driven propensity, and not necessarily the outcome of a forward-looking calculation.

For these reasons it is preferable to regard habit formation as an endogenous change of preferences rather than an outcome of decisions governed by a meta-preference function that deals with a number of variables over a series of time periods.[15]

10.6 DISCUSSION – DOWNWARD CAUSATION

Another use of our model is that it provides a heuristic framework to consider the nuanced interpretations and meanings of the idea of 'downward causation' – a concept largely unfamiliar to economists but quite well known in the philosophy of psychology and the philosophy of biology (Andersen *et al.*, 2000; Campbell, 1974; Sperry, 1969, 1991; Popper and Eccles, 1977; Mayr, 1985).

The concept of downward causation depends upon the ontological notion that any complex system has 'higher level' systemic properties as well as 'lower level' components. At the systemic level there may exist 'emergent properties' that are, by definition, additional properties that depend upon but are not explicable or predictable from an analysis of the components at the lower level. The concept of emergent properties has recently become prominent in discussions of the complex simulations, pioneered in Santa Fe and elsewhere (Lane, 1993).[16]

Downward causation refers to possible effects of higher-level properties on lower-level components. As noted in the preceding chapter, 'downward causation' has weak and strong forms.

---

15 There is a some similarity between our concept of habit and the idea of reinforcement in the works of Ido Erev and Alvin Roth (Erev and Roth, 1998; Roth and Erev, 1995). In their reinforcement model and our habit model, past behaviour influences current behaviour through more than expectations. Our habit function is thus close to the function typically used to model simple reinforcement, but it is not identical. Crucially, the force of the past in our habit function does not decay due to forgetfulness as in Roth and Erev (1995). In our formulation of habituation the force of the past accumulates as time unfolds. Erev and Roth (1998) later generalized their reinforcement model to unify reinforcement learning and probabilistic fictitious play. In this generalization, they defined a 'subjective reinforcement' of a player's initial beliefs as the sum of initial expectations and accumulated experience. According to the function used to model this idea, the initial expectations were modified by a time-dependent term defined as the average return of action k at time t divided by the number of times that the strategy associated with k has been played up to t. This formulation is quite close to the habit function used in our model where habits are built up steadily, and once acquired they are more difficult to reverse. Consequently, our concept of habituation is close to that of reinforcement in their generalized model.

16 On the concept of emergent properties and its history see Beckerman *et al.* (1992), Blitz (1992), Emmeche *et al.* (1997), Humphreys (1997), Cunningham (2000) and Hodgson (2004a).

In our model, this weaker form of downward causation is clearly present. As a left/right driving convention begins to be formed, more and more cars drive in conformity with that emerging convention. If a convention begins to emerge, then those that survive tend to be those that conform. Evolutionary selection acts on the population of agents, causing a shift in the characteristics of the population as a whole. This is an outcome of 'natural selection' and amounts to weak downward causation.

In the population as a whole, this evolutionary selection works on both the four fixed parameters and the single variable expressing habit. The set of values in the population as a whole changes by means of the death of the unsuccessful and the birth of the new agents. However, for any individual agent, evolutionary selection does not cause a change in the values of the four fixed parameters.

The stronger notion of 'reconstitutive downward causation', involves changing individuals as well as populations as a result of causal powers associated with higher levels (Hodgson, 2004a). However, Sperry (1991) and other authors insist that explanations based on downward causation should be carefully focused on real causal mechanisms. This is the problem: while it is tempting to explain the behaviour of units in terms of collectives or wholes, the precise causal mechanism is difficult to determine.

If there is some mechanism whereby an actual or emerging convention can affect or 'reconstitute' the characteristics of the individual units, then this would amount to reconstitutive downward causation. System-wide outcomes (at a 'higher' level) would affect the characteristics of individual units (at a lower level).

In our model, this stronger form of downward causation is also present and is associated with a discernible causal mechanism because as the left/right convention begins to emerge, more and more surviving cars develop the habit to drive on the left or the right, according to that convention. Strength of habit is based on two of the five variables that form the 'preference function' of each agent. For each individual, one of these preference elements ($Habituation_{n,t}$) can change. In this way, emerging and enduring systemic properties reconstitute 'downwards' the preferences of the agent. Part of the achievement here is to show that both forms of downward causation can be represented in an agent-based model. In particular, we can identify a specific causal mechanism of reconstitutive downward causation.

Another crucial point to recognize is the specific mechanism by which reconstitutive downward causation operates. It is on *habits* rather than merely on behaviour, intentions or other preferences. Clearly, the definitional distinction between habit (as a propensity or disposition) and behaviour (or action) is essential to make sense of this statement.

The existence of a viable mechanism of reconstitutive downward causation contrasts with other, untenable 'top down' or 'methodologically collectivist' explanations in the social sciences where there are unspecified 'structural', 'cultural', or 'economic' forces controlling individuals. Crucially, the mechanism of reconstitutive downward causation that is outlined here affects the dispositions, thoughts, and actions of human actors. It is highly inadequate to regard preferences or purposes as changing simply as a result of unspecified cultural or social forces. What does happen is that the framing, shifting and constraining capacities of social institutions give rise to new perceptions and dispositions within individuals. Upon new habits of thought and behaviour, new preferences and intentions emerge.

Hence the concept of reconstitutive downward causation does not rely on new or mysterious types of cause or causality. We exclude any version of methodological collectivism or holism where an attempt is made to explain individual dispositions or behaviour entirely in terms of institutions or other system-level characteristics. Instead, we are obliged to explain particular human behaviour in terms of causal processes operating at the individual level, such as individual aspirations, dispositions or constraints.

As explained in the preceding chapter, when an institutional structures gives rise to new or changed habits, then we have a possible and acceptable mechanism of reconstitutive downward causation. Of course, institutions may directly affect our intentions by providing incentives, sanctions or constraints. In contrast, a reconstitutive causal mechanism involves factors that are foundational to purposes, preferences and deliberation as a whole (Margolis, 1987). By affecting habits, institutions can eventually and indirectly influence our intentions.

10.7 CONCLUSION

The model discussed in this chapter shows how a left/right traffic convention may emerge in an agent-based model. The main factor inhibiting this convergence is error. Also, in limited circumstances, agile avoidance behaviour can lead to recurrent, cycling patterns of behaviour with no emergent left/right convention. The simulation results show that increases in the 'strength of habit' of agents in the model when combined with evolutionary selection pressure can help to suppress both of these disturbing factors.

This simulation points to some of the deeper conceptual issues involved in the evolution of conventions, particularly the nature of rational decision-making and its reliance upon habit. Overall, the simulations show that the systemic convergence to a left/right convention is often improved and sustained by strength of habit. Accordingly, habit plays an important part alongside the 'intelligent' and calculative aspects of agent behaviour, particularly in cases where information is limited.

In contrast, the analyses of Stephen Jones (1984) and Ekkehart Schlicht (1998) maintain that conventions and customs emerge principally because individuals have a preference for them. In our simulations, this is not generally the case where information is limited. In these circumstances, habit is additionally and vitally important because it can often enhance stable behaviour and help to create stable outcomes.

The specification of habit in the model is redolent of the concept in the works of pragmatist philosophers such as Peirce and James. Habit acts in the model as if it were the foundation of a 'conviction' or firmly held 'belief'. This suggests that the evolution of conventions may depend not only on the rational calculations of actors but also on the widespread development of convictions or norms concerning appropriate behaviour.

This model also has implications for an understanding of the nature and role of habit. In the specification here, the conception of habit is clearly distinguished from serially correlated behaviour. This definition contrasts significantly with that in the work of Becker and others.

We also identify a mechanism of 'reconstitutive downward causation' among agents. Although each car has four inert 'instincts', the fifth variable concerning habituation changes as agent behaviour changes. As a left/right convention emerges among the population as a whole, this provides a channel of movement for every individual. Accordingly, individual habits reflect the emergent convention among the whole population. As a result, the formation of individual habits is guided by systemic conventions. This is tantamount to a change of preferences, and it results from a 'downwards' causal process from the emergent institution to the individual.

A possible criticism of this thesis could stem from a Beckerian approach where each agent has a meta-preference function with arguments representing all relevant temporal and other variables. We have shown that this approach comes up against the problem of computational limitations of agents required to deal with large and increasing amounts of information concerning their past. It makes more sense to treat preferences as partially endogenous and malleable. Furthermore, in contrast to the idea of a meta-preference function, the conception of habit defined here greatly reduces the number of variables that each agent has to take into account.

Given the powerful effect of habituation in our model, reconstitutive downward causation may provide a degree of durability and stability in institutional structure that is not explained adequately in standard models. The circular, positive feedback from institution to individuals and from individuals to institutions can help to enhance the durability of the institutional unit. There may be stable emergent properties that exist *not despite*, but *because of*, endogenous preference formation.

With the theoretical framework proposed here, it may also be possible to overcome the dilemma between methodological individualism and methodological collectivism. By acting not directly on individual decisions, but on habitual dispositions, institutions exert reconstitutive downward causation without reducing the role of individual agency. Upward causation, from individuals to institutions, is still possible, without assuming that the individual is given or immanently conceived. Explanations of socio-economic phenomena are reduced neither to individuals nor to institutions alone.

11. The Nature and Replication of Routines

> In our evolutionary theory, these routines play the role that genes play in biological evolutionary theory. They are a persistent feature of the organism and determine its possible behavior (though *actual* behavior is determined also by the environment); they are heritable in the sense that tomorrow's organisms generated from today's (for example, by building a new plant) have many of the same characteristics, and they are selectable in the sense that organisms with certain routines may do better than others, and, if so, their relative importance in the population (industry) is augmented over time.
>
> Richard Nelson and Sidney Winter,
> *An Evolutionary Theory of Economic Change* (1982)

11.1 INTRODUCTION

Routines are vital to all organizations and their significance is widely appreciated.[1] It is important to understand both how they can be built and how they can be changed. Such awareness is essential to any analysis of how knowledge is retained and transferred, for the development of business strategy, and for the creation of policies to encourage more beneficial business practices.

Detailed empirical investigation is essential in this regard, but detailed taxonomic studies based on empirical evidence are relatively rare. One reason why empirical investigations have so far remained rather limited is that the conceptual specification of a routine remains obscure. Greater conceptual precision is an essential precondition of fruitful empirical enquiry.

This chapter attempts to illuminate the concept of the routine, by citing relevant insights from philosophy, social theory and psychology, and by focusing on some milestone contributions in this area. The second section of this chapter addresses the analogous and component concept of habit, with a view to making a distinction between habits and routines. The third section explores the metaphor of 'routines as genes' and argues that routines must be treated as capacities or dispositions, rather than behaviours. The fourth section considers how routines persist and carry information through time.

[1] Thanks are due to participants at the Second Routines Workshop in Sophia-Antipolis, France in January 2005 for comments on some of the ideas in this paper. Use is made of material from Hodgson (forthcoming).

The fifth section raises the issue of what is meant by the replication of routines, after briefly citing some theoretical and empirical studies in the area. The sixth section concludes the chapter.

11.2 HABITS AS THE BASIS AND INDIVIDUAL ANALOGUE OF ROUTINES

To understand the concept of a routine we need to appreciate the idea of a habit. First, routines operate through the triggering of individual habits. Second, routines are the organizational analogue of individual habits. So the analysis starts here with the habit concept.

Pragmatist philosophers and institutional economists such as Thorstein Veblen (1919) regarded habit as an acquired proclivity or capacity, which may or may not be actually expressed in current behaviour (Hodgson, 2004a). As noted in Chapter 8 above, a habit is a propensity to behave in a particular way in a particular class of situations.

Habit is not the negation of deliberation, but its necessary foundation. Reasons and beliefs are often the rationalizations of deep-seated feelings and emotions that spring from habits that are laid down by repeated behaviours. This interplay of behaviour, habit, emotion and rationalization helps to explain the normative power of custom in human society.

Habits are socially acquired, not genetically transmitted. In this respect they are distinguished from instincts. Instincts are blunt instruments to deal with changing, complex and unpredictable circumstances. Humans developed the capacity to acquire habits concomitantly with the evolution of a cultural apparatus by which adaptive solutions to problems of survival could be preserved and passed on.[2]

By accepting the foundational role of habit in sustaining rule-following behaviour, we can begin to build an alternative ontology of institutions and routines, in which we avoid the conceptual problems of an account based primarily on intentionality. This is not to deny the importance of intentionality, but to regard it as a consequence as much as a cause, and to place it in the broader context of other, non-deliberative behaviours.

Importantly, all learning, and the attainment of all skills, depends on the acquisition of habits. Knowledge and skills involve the capacity to address a complex problem and to identify rapidly the means of dealing with it. Experience and intuition are crucial here, and these must be grounded in acquired habits of thought or behaviour that dispose the agent to identify the crucial aspects of or responses to the problem. All skills, from knowledge of

---

[2] See Veblen (1914, pp. 6–7), Richerson *et al.* (2001), Richerson and Boyd (2001, 2004), Hodgson (2004a).

mathematics through competence with languages to ability with a musical instrument, depend on habits. Habits are the necessary means of avoiding full reflection over every detail, so that the more deliberative levels of the mind are freed up for more strategic issues. If all details were necessarily the subject of conscious deliberation, then the mind would be overwhelmed and paralyzed by minutiae.

We briefly consider two possible types of mechanism by which habit may be replicated from person to person. The first is by incentive or constraint. These can provide reasons to acquire specific customs, follow particular traffic conventions and use specific linguistic terms. In these cases, because others are acting in a particular way we can have powerful incentives to behave accordingly. In doing so, we too build up habits associated with these behaviours. The behaviours are reproduced and also the habits giving rise to them are replicated.

Another possible mechanism is imitation. Imitation need not be fully conscious, and it will also involve some 'tacit learning' (Polanyi, 1967; Reber, 1993; Knudsen, 2002). Perhaps imitation can occur even without strong incentives, on the grounds that the propensity to imitate is instinctive, and this instinct has itself evolved for efficacious reasons among social creatures (James, 1892; Veblen, 1899; Campbell, 1975; Boyd and Richerson, 1985; Simon, 1990; Tomasello, 2000; Henrich, 2004). However, an imitation instinct would require an existing set of common behaviours in the group, otherwise an emerging propensity to imitate might not have a selection advantage. For instinctive imitation to take off, common behaviours may have to emerge for other reasons. Furthermore, if imitation is more than mimicry, then the rules and understandings associated with it also have to be transmitted. Imitation is more problematic than it appears. Nevertheless, there are provisional grounds to consider a partially instinctive propensity to imitate as a strong element in the complex social glue, and hence a force behind the replication of habits.

If habits replicate, then this means that multiple habits exist with similar characteristics. With genes, replicative similarity is at the level of the generative structure. However, there is no obvious reason why two people with similar habits have similar neural patterns in the brain. Habit similarity is at the level of descriptions of the rule-like dispositions that give rise to the behaviour, not of some neural structure.

Having established the concept of habit, and for reasons that should become clearer below, we are now in a stronger position to turn to the concept of a routine. In the following section it will be explained how routines play a similar role for organizations that habits play for individuals.

11.3 ROUTINES AS ORGANIZATIONAL GENES

In everyday parlance the word ‘routine’ is used loosely to refer to repeated sequences of behaviour, by individuals as well as by organizations. However, when Richard Nelson and Sidney Winter (1982) used the metaphor of ‘routines as genes’, they suggested a more specific and technical meaning for the term, which is further clarified here.

In evolutionary and institutional economics a consensus has emerged that routines relate to groups or organizations, whereas habits relate to individuals (Cohen *et al.*, 1996; Dosi *et al.*, 2000). Individuals have habits; groups have routines. Routines are the organizational analogue of habits. But routines do not simply refer to habits that are shared by many individuals in an organization or group. If this were the case there would be no need for the additional concept of a routine. Routines are not reducible to habits alone: they are organizational meta-habits, existing on a substrate of habituated individuals in a social structure. Routines are one ontological layer above habits themselves.

The causal connection between habits and routines will be examined in more detail in the next section. It is first necessary to address an important question concerning routines: are they organizational dispositions or organizational behaviours?

Confusingly, in their 1982 book, Nelson and Winter sometimes treat routines as dispositions, but otherwise described them as behaviours. For example, Nelson and Winter (1982, p. 15) write: ‘It is that most of what is *regular and predictable* about business behaviour is plausibly subsumed under the heading “routine”’. But they go on in the same sentence to describe routines as ‘dispositions … that shape the approach of the firm’ to problems. Routines are also treated as ‘organizational memory’, which refers more to capabilities than to behaviour.

Another passage introduces the useful analogy between a routine and a computer program, but repeats the same confusion. Nelson and Winter (1982, p. 97) see a ‘routine’ as being like a computer ‘program’, referring thereby ‘to a repetitive pattern of activity in an entire organization’ as well as to skills or capacities. But there is a difference between a computer program and the computer’s output or behaviour. The computer program is a rule-based system, with a generative coding that, along with other inputs, determines the computer’s output. Nelson and Winter conflate generative and dispositional factors such as the computer program with outputs such a ‘repetitive pattern of activity’ or ‘performance’.

The idea of ‘routines as genes’ is a useful analogy. But routines are very different from genes. Routines do not replicate biologically and they are much less enduring. All analogies are inexact in some respects and must be handled with care, as Nelson and Winter are fully aware. The gene analogy usefully points to routines as relatively durable carriers of information through shorter periods of time (Knudsen, forthcoming), with the algorithmic capacity to generate particular outcomes in given circumstances. Routines are like genes in the sense that they are both generative, rule-like structures and potentialities. However, routines (like genes) cannot be both generative structures and outcomes of such structures. This point is not about the appropriateness or otherwise of biological analogies, but about the clear meanings of words and their ontological references.

Winter (1995, pp. 149–50) distinguishes between a 'routine in operation at a particular site ... a web of coordinating relationships connecting specific resources' and the 'routine *per se* – the abstract activity pattern'. But the one term 'routine' cannot usefully apply to both the 'web of coordinating relationships' and the 'activity pattern' that is the outcome of the coordinating structure and its environmental triggers; it cannot helpfully denote both potentiality and actuality. It should denote one or the other, but not both.

At root there is a philosophical contention here: the essence of what an entity *is* cannot be conflated with what an entity *does*. If we make this conflation, then we wrongly imply that when the entity interrupts its characteristic activity, then it ceases to exist. Birds fly. But what defines a bird is descent from a genus with the *capacity* to fly, not flying itself. If a bird were wrongly defined as a flying animal, then any bird sitting on a branch or pecking on the ground would cease to be a bird.

Accordingly routines are not behaviour; they are stored behavioural capacities or capabilities. Consider a firm in which all employees and managers work between 9am and 5pm only. During this working day a number of organizational routines can be energized. At other times the firm is inactive. But the routines do not all disappear at 5pm, to reappear mysteriously the next day. The routines-as-capacities remain, as long as the individuals have the capacity and disposition to work again together in the same context. Subject to this condition, the routines can be triggered the next day by appropriate stimuli.

Making the central philosophical point here, Aristotle (1956, pp. 227–8) in his *Metaphysics* criticized Eucleides of Megara – a disciple of Socrates – and his school

> who maintain that a thing *can act* only when it *is acting*. But the paradoxes attending this view are not far to seek. … Now if a man cannot have an art without having at some time learned it, and cannot later be without it unless he has lost it, are we to suppose that the moment he stops building he has lost his art? If so, how will he have recovered it if he immediately resumes building? The same is true of inanimate objects. … The Megaric view, in fact, does away with all change. On their theory that which stands will *always* stand, that which sits

> will *always* sit; ... Since we cannot admit this view ... we must obviously draw a distinction between potentiality and actuality.

An enduringly relevant point here is that definitions or ontologies that are based on behaviour cannot cope with instances where the behaviour changes or ceases. Even when an entity with a particular behavioural propensity is inert, the capacity to produce the characteristic behaviour remains, and this capacity, not the outcome, continues to define part of the essence of the entity. Although ancient, this point is not arcane; it is widely utilized in modern realist philosophy of science. Central to most strands of modern realist philosophy is the distinction between the *potential* and the *actual*, between dispositions and outcomes, where in each case the former are more fundamental than the latter.[3]

Science is about the discovery of causal laws or principles. Causes are not events; they are generative mechanisms that can under specific conditions give rise to specific events. For example, a force impinging on an object does not always make that object move. The outcome also depends on friction, countervailing forces, and other factors. As Veblen (1919, p. 89) put it: 'The laws of nature are ... of the nature of a propensity'. Hence there must be a distinction between an observed empirical regularity and any causal law that lies behind it. Similarly there must be a distinction between the capacities and behaviours of an entity.

In biology, genes and genotypes are potentialities; they are not behaviours. In the socio-economic domain, the closest analogies to genotypes are the generative rule-like structures inherent in ingrained individual habits and in organizational routines. Habits and routines are thus understood as conditional, rule-like potentialities or dispositions, rather than behaviour as such. The key distinction in the socio-economic sphere is between habits and routines as dispositions, on the one hand, and manifest behaviour, on the other hand.

Similarly, it is appropriate to treat routines as behavioural propensities of organizations, rather than behaviour as such. In this light, any emphasis on the allegedly *predictable* character of routines is misplaced. Predictions relate to outcomes or events, not to causal laws, rules or generative structures. The moderately dependable feature of a routine, rule or computer program is not one of predictability but of durability. Routines (or rules or computer programs) are usually conditional on other inputs or events. As a result any predictability does not stem from the routine alone but from the predictability

---

[3] For realist accounts upholding a distinction between generative mechanisms or causal powers, on the one hand, and outcomes or events, on the other, see for example Bhaskar (1975), Harré and Madden (1975), Popper (1990). Critical realism, to its credit, emphasizes this point. But it is not original to critical realism.

of these other inputs. For example, a firm may have a fixed mark-up pricing routine of adding 20 per cent to the unit cost of its products. If costs were capricious and highly variable, as they might be under some circumstances, then the resulting price would be equally unreliable. The relatively enduring and persistent quality of a routine is not its outcome but its generative, rule-like structure.

While a consensus has been established that a routine is an organizational rather than an individual phenomenon, some confusion remains on the above points, and this has led to some conceptual and empirical difficulties.[4] Some of these difficulties can be overcome by consistently treating a routine as an organizational capacity and generative structure, analogous to biological genes or computer programs, but having distinctive features of their own.

To their credit, both Nelson and Winter are now more inclined to describe the routine in terms of a capacity. Nelson and Winter (2002, p. 30) 'treat *organizational routine* as the organizational analogue of individual skill'. Similarly, Barbara Levitt and James March (1988, p. 320) write that the 'generic term "routines" includes the forms, rules, procedures, conventions, strategies, and technologies around which organizations are constructed and through which they operate'. Another useful definition of a routine as a potentiality or capability, rather than behaviour, is found in the discussion by Michael Cohen *et al.* (1996, p. 683) who declare that a 'routine is an executable *capability* for repeated performance in some *context* that [has] been *learned* by an organization in response to *selective pressures*'.

A routine is here defined as a generative structure or capacity within an organization. *Routines are organizational dispositions to energize conditional patterns of behaviour within an organized group of individuals, involving sequential responses to cues.* The next section raises the general questions of how routines work within organizations and how they carry information.

11.4 HOW DO ROUTINES CARRY INFORMATION?

The analysis of how routines endure and replicate is enormous and incomplete (Hodgson, 2003a). At present, our general understanding is limited, and progress depends largely on the accumulation of detailed case studies. As Winter (1990, p. 270) notes, so far 'little attention has been paid to the mechanism by which whatever-it-is-called is transmitted' and to its 'replication mechanism'. For Winter (1990, p. 294 n.) this amounts to a regrettable 'vagueness on a key issue'. Winter (1990, pp. 270–275) insisted:

---

[4] For discussions of some of these difficulties see Cohen *et al.* (1996), Reynaud (2000), M. Becker (2001, 2005) and Lazaric (2000).

'The question of what is "inherited" and how the inheritance mechanisms works is, however, ... central and ... far from definitive resolution ... To develop the routines as genes approach fully, the problem of inheritance mechanisms needs to be dealt with convincingly'.

To understand how routines work it is necessary to consider how any tacit or other information associated with a routine is preserved and replicated. A very useful study in this regard is by Michael Cohen and Paul Bacdayan (1994). They use the distinction in psychology between procedural and other, more cognitive forms of memory, such as semantic, episodic or declarative memory. As psychologists Endel Tulving and Daniel Schacter (1990, p. 301) put it:

> Cognitive memory systems have the capability of modeling the external world – that is, of storing representations of objects, events, and relations among them – whereas procedural memory does not have this capacity.

Procedural memory is triggered by preceding events and stimuli. It typically leads to behavioural responses and has a major tacit component. It is potential action that is energized by social or other cues, often involving physical artefacts. 'Procedural knowledge is less subject to decay, less explicitly accessible, and less easy to transfer to novel circumstances' (Cohen and Bacdayan, 1994, p. 557).

Routines depend upon a structured group of individuals, each with habits of a particular kind, where many of these habits depend upon procedural memory. The behavioural cues by some members of a structured assembly of habituated individuals triggers specific habits in others. Hence various individual habits sustain each other in an interlocking structure of reciprocating individual behaviours. Together these behaviours take on collective qualities associated with teams. But both individuals and structures are involved throughout. The organization or group provides a structured social and physical environment for each individual, including rules and norms of behaviour, of both the explicit and the informal kind. This environment is made up of the other individuals, the relations between them and the technological and physical artefacts that they may use in their interactions. This social and physical environment enables, stimulates and channels individual activities, which in turn can help trigger the behaviour of others, produce or modify some artefacts, and help to change or replicate parts of this social and physical environment.

Partly because of procedural memory, organizations can have important additional properties and capacities that are not possessed by individuals, taken severally. The organization provides the social and physical environment that is necessary to enable specific activities, cue individual habits and deploy individual memories. If one person leaves the organization and is replaced by another, then the new recruit may have to learn the habits that are required to maintain specific routines. Just as the human body has a life in addition to its constituent cells, the organization thus has a life in addition to its members. Generally, the organizational whole is greater than the sum of the properties its individual members, taken severally. The additional properties of the whole stem from the structured relations and causal interactions between the individuals involved. This is a central proposition in the emergentist tradition of philosophy and social theory (Blitz, 1992; Kontopoulos, 1993; Hodgson, 2004a; Weissman, 2000).

A routine derives from the capacity of an organization to provide conditions to energize a series of conditional, interlocking, sequential behaviours among several individuals within the organization. Cohen and Bacdayan (1994, p. 557) write: 'The routine of a group can be viewed as the concatenation of such procedurally stored actions, each primed by and priming the actions of others'. This statement captures the dependence of routines on procedural memory, but is somewhat ambiguous concerning the genotypic or phenotypic status of a routine.

As argued above, routines are not behaviour; they are stored behavioural capacities or capabilities. These capacities involve knowledge and memory. They involve organizational structures and individual habits which, when triggered, lead to sequential behaviours. But this does not mean that a routine can be fully codified. Routines are not necessarily nominal, codified or officially approved procedures. Routines generally rely on informal and tacit knowledge, and this fact is clearly relevant for understanding their replication.

The temporal durability of routines and the way that they can embody knowledge 'forgotten' by individuals is illustrated by an anecdote related by Elting Morison (1966). A time-and-motion expert was studying film footage of Second World War motorized artillery crews. He was puzzled by a recurring three-second pause just before the guns were fired. An old soldier also watching the film suddenly realized that the three-second pause had originated from the earlier era in which the guns were drawn by horses, and the horses had to be held and calmed in the seconds just before the guns went off. Despite its eventual redundancy, this part of the routine had survived the transition from horse-driven to motorized artillery. Part of the knowledge held in a routine can become obsolete, yet still be reproduced, like the examples of 'rudimentary organs' discussed by Charles Darwin (1859, pp. 450–458).

In sum, the explanation of the persistence of routines is a story of both the persistence of organizations and the persistence of the habits of the individuals involved. The explanation of the latter is in large part a psychological matter, referring to the nature of individual habits. By contrast, explanations of the former must answer the question of why organizations are often resistant to change, which has been an important question within organization theory since its inception (Simon, 1947; March and Simon, 1958; Stinchcombe, 1965). There is no attempt to develop such an account here: it is simply identified as a necessary component of the explanation of the persistence of routines.

11.5 THE REPLICATION OF ROUTINES

Just as habits replicate from individual to individual, routines replicate from group to group and from organization to organization. In studies of technological diffusion, organization studies and the strategic management literature there is some discussion of the diffusion or replication of routines.[5] Prominent mechanisms for the diffusion of routines involve the movement of employees from organization to organization, or independent experts or consultants that help to transfer knowledge and experience gained in one context to another. The above authors cite case studies involving the transfer of technologies, management procedures, corporate multidivisional structures, accounting conventions and much else. What is central to these transfers is the replication of practices and organizational relationships. What is generally critical is the capacity of the receiving organization to accommodate and utilize these practices and relationships in the context of its own ingrained culture of habits and beliefs.

Are these examples of routine replication, analogous to the replication of genes in biology? To answer this question we need to employ the general distinction between a 'replicator' and an 'interactor', as found in the philosophy of evolutionary systems (Hull, 1988). The concept of replication, as developed by Kim Sterelny *et al.* (1996), Peter Godfrey-Smith (2000), Dan Sperber (2000) and Robert Aunger (2002), involves the following three conditions.

- *Causation*: the source must be causally involved in the production of the copy, at least in the sense that without the source the particular copy would not be created.
- *Similarity*: the copy must also possess the capacity to replicate and be like its source in other relevant respects.

---

[5] See for example Aldrich and Martinez (2003), Becker and Lazaric (2003), DiMaggio and Powell (1983), Hannan and Freeman (1984, 1989), Lazaric and Denis (2001), Levitt and March (1988), Rogers (1995), Stinchcombe (1990), Szulanski (1996, 2000), Zucker (1987).

- *Information transfer*: the process that generates the copy must obtain the information that makes the copy similar to its source from that same source.

Sperber (2000) emphasizes that the third condition is critical. Cases where the third condition is absent include the diffusion of behaviour, such as contagious laughter, where A triggers B, but where the propensity to that behaviour is already present in B. Sperber argues convincingly that many examples of so-called 'memes' do not satisfy the third condition and thus are not true replicators.[6]

Relevant 'contagious' behaviour in the socio-economic context would be the spread of trustworthy/untrustworthy, civil/uncivil, or cooperative/uncooperative behaviours. These behaviours are triggered by external stimuli, but generally the behaviour is already latent in the individual involved. Such diffusions of similar behaviour do not obtain their characteristics of similarity from the stimulus that each receives. For true replication to occur, the capacity to produce the similar behaviour must itself be replicated. Again this points to the importance of making a distinction between capacity or disposition, on the one hand, and behaviour on the other hand.

In addition, more must be involved than the replication of the individual habits associated with the routine. The replication of routines must involve the replication of the generative structures and capacities that are additional to the habits of the individuals involved, taken severally. Furthermore, given that the structures associated with the routine are constitutive of the routine itself, and contain some of the 'information' embodied in the routine, these structures must play a causal role in a true process of replication.

The transfer of skills from a master to an apprentice is typically a case of habit replication, rather than the replication of routines. For routine replication to occur, not only the individual skills must be replicated, but also the manner in which they are organized together into an effective structured relationship between several individuals.

The replication of individual skills and habits involves the transfer of tacit as well as codifiable knowledge. Tacit knowledge is transferred as a result of repeated practice, often with similar stimuli and constraints. Because routines are partly made up of individual skills, tacit knowledge is unavoidably involved at the level of routines as well (Polanyi, 1967; Nelson, and Winter,

[6] The term 'meme' was made famous by Dawkins (1976). However, the enthusiasm for 'memes' far outstrips the achieved degree of clarity and consensus of meaning. A meme has been variously described as a unit of cultural imitation (Dawkins, 1976), a unit of information residing in a brain (Dawkins, 1982), units of culturally transmitted instructions (Dennett, 1995), neural patterns (Aunger, 2002) and much else.

1982; Hannan and Freeman, 1989; Cohen and Bacdayan, 1994; Cohen *et. al.*, 1996). This tacit dimension, combined with its structured nature of a routine, makes it a complex and elusive entity, which is often difficult to replicate.

As with habits, replicative similarity is at the level of descriptions of the rule-like dispositions that give rise to the behaviour, rather than at the level of the neural patterns of the individuals involved.[7] The facilitation of the process of routine replication is a key area for management practice and enquiry. It may be possible to replicate some routines through descriptions of their essentials in a manual or textbook, but these cases are relatively simple and rare, and will often rely on subsequent practice and advice.

In the organization studies literature, examples of successful routine replication typically involve the combination of codifiable information and instructions with extensive personal example, advice and contact, where the receiving organization has sufficient plasticity to usefully absorb and accommodate the routine. Sometimes routines are spread as a result of laws or rules that emanate from a third organization, such as the state, or an association of employers. Otherwise the replication of routines can occur as the result of the strategy of its receiving organization, or it can result from lower-level contact, stimulation and imitation. Routines replicate, and they do so on a substrate of organized and habituated individuals.

Another question that arises concerns the propensities of organizations to replicate their routines. At the individual level, habits replicate largely because individuals have an instinctive propensity to imitate some behaviours. This involves the ability to sense the more significant actions, and the tacit rules and meanings associated with behaviour (Tomasello, 2000). There is no equivalent to this individual instinct at the level of the organization. On the contrary, firms are often conservative and difficult to change. The structure and culture of the organization often discourages innovation, as this would challenge individual vested interests and the 'groupthink' of the collective. Rather than to imitate others, organizations will often carry on in the same old way, unless their internal perception of a crisis prompts an extreme or energetic survival strategy. Complex organizations are extremely recent in human history, so despite the possible survival advantages of organizational imitation, the evolution of selective capacities to imitate at the organizational level have had little time to develop.

---

[7] It is possible that two routines with very similar sets of rules may lead to different behavioural outcomes, because of different information inputs or stimuli. Obversely, behaviourally similar routines may emanate from very different rule structures. Related possibilities exist in biology with genes and behaviour. In all cases, with genes, habits and routines, relevant similarity exists at the level of description of conditional, rule-like dispositions.

Empirical studies illuminate the degree of organizational conservatism in reality. Michael Hannan and John Freeman (1989) are leading proponents of the view that the capacity to change routines within organizations is relatively limited, and that changes in the population of routines within industries or societies largely comes about through the survival or extinction of specific organizations, and the consequence persistence or disappearance of the routines they carry, rather than through modifications in the routines themselves. This is an important area of ongoing empirical enquiry.[8]

What then are the corresponding interactors? David Hull (1988, p. 408) defines an interactor as 'an entity that directly interacts as a cohesive whole with its environment in such a way that this interaction *causes* replication to be differential'. The term 'cohesive whole' indicates that its components stick together and remain united. This must mean at least that all the components depend critically on the survival of the whole, and that to some degree the components depend on the survival of each other. Refining this definition still further, Hodgson and Knudsen (2004b) argue that a firm may be regarded as an interactor, and consequently as a 'vehicle' for its inherent habits and routines. The fate of a routine is often dependent on the fate of its host firm. It should be pointed out, however, that although this type of evolutionary approach has a long history (Hodgson, 2004a), at least in its present form and context it is in the early stages of its development, and many outstanding conceptual problems remain to be resolved.

11.6 CONCLUSION

This chapter explores the concept of a routine in fundamental terms, using insights from philosophy, psychology and social theory. A routine is here defined as a generative structure or capacity within an organization. *By definition, routines are organizational dispositions to energize conditional patterns of behaviour within an organized group of individuals, involving sequential responses to cues.* There are important philosophical reasons, endorsed by modern philosophy of science, for defining routines as organizational dispositions or capacities, rather than behaviour as such.

Just as habits relate to individuals, routines relate to organizations. Both are socially transmitted dispositions, formed through repeated behaviours. Routines themselves are structures of interlocking individual habits. But routines are more than mere aggregations of habits, because they also depend

[8] Usher and Evans (1996) provide a useful review of this literature, with further evidence. However, it has been argued elsewhere that their characterization of this debate as between 'Darwinian' and 'Lamarckian' concepts of change is at best highly misleading (Hodgson and Knudsen, forthcoming).

on the emergent properties of organization itself, emanating from structured causal relations and interactions between individuals.

One of the reasons why the study of routines is important for the study of business practice is that they are repositories and carriers of knowledge and skill. The routine is often the means through which individual skills are triggered and energized. One psychological mechanism that is important here is procedural memory, which means that some powers of recall can be enhanced when triggered by cues provided by others. In this manner the routine as a whole becomes more than the sum of the capacities of the individuals involved, taken severally.

The study of routines is part of a broader project to apply evolutionary principles to the analysis of social and economic development. This project must involve an alliance of conceptual development, formal theory and empirical enquiry. It is unlikely that significant overall progress will be made without some advancement on all of these three fronts. Hence to emphasize one to the exclusion of the others would be to impair the development of institutional and evolutionary economics.

References

Ackerman, Robert (1976) *The Philosophy of Karl Popper* (Amherst, MA: University of Massachusetts Press).

Adaman, Fikret and Devine, Patrick (1996) 'The Economic Calculation Debate: Lessons for Socialists', *Cambridge Journal of Economics*, **20**(5), September, pp. 523–37.

Adaman, Fikret and Devine, Patrick (1997) 'On the Economic Theory of Socialism', *New Left Review,* no. 221, January–February, pp. 54–80.

Akerlof, George A. (1970) 'The Market for "Lemons": Quality Uncertainty and the Market Mechanism', *Quarterly Journal of Economics*, **84**(3), August, pp. 488–500.

Akerlof, George A. and Kranton, Rachel E. (2005) 'Identity and the Economics of Organizations', *Journal of Economic Perspectives,* **19**(1), Winter, pp. 9–32.

Aldrich, Howard E. and Martinez, Martha (2003) 'Entrepreneurship as Social Construction: A Multi-Level Evolutionary Approach', in Acs, Z. C. and Audretsch, David B. (eds) (2003) *Handbook of Entrepreneurial Research* (Boston: Kluwer), pp. 359–99.

Alessie, Rob and Kapteyn, Arie (1991) 'Habit Formation, Interdependent Preferences and Demographic Effects in the Almost Ideal Demand System', *Economic Journal*, **101**(3), May, pp. 404–19.

Allen, E. *et al.* (35 authors comprising the Sociobiology Study Group of Science for the People) (1976) 'Sociobiology – Another Biological Determinism', *Bioscience*, **26**(3), pp. 182–6.

Amin, Ash (1999) 'An Institutionalist Perspective on Regional Economic Development', *International Journal of Urban and Regional Research*, **23**(2), June, pp. 365–78.

Andersen, Peter Bøgh, Emmeche, Claus, Finnemann, Niels Ole and Christiansen, Peder Voetman (eds) (2000) *Downward Causation: Minds, Bodies and Matter* (Aarhus: Aarhus University Press).

Aoki, Masahiko (2001) *Toward a Comparative Institutional Analysis* (Cambridge, MA: MIT Press).

Archer, Margaret S. (1995) *Realist Social Theory: The Morphogenetic Approach* (Cambridge: Cambridge University Press).

Archer, Margaret S., Bhaskar, Roy, Collier, Andrew, Lawson, Tony and Norrie, Alan (eds) (1998) *Critical Realism: Essential Readings* (London: Routledge).

Aristotle (1956) *Metaphysics,* edited and translated by John Warrington with an introduction by W. David Ross (London: Dent).

Aronowitz, Stanley (1988) *Science As Power: Discourse and Ideology in Modern Society* (Minneapolis: University of Minnesota Press).

Arrow, Kenneth J. (1986) 'Rationality of Self and Others in an Economic System', *Journal of Business*, **59**(4.2), October, pp. S385–S399.

Arthur, W. Brian (1994) *Increasing Returns and Path Dependence in the Economy* (Ann Arbor, MI: University of Michigan Press).

Ashby, W. Ross (1952) *Design for a Brain* (New York: Wiley).

Ashby, W. Ross (1956) *An Introduction to Cybernetics* (New York: Wiley).

Aunger, Robert (2002) *The Electric Meme: A New Theory of How We Think* (New York: Free Press).

Axelrod, Robert M. (1984) *The Evolution of Cooperation* (New York: Basic Books).

Baert, Patrick (1996) 'Realist Philosophy of the Social Sciences and Economics: A Critique', *Cambridge Journal of Economics*, **20**(5), September, pp. 513–22.

Bagehot, Walter (1872) *Physics and Politics, or, Thoughts on the Application of the Principles of 'Natural Selection' and 'Inheritance' to Political Society* (London: Henry King).

Bain, Read (1936) Review of *Thorstein Veblen and His America* by Joseph Dorfman and *What Veblen Taught* edited by Wesley Mitchell, *American Sociological Review,* **1**(3), June, pp. 485–87.

Bain, Read (1940) Review of *The Individual and Its Society* by Abram Kardiner and Ralph Linton, *American Sociological Review*, **5**(2), April, pp. 254–7.

Baldwin, James Mark (1909) *Darwin and the Humanities* (Baltimore: Review Publishing).

Ball, Terence (1994) *Reappraising Political Theory – Revisionist Studies in the History of Political Thought* (Oxford: Oxford University Press).

Bannister, Robert C. (1973) 'William Graham Sumner's Social Darwinism: A Reconsideration', *History of Political Economy*, **5**(1), Spring, pp. 89–108.

Bannister, Robert C. (1979) *Social Darwinism; Science and Myth in Anglo-American Social Thought* (Philadelphia: Temple University Press).

Barnes, Harry Elmer (1921) 'Some Contributions of Sociology to Modern Political Theory', *American Political Science Review*, **15**(4), November, pp. 487–533.

Barnes, Harry Elmer (1932) 'The Development of Sociology', *Scientific Monthly*, **35**(6), December, pp. 543–53.

Becker, Gary S. (1962) 'Irrational Behavior and Economic Theory', *Journal of Political Economy*, **70**(1), February, pp. 1–13.

Becker, Gary S. (1992) 'Habits, Addictions and Traditions', *Kyklos*, 45, pp. 327–46.

Becker, Gary S. (1996) *Accounting for Tastes* (Cambridge, MA: Harvard University Press).

Becker, Gary S. and Murphy, Kevin M. (1988) 'A Theory of Rational Addiction', *Journal of Political Economy*, **96**(4), pp. 675–700.

Becker, Markus C. (2001) 'The Role of Routines in Organisations: An Empirical and Taxonomic Investigation', Ph.D. Thesis, University of Cambridge.

Becker, Markus C. (2005) 'The Concept of Routines: Some Clarifications', *Cambridge Journal of Economics*, **29**(2), March, pp. 249–62.

Becker, Markus C. and Lazaric, Nathalie (2003) 'The Influence of Knowledge in the Replication of Routines', *Économie appliquée*, **56**(3), septembre, pp. 65–94.

Beckerman, Ansgar, Flohr, Hans and Kim, Jaegwon (eds) (1992) *Emergence or Reduction? Essays on the Prospects of Nonreductive Physicalism* (Berlin: De Gruyter).

Beer, Max (1940) *A History of British Socialism*, 2 vols (London: Allen and Unwin).

Beer, Stafford (1972) *Brain of the Firm* (London: Allen Lane).

Bellomy, Donald C. (1984) '"Social Darwinism" Revisited', *Perspectives in American History*, New Series, **1**, pp. 1–129.

Benacerraf, Paul and Putnam, Hilary (eds) (1984) *Philosophy of Mathematics: Selected Readings* (Cambridge and New York: Cambridge University Press).

Benton, Ted (1982) 'Social Darwinism and Socialist Darwinism in Germany: 1860–1900', *Revista di filosofia,* **73**, pp. 79–121.

Bertalanffy, Ludwig von (1950) 'The Theory of Open Systems in Physics and Biology', *Science*, **111**, pp. 23–9.

Bertalanffy, Ludwig von (1971) *General Systems Theory: Foundation Development Applications* (London: Allen Lane).

Best, Michael H. (1982) 'The Political Economy of Socially Irrational Products', *Cambridge Journal of Economics,* **6**(1), March, pp. 53–64.

Bhaskar, Roy (1975) *A Realist Theory of Science* (Leeds: Leeds Books).

Bhaskar, Roy (1986) *Scientific Realism and Human Emancipation* (London: Verso).

Bhaskar, Roy (1989a) *The Possibility of Naturalism: A Philosophic Critique of the Contemporary Human Sciences*, 2nd edn (Brighton: Harvester).

Bhaskar, Roy (1989b) *Reclaiming Reality: A Critical Introduction to Contemporary Philosophy* (London: Verso).

Bhaskar, Roy (1991) *Philosophy and the Idea of Freedom* (Oxford: Basil Blackwell).

Bhaskar, Roy (1993) *Dialectic: The Pulse of Freedom* (London: Verso).

Bhaskar, Roy (1994) *Plato, Etc.* (London: Verso).

Bhaskar, Roy and Collier, Andrew (1998) 'Introduction: Explanatory Critiques', in Archer *et al.* (1998, pp. 385–94).

Binmore, Kenneth (1994) *Playing Fair: Game Theory and the Social Contract. Volume I* (Cambridge, MA: MIT Press).

Binmore, Kenneth (1998a) *Just Playing: Game Theory and the Social Contract. Volume 2* (Cambridge, MA: MIT Press).

Binmore, Kenneth (1998b) 'Review of *Complexity and Cooperation* by Robert Axelrod', *Journal of Artificial Societies and Social Situations,* **1**(1) <http://jasss.soc.surrey.ac.uk/JASSS/1/1/review1.html>

Black, Max (1962) *Models and Metaphors: Studies in Language and Philosophy* (Ithaca: Cornell University Press).

Blanciforti, L. and Green, R. (1983) 'An Almost Ideal System Incorporating Habits: An Analysis of Expenditures on Food and Aggregate Commodity Groups', *Review of Economics and Statistics*, **65**, pp. 511–15.

Blaug, Mark (1980) *A Methodological Appraisal of Marxian Economics* (Amsterdam: North-Holland).

Blaug, Mark (1997a) *Economic Theory in Retrospect*, 5th edn (Cambridge: Cambridge University Press).

Blaug, Mark (1997b) 'Ugly Currents in Modern Economics', *Options politiques*, **18**(17), September, pp. 3–8.

Blaug, Mark (1999) 'The Formalist Revolution or What Happened to Orthodox Economics After World War II?', in Backhouse, Roger E. and Creedy, John (eds) (1999) *From Classical Economics to the Theory of the Firm: Essays in Honour of D. P. O'Brien* (Cheltenham: Edward Elgar), pp. 257–80.

Blaug, Mark (2003) 'The Formalist Revolution of the 1950s', in Samuels, Warren J., Biddle, Jeff E. and Davis, John B. (eds) (2003) *A Companion to the History of Economic Thought* (Malden, MA and Oxford, UK: Blackwell), pp. 395–410.

Blinder, Alan (1990) 'Discussion', *American Economic Review,* **80**, May, pp. 445–7.

Blitz, David (1992) *Emergent Evolution: Qualitative Novelty and the Levels of Reality* (Dordrecht: Kluwer).

Block, Walter (ed.) (1989) *Economics and the Environment: A Reconciliation* (Vancouver, BC: Fraser Institute).

Bode, B. H. (1922) 'Critical Realism', *Journal of Philosophy*, **19**(3), February, pp. 68–78.

Boettke, Peter J. (ed.) (2000) *Socialism and the Market: The Calculation Debate Revisited* (London and New York: Routledge).

Boguslaw, Robert (1965) *The New Utopians: A Study of System Design and Social Change* (Englewood Cliffs, NJ: Prentice-Hall).

Boland, Lawrence A. (1981) 'On the Futility of Criticizing the Neoclassical Maximization Hypothesis', *American Economic Review*, **71**(5), December, pp. 1031–6.

Bowler, Peter J. (1983) *The Eclipse of Darwinism: Anti-Darwinian Evolution Theories in the Decades around 1900* (Baltimore: Johns Hopkins University Press).

Bowler, Peter J. (1988) *The Non-Darwinian Revolution: Reinterpreting a Historical Myth* (Baltimore: Johns Hopkins University Press).

Bowles, Samuel (1981) 'Technical Change and the Profit Rate: A Simple Proof of the Okishio Theorem', *Cambridge Journal of Economics*, **5**(2), June, pp. 183–6.

Bowles, Samuel (1998) 'Endogenous Preferences: The Cultural Consequences of Markets and Other Economic Institutions', *Journal of Economic Literature*, **36**(1), March, pp. 75–111.

Bowles, Samuel (2004) *Microeconomics: Behavior, Institutions and, Evolution* (Princeton, NJ and New York: Princeton University Press and Russell Sage Foundation).

Boyd, Robert and Richerson, Peter J. (1980) 'Sociobiology, Culture and Economic Theory', *Journal of Economic Behavior and Organization*, **1**(1), March, pp. 97–121.

Boyd, Robert and Richerson, Peter J. (1985) *Culture and the Evolutionary Process* (Chicago: University of Chicago Press).

Boyer, Robert (2005) 'Coherence, Diversity, and the Evolution of Capitalisms – The Institutional Complementarity Hypothesis', *Evolutionary and Institutional Economics Review*, **2**(1), October, pp. 43–80.

Braverman, Harry (1974) *Labor and Monopoly Capital: The Degradation of Work in the Twentieth Century* (New York: Monthly Review Press).

Brown, Andrew, Fleetwood, Steve and Roberts, John Michael (eds) (2001) *Critical Realism and Marxism* (London and New York: Routledge).

Bunge, Mario A. (1979) *Treatise on Basic Philosophy*, vol. 4, *Ontology II: A World of Systems* (Dordrecht, Holland: Reidel).

Bunge, Mario A. (1980) *The Mind-Body Problem: A Psychobiological Approach* (Oxford: Pergamon).

Burke, Edmund (1757) *A Philosophical Enquiry Into the Origin of Our Ideas of the Sublime and the Beautiful* (London: Dodsley).

Burke, Edmund (1790) *Reflections on the Revolution in France and on the Proceedings in Certain Societies in London* (London: Dodsley).

Caldwell, Bruce J. (1982) *Beyond Positivism: Economic Methodology in the Twentieth Century* (London: Allen and Unwin).

Callinicos, Alex (1999) *Social Theory: A Historical Introduction* (Cambridge: Polity Press).

Camic, Charles (1986) 'The Matter of Habit', *American Journal of Sociology*, **91**(5), pp. 1039–87.

Camic, Charles (1987) 'The Making of a Method: A Historical Reinterpretation of the Early Parsons', *American Sociological Review*, **52**(4), August, pp. 421–39.

Camic, Charles (ed.) (1991) *Talcott Parsons: The Early Essays* (Chicago: University of Chicago Press).

Campbell, Donald T. (1965) 'Variation, Selection and Retention in Sociocultural Evolution', in Barringer, H. R., Blanksten, G. I. and Mack, R. W. (eds) (1965) *Social Change in Developing Areas: A Reinterpretation of Evolutionary Theory* (Cambridge, MA: Schenkman), pp. 19–49. Reprinted in *General Systems*, **14**, 1969, pp. 69–85.

Campbell, Donald T. (1974) '"Downward Causation" in Hierarchically Organized Biological Systems', in Ayala, Francisco J. and Dobzhansky, Theodosius (eds) (1974) *Studies in the Philosophy of Biology* (London, Berkeley and Los Angeles: Macmillan and University of California Press), pp. 179–86.

Campbell, Donald T. (1975) 'On the Conflicts Between Biological and Social Evolution and Between Psychology and Moral Tradition', *American Psychologist*, **30**(12), December, pp. 1103–26.

Case, Clarence Marsh (1922) 'Instinctive and Cultural Factors in Group Conflicts', *American Journal of Sociology,* **28**(1), July, pp. 1–20.

Caves, Richard E. (1980) 'Productivity Differences Among Industries', in Caves, Richard E. and Krause, Lawrence B. (eds) (1980) *Britain's Economic Performance* (Washington, DC: Brookings Institution), pp. 135–98.

Chick, Victoria (1998) 'On Knowing One's Place: The Role of Formalism in Economics', *Economic Journal,* **108**(6), November, pp. 1859–69.

Chick, Victoria and Dow, Sheila C. (2001) 'Formalism, Logic and Reality: A Keynesian Analysis', *Cambridge Journal of Economics*, **25**(6), November, pp. 705–21.

Chick, Victoria and Dow, Sheila C. (2005) 'The Meaning of Open Systems', *Journal of Economic Methodology*, **13**(3), September, pp. 363–81.

Choi, Kwang (1983) 'A Statistical Test of Olson's Model', in Mueller, Dennis C. (ed.) (1983) *The Political Economy of Growth* (New Haven: Yale University Press), pp. 57–78.

Churchland, Patricia S. (1986) *Neurophilosophy: Toward a Unified Science of the Mind-Brain* (Cambridge, MA: MIT Press).

Churchland, Paul M. (1984) *Matter and Consciousness* (Cambridge, MA: MIT Press).

Churchland, Paul M. (1989) *A Neurocomputational Perspective: The Nature of Mind and the Structure of Science* (Cambridge, MA: MIT Press).

Claeys, Gregory (2000) 'The "Survival of the Fittest" and the Origins of Social Darwinism, *Journal of the History of Ideas,* **61**(2), pp. 223–40.

Clark, Andy (1997a) 'Economic Reason: The Interplay of Individual Learning and External Structure', in Drobak, John N. and Nye, John V. C. (eds) (1997) *The Frontiers of the New Institutional Economics* (San Diego and London: Academic Press), pp. 269–90.

Clark, Andy (1997b) *Being There: Putting the Brain, Body and World Together Again* (Cambridge, MA: MIT Press).

Clark, Evalyn A. (1940) 'Adolph Wagner: From National Economist to National Socialist', *Political Science Quarterly*, **55**(3), September, pp. 378–411.

Clark, Linda L. (1985) *Social Darwinism in France* (Tuscaloosa: University of Alabama Press).

Clemens, Elisabeth S. and Cook, James M. (1999) 'Politics and Instititutions: Explaining Durability and Change', *Annual Review of Sociology*, **25**, pp. 441–66.

Coase, Ronald H. (1937) 'The Nature of the Firm', *Economica*, **4**, November, pp. 386–405.

Coates, David and Hillard, John (eds) (1986) *The Economic Decline of Modern Britain: The Debate Between Left and Right* (Brighton: Harvester).

Coats, A. W. (1954) 'The Influence of Veblen's Methodology', *Journal of Political Economy*, **62**(6), December, pp. 529–37.

Cockshott, W. Paul and Cottrell, Allin F. (1993) *Towards a New Socialism* (Nottingham: Spokesman).

Cohen, Michael D. and Bacdayan, Paul (1994) 'Organizational Routines are Stored as Procedural Memory – Evidence from a Laboratory Study', *Organization Science*, **5**(4), November, pp. 554–68.

Cohen, Michael D., Burkhart, Roger, Dosi, Giovanni, Egidi, Massimo, Marengo, Luigi, Warglien, Massimo, and Winter, Sidney (1996) 'Routines and Other Recurring Action Patterns of Organizations: Contemporary Research Issues', *Industrial and Corporate Change*, **5**(3), pp. 653–98.

Colander, David C. (2005a) 'The Making of an Economist Redux', *Journal of Economic Perspectives,* **19**(1), Winter, pp. 175–98.

Colander, David C. (2005b) 'The Future of Economics: The Appropriately Educated in Pursuit of the Knowable', *Cambridge Journal of Economics*, **29**(6), November, pp. 927–41.

Colander, David C., Holt, Richard P. F. and Rosser, J. Barkley, Jr (2004a) *The Changing Face of Economics: Interviews with Cutting Edge Economists* (Ann Arbor, MI: University of Michigan Press).

Colander, David C., Holt, Richard P. F. and Rosser, J. Barkley, Jr (2004b) 'The Changing Face of Economics', *Review of Political Economy*, **16**(4), October, 485–499.

Coleman, James S. (1982) *The Asymmetric Society* (Syracuse: Syracuse University Press).

Collier, Andrew (1989) *Scientific Realism and Socialist Thought* (Hemel Hempstead: Harvester Wheatsheaf).

Collier, Andrew (1994) *Critical Realism: An Introduction to Roy Bhaskar's Philosophy* (London: Verso).

Colp, Ralph (1974) 'The Contacts Between Karl Marx and Charles Darwin', *Journal of the History of Ideas*, **35**(2), April–June, pp. 329–38.

Colp, Ralph (1982) 'The Myth of the Marx-Darwin Letter', *History of Political Economy*, **14**(4), Winter, pp. 416–82.

Commons, John R. (1925) 'Law and Economics', *Yale Law Journal*, **34**(1), February, pp. 371–82.

Commons, John R. (1934) *Institutional Economics – Its Place in Political Economy* (New York: Macmillan).

Conquest, Robert (1986) *The Harvest of Sorrow: Soviet Collectivization and the Terror-Famine* (Oxford: Oxford University Press).

Cosmides, Leda and Tooby, John (1994) 'Beyond Intuition and Instinct Blindness: Towards an Evolutionary Rigorous Cognitive Science', *Cognition*, **50**(1–3), April–June, pp. 41–77.

Cravens, Hamilton (1978) *The Triumph of Evolution: American Scientists and the Hereditary-Environment Controversy, 1900–1941* (Philadelphia: University of Pennsylvania Press).

Crawford, Sue E. S. and Ostrom, Elinor (1995) 'A Grammar of Institutions', *American Political Science Review*, **89**(3), September, pp. 582–600.

Crook, Paul (1994) *Darwinism, War and History: The Debate over the Biology of War from the 'Origin of Species' to the First World War* (Cambridge: Cambridge University Press).

Cunningham, Bryan (2000) 'The Re-emergence of "Emergence"', *Philosophy of Science*, **68**, pp. S62–S74.

Cziko, Gary (1995) *Without Miracles: Universal Selection Theory and the Second Darwinian Revolution* (Cambridge, MA: MIT Press).

Damasio, Antonio R. (1994) *Descartes' Error: Emotion, Reason, and the Human Brain* (New York: Putnam).

Darwin, Charles R. (1845) *Journal of Reserches into the Natural History and Geology of the Countries Visited During the Voyage of H. M. S. Beagle Round the World Under the Command of Capt. FitzRoy, R. N.* (London: Murray).

Darwin, Charles R. (1859) *On the Origin of Species by Means of Natural Selection, or the Preservation of Favoured Races in the Struggle for Life*, first edn (London: Murray).

Darwin, Charles R. (1871) *The Descent of Man, and Selection in Relation to Sex*, 2 vols (London: Murray and New York: Hill).

Darwin, Francis (ed.) (1887) *Life and Letters of Charles Darwin,* 3 vols (London: John Murray).

Davis, John B. (2006) 'The Turn in Economics: Neoclassical Dominance to Mainstream Pluralism?' *Journal of Institutional Economics*, **2**(1), April, pp. 1–20.

Dawkins, Richard (1976) *The Selfish Gene* (Oxford: Oxford University Press).

Dawkins, Richard (1982) *The Extended Phenotype: The Gene as the Unit of Selection* (Oxford: Oxford University Press).

Dawson, Doyne (2002) 'The Marriage of Marx and Darwin?', *History and Theory*, **41**(1), February, pp. 43–59.

De Sarlo, Francesco (1887) *Studi sul Darwinismo* (Napoli: Tocco).

Degler, Carl N. (1991) *In Search of Human Nature: The Decline and Revival of Darwinism in American Social Thought* (Oxford and New York: Oxford University Press).

Dennett, Daniel C. (1995) *Darwin's Dangerous Idea: Evolution and the Meanings of Life* (London: Allen Lane).

Denzau, Arthur T. and North, Douglass, C. (1994) 'Shared Mental Models: Ideologies and Institutions', *Kyklos*, **47**, Fasc. 1, pp. 3–31.

Department of Philosophy University of Colorado (eds) (1952). *Readings on Fascism and National Socialism* (Denver, CO: Alan Swallow).

Depew, David J. and Weber, Bruce H. (1995) *Darwinism Evolving: Systems Dynamics and the Genealogy of Natural Selection* (Cambridge, MA: MIT Press).

Desmond, Adrian and Moore, James R. (1991) *Darwin* (London: Michael Joseph).

Devine, Patrick (1988) *Democracy and Economic Planning: The Political Economy of a Self-Governing Society* (Cambridge: Polity Press).

Dewey, John (1922) *Human Nature and Conduct: An Introduction to Social Psychology* (New York: Holt).

DiMaggio, Paul J. and Powell, Walter W. (1983) 'The Iron Cage Revisited: Institutional Isomorphism and Collective Rationality in Organizational Fields', *American Sociological Review*, **48**(2), April, pp. 147–160.

Dopfer, Kurt (ed.) (2004) 'The Economic Agent as Rule Maker and Rule User: *Homo Sapiens Oeconomicus*', *Journal of Evolutionary Economics*, **14**(20), May, pp. 177–95.

Dopfer, Kurt, Foster, John and Potts, Jason (2004) 'Micro-Meso-Macro', *Journal of Evolutionary Economics*, **14**(3), July, pp. 263–79.

Dorfman, Joseph (1934) *Thorstein Veblen and His America* (New York: Viking Press).

Dosi, Giovanni and Metcalfe, J. Stanley (1991) 'On Some Notions of Irreversibility in Economics', in Saviotti and Metcalfe (1991, pp. 133–59).

Dosi, Giovanni, Nelson, Richard R. and Winter, Sidney G. (2000) 'Introduction: The Nature and Dynamics of Organizational Capabilities' in Dosi, Giovanni, Nelson, Richard R. and Winter, Sidney G. (eds) (2000) *The Nature and Dynamics of Organizational Capabilities* (Oxford: Oxford University Press), pp. 1–22.

Douglas, Mary (1987) *How Institutions Think* (London and Syracuse: Routledge and Kegan Paul and Syracuse University Press).

Douglas, Mary T. and Isherwood, Baron (1980) *The World of Goods: Towards an Anthropology of Consumption* (Harmondsworth: Penguin).

Downward, Paul (2000) 'A Realist Appraisal of Post-Keynesian Pricing Theory', *Cambridge Journal of Economics,* **24**(2), March, pp. 211–24.

Downward, Paul (ed.) (2003) *Applied Economics: A Critical Realist Approach* (London and New York: Routledge).

Drummond, Henry (1894) *The Ascent of Man* (London: Hodder and Stoughton).

Duesenberry, James S. (1949) *Income, Saving and the Theory of Consumer Behavior* (Cambridge MA: Harvard University Press).

Duffy, John and Ochs, Jack (1999) 'Emergence of Money as a Medium of Exchange: An Experimental Study', *American Economic Review,* **89**(4), September, pp. 847–77.

Dugger, William M. and Sherman, Howard J. (2000) *Reclaiming Evolution: A Dialogue Between Marxism and Institutionalism on Social Change* (London and New York: Routledge).

Durham, William H. (1991) *Coevolution: Genes, Culture, and Human Diversity* (Stanford: Stanford University Press).

Durkheim, Émile (1895) *Les règles de la méthode sociologique*, 1st edn (Paris :Alcan).

Durkheim, Émile (1984) *The Division of Labour in Society*, translated from the French edition of 1893 by W. D. Halls with an introduction by Lewis Coser (London: Macmillan).

Earman, John (1986) *A Primer on Determinism* (Boston: Reidel).

Edelman, Gerald M. (1987) *Neural Darwinism: The Theory of Neuronal Group Selection* (New York: Basic Books).

Eiser, J. Richard, Pahl, Sabine and Prins, Yvonne R. A. (2001) 'Optimism, Pessimism, and the Direction of Self-Other Comparisons', *Journal of Experimental Social Psychology*, **37**(1), January, pp. 77–84.

Elbaum, Bernard and Lazonick, William (eds) (1986) *The Decline of the British Economy* (Oxford: Oxford University Press).

Elder-Vass, Dave (2005) 'Emergence and the Realist Account of Cause', *Journal of Critical Realism*, **4**(2), pp. 315–38.

Ellwood, Charles A. (1938) *A History of Social Philosophy* (New York: Prentice-Hall).

Elson, Diane (1988) 'Market Socialism or Socialisation of the Market?' *New Left Review,* No. 172, November/December, pp. 3–44.

Elster, Jon (1983) *Sour Grapes: Studies in the Subversion of Rationality* (Cambridge: Cambridge University Press).

Emmeche, Claus, Køppe, Simo and Stjernfelt, Frederik (1997) 'Explaining Emergence: Towards an Ontology of Levels', *Journal for General Philosophy of Science,* **28**(1), pp. 83–119.

Emmeche, Claus, Køppe, Simo and Stjernfelt, Frederik (2000) 'Levels, Emergence, and Three Versions of Downward Causation', in Andersen *et al.* (2000, pp. 13–34).

Engels, Frederick (1962) *Anti-Dühring: Herr Eugen Dühring's Revolution in Science,* translated from the 3rd German edition of 1894 (London: Lawrence and Wishart).

Engels, Frederick (1964) *Dialectics of Nature* (London: Lawrence and Wishart).

Epstein, Joshua M. (2001) 'Learning to be Thoughtless: Social Norms and Individual Computation', *Computational Economics*, **18**, pp. 9–24.

Erev, Ido and Roth, Alvin E. (1998) 'Predicting How People Play Games: Reinforcement Learning in Experimental Games with Unique, Mixed Strategy Equilibria', *American Economic Review*, **88**(4), December, pp. 848–81.

Faulkner, Philip (2002) 'Some Problems With the Conception of the Human Subject in Critical Realism', *Cambridge Journal of Economics,* **26**(6), November, pp. 739–51.

Favereau, Olivier and Lazega, Emmanuel (eds) (2002) *Conventions and Structures in Economic Organization: Markets, Networks and Hierarchies* (Cheltenham, UK and Northampton, MA: Edward Elgar).

Fay, Margaret A. (1978) 'Did Marx Offer to Dedicate *Capital* to Darwin?', *Journal of the History of Ideas*, **39**(1), January–March, pp. 133–46.

Festinger, Leon (1957) *A Theory of Cognitive Dissonance* (Stanford, CA: California University Press).

Feuer, Lewis S. (1975) 'Is the Darwin-Marx Correspondence Authentic?', *Annals of Science*, **32**, pp. 11–12.

Field, Alexander J. (1979) 'On the Explanation of Rules Using Rational Choice Models', *Journal of Economic Issues*, **13**(1), March, pp. 49–72.

Field, Alexander J. (1984) 'Microeconomics, Norms and Rationality', *Economic Development and Cultural Change*, **32**(4), July, pp. 683–711.

Fiori, Stefano (2002) 'Alternative Visions of Change in Douglass North's New Institutionalism', *Journal of Economic Issues* **36**(4), December, pp. 1025–43.

Fleetwood, Steven (1995) *Hayek's Political Economy: The Socio-Economics of Order* (London: Routledge).

Fleetwood, Steven (1996) 'Order Without Equilibrium: A Critical Realist Interpretation of Hayek's Notion of Spontaneous Order', *Cambridge Journal of Economics,* **20**(6), November, pp. 729–47.

Fleetwood, Steven (ed.) (1998) *Critical Realism in Economics: Development and Debate* (London: Routledge).

Foster, John Fagg (1981) 'The Papers of J. Fagg Foster', *Journal of Economic Issues*, **15**(4), December, pp. 857–1012.

Fracchia, Joseph and Lewontin, Richard C. (1999) 'Does Culture Evolve?', *History and Theory,* **38**(4), pp. 52–78.

Friedman, Milton (1953) 'The Methodology of Positive Economics', in M. Friedman, *Essays in Positive Economics* (Chicago: University of Chicago Press), pp. 3–43.

Furubotn, Eirik G. and Pejovich, Svetozar (eds) (1974) *The Economics of Property Rights* (Cambridge, MA: Ballinger).

Galbraith, John Kenneth (1969) *The Affluent Society,* 2nd edn (London: Hamilton).

Gasman, Daniel (1971) *The Scientific Origins of National Socialism: Social Darwinism in Ernst Haeckel and the German Monist League* (London: Macdonald).

Gasman, Daniel (1998) *Haeckel's Monism and the Birth of Fascist Ideology* (New York: Lang).

Gide, Charles and Rist, Charles (1915) *A History of Economic Doctrines From the Time of the Physiocrats to the Present Day,* translated from the French edition of 1913 by William Smart and R. Richards (London: George Harrap).

Gintis, Herbert and Bowles, Samuel (2006) *A Cooperative Species: Human Reciprocity and its Evolution* (Chicago: University of Chicago Press), forthcoming.

Gittler, Joseph B. (1942) 'Schema for Studying the Social Effects of Inventions', *Sociometry*, **5**(4), November, pp. 382–94.

Glyn, Andrew and Sutcliffe, Robert (1972) *British Capitalism, Workers and the Profits Squeeze* (Harmondsworth: Penguin).

Gode, Dhananjay K. and Sunder, Shyam (1993) 'Allocative Efficiency of Markets with Zero-Intelligence Traders: Market as a Partial Substitute for Individual Rationality', *Journal of Political Economy*, **101**, February, pp. 119–37.

Godfrey-Smith, Peter (2000) 'The Replicator in Retrospect', *Biology and Philosophy*, **15**, pp. 403–23.

Gould, Stephen Jay (1978) *Ever Since Darwin: Reflections in Natural History* (London: Burnett Books).

Gould, Stephen Jay (1996) *Life's Grandeur: The Spread of Excellence from Plato to Darwin* (London: Cape).

Grandmont, Jean-Michel (1992) 'Transformations of the Commodity Space, Behavioral Heterogeneity and the Aggregation Problem', *Journal of Economic Theory*, **57**(1), pp. 1–35.

Granger, Clive W. J. (2004) 'Critical Realism and Econometrics: An Econometrician's Viewpoint', in Lewis (2004, pp. 96–106).

Grant, John E. (1922) *The Problem of War and Its Solution* (New York: Dutton).

Green, Francis (1979) 'The Consumption Function: A Study in the Failure of Positive Economics', in Green, Francis and Nore, Petter (1979) *Issues in Political Economy: A Critical Approach* (London: Macmillan), pp. 33–60.

Greif, Avner (1993) 'Contract Enforceability and Economic Institutions in Early Trade: The Maghribi Traders' Coalition', *American Economic Review*, **83**(3), pp. 525–48.

Grinyer, J., Russell, A. and Collison, D. (1998) 'Evidence of Managerial Short-Termism in the UK', *British Journal of Management*, **9**(1), pp. 13–22.

Haeckel, Ernst (1874) *Anthropogenie oder Entwicklungsgeschichte des Menschen* (Leipzig: Engelmann).

Hall, Peter A. and Soskice, David (2001) *Varieties of Capitalism: The Institutional Foundations of Comparative Advantage* (Oxford: Oxford University Press).

Hamilton, Walton H. (1919) 'The Institutional Approach to Economic Theory', *American Economic Review*, **9**, Supplement, pp. 309–18.

Hamilton, Walton H. (1932) 'Institution' in Seligman, Edwin R. A. and Johnson, Alvin (eds) (1932) *Encyclopaedia of the Social Sciences* (New York: Macmillan) Vol. 8, pp. 84–89.

Hands, D. Wade (2001) *Reflection Without Rules: Economic Methodology and Contemporary Science Theory* (Cambridge and New York: Cambridge University Press).

Hannan, Michael T. and Freeman, John (1984) 'Structural Inertia and Organizational Change', *American Sociological Review*, **49**(2), April, pp. 149–64.

Hannan, Michael T. and Freeman, John (1989) *Organizational Ecology* (Cambridge, MA: Harvard University Press).

Harcourt, Geoffrey C. (1972) *Some Cambridge Controversies in the Theory of Capital* (Cambridge, Cambridge University Press).

Hardin, Garrett (1968) 'The Tragedy of the Commons', *Science*, **162**, pp. 1243–8.

Harré, Rom and Madden, Edward H. (1975) *Causal Powers: A Theory of Natural Necessity* (Oxford: Basil Blackwell).

Hawkins, Mike (1997) *Social Darwinism in European and American Thought, 1860–1945: Nature as Model and Nature as Threat* (Cambridge: Cambridge University Press).

Hayek, Friedrich A. (ed.) (1935) *Collectivist Economic Planning* (London: George Routledge).

Hayek, Friedrich A. (1944) *The Road to Serfdom* (London: George Routledge).

Hayek, Friedrich A. (1948) *Individualism and Economic Order* (London and Chicago: George Routledge and University of Chicago Press).

Hayek, Friedrich A. (1967) 'Notes on the Evolution of Systems of Rules of Conduct', in Hayek, Friedrich A. (1967) *Studies in Philosophy, Politics and Economics* (London: Routledge and Kegan Paul), pp. 66–81.

Hayek, Friedrich A. (1973) *Law, Legislation and Liberty; Volume 1: Rules and Order* (London: Routledge and Kegan Paul).

Hayek, Friedrich A. (1979) *Law, Legislation and Liberty; Volume 3: The Political Order of a Free People* (London: Routledge and Kegan Paul).

Hayek, Friedrich A. (1988) *The Fatal Conceit: The Errors of Socialism. The Collected Works of Friedrich August Hayek, Vol. I*, edited by William W. Bartley III (London: Routledge).

Henrich, Joseph (2004) 'Cultural Group Selection, Coevolutionary Processes and Large-Scale Cooperation', *Journal of Economic Behavior and Organization*, **53**(1), February, pp. 3–35.

Hesse, Mary B. (1966) *Models and Analogies in Science* (Notre Dame: University of Notre Dame Press).

Hildenbrand, Werner (1994) *Market Demand: Theory and Empirical Evidence* (Princeton, NJ: Princeton University Press).

Himmelfarb, Gertrude (1959) *Darwin and the Darwinian Revolution* (London: Chatto and Windus).

Hindess, Barry (1989) *Political Choice and Social Structure: An Analysis of Actors, Interests and Rationality* (Aldershot: Edward Elgar).

Hobsbawm, Eric J. (1968) *Industry and Empire* (London: Weidenfeld and Nicolson).

Hodgson, Geoffrey M. (1974) 'The Theory of the Falling Rate of Profit', *New Left Review*, no. 84, March/April, pp. 55–82. Reprinted in Hodgson (1991).

Hodgson, Geoffrey M. (1982a) 'On the Political Economy of the Socialist Transformation', *New Left Review*, no. 133, May/June, pp. 52–66.

Hodgson, Geoffrey M. (1982b) *Capitalism, Value and Exploitation: A Radical Theory* (Oxford: Martin Robertson).

Hodgson, Geoffrey M. (1984) *The Democratic Economy: A New Look at Planning, Markets and Power* (Harmondsworth: Penguin).

Hodgson, Geoffrey M. (1988) *Economics and Institutions: A Manifesto for a Modern Institutional Economics* (Cambridge and Philadelphia: Polity Press and University of Pennsylvania Press).

Hodgson, Geoffrey M. (1989) 'Institutional Rigidities and Economic Growth', *Cambridge Journal of Economics*, **13**(1), March, pp. 79–101. Reprinted in Hodgson (1991).

Hodgson, Geoffrey M. (1991) *After Marx and Sraffa: Essays in Political Economy* (London: Macmillan).

Hodgson, Geoffrey M. (1993) *Economics and Evolution: Bringing Life Back Into Economics* (Cambridge, UK and Ann Arbor, MI: Polity Press and University of Michigan Press).

Hodgson, Geoffrey M. (1996) 'An Evolutionary Theory of Long-Term Economic Growth', *International Studies Quarterly*, **40**, pp. 393–412.

Hodgson, Geoffrey M. (1997) 'The Ubiquity of Habits and Rules', *Cambridge Journal of Economics,* **21**(6), November, pp. 663–84.

Hodgson, Geoffrey M. (1998a) 'The Approach of Institutional Economics', *Journal of Economic Literature,* **36**(1), March, pp. 166–92.

Hodgson, Geoffrey M. (1998b) 'Competence and Contract in the Theory of the Firm', *Journal of Economic Behavior and Organization*, **35**(2), April, pp. 179–201.

Hodgson, Geoffrey M. (1999a) *Economics and Utopia: Why the Learning Economy is not the End of History* (London: Routledge).

Hodgson, Geoffrey M. (1999b) *Evolution and Institutions: On Evolutionary Economics and the Evolution of Economics* (Cheltenham: Edward Elgar).

Hodgson, Geoffrey M. (1999c) 'Marching to the Promised Land?: Some Doubts on the Theoretical and Policy Affinities of Critical Realism' with a response by Andrew Collier and a rejoinder, *Alethia,* **2**(2), October, pp. 2–13.

Hodgson, Geoffrey M. (2001a) 'Is Social Evolution Lamarckian or Darwinian?' in Laurent, John and Nightingale, John (eds) (2001) *Darwinism and Evolutionary Economics* (Cheltenham: Edward Elgar), pp. 87–118.

Hodgson, Geoffrey M. (2001b) *How Economics Forgot History: The Problem of Historical Specificity in Social Science* (London and New York: Routledge).

Hodgson, Geoffrey M. (2001c) 'The Evolution of Capitalism from the Perspective of Institutional and Evolutionary Economics', in Hodgson, Geoffrey M., Itoh, Makoto and Yokokawa, Nobuharu (eds) (2001) *Capitalism in Evolution: Global Contentions – East and West* (Cheltenham: Edward Elgar), pp. 63–82.

Hodgson, Geoffrey M. (2002a) 'The Legal Nature of the Firm and the Myth of the Firm-Market Hybrid', *International Journal of the Economics of Business*, **9**(1), February, pp. 37–60.

Hodgson, Geoffrey M. (2002b) 'Darwinism in Economics: From Analogy to Ontology', *Journal of Evolutionary Economics,* **12**(2), June, pp. 259–81.

Hodgson, Geoffrey M. (2002c) 'The Evolution of Institutions: An Agenda for Future Theoretical Research', *Constitutional Political Economy*, **13**(2), June, pp. 111–27.

Hodgson, Geoffrey M. (2002d) 'Reconstitutive Downward Causation: Social Structure and the Development of Individual Agency' in Fullbrook, Edward (ed.) (2002) *Intersubjectivity in Economics: Agents and Structures* (London and New York: Routledge), pp. 159–80.

Hodgson, Geoffrey M. (2003a) 'The Mystery of the Routine: The Darwinian Destiny of *An Evolutionary Theory of Economic Change*', *Revue économique*, **54**(2), mars, pp. 355–84.

Hodgson, Geoffrey M. (2003b) 'The Hidden Persuaders: Institutions and Individuals in Economic Theory', *Cambridge Journal of Economics*, **27**(2), March, pp. 159–75.

Hodgson, Geoffrey M. (2003c) 'The Enforcement of Contracts and Property Rights: Constitutive versus Epiphenomenal Conceptions of Law', *International Review of Sociology,* **13**(2), July, pp. 373–89.

Hodgson, Geoffrey M. (2004a) *The Evolution of Institutional Economics: Agency, Structure and Darwinism in American Institutionalism* (London and New York: Routledge).

Hodgson, Geoffrey M. (2004b) 'Some Claims Made for Critical Realism in Economics: Two Case Studies', *Journal of Economic Methodology*, **11**(1), March, pp. 71–91.

Hodgson, Geoffrey M. (2004c) 'Hayekian Evolution Reconsidered: A Reply to Caldwell', *Cambridge Journal of Economics,* **28**(2), March, pp. 291–300.

Hodgson, Geoffrey M. (2004d) 'Social Darwinism in Anglophone Academic Journals: A Contribution to the History of the Term', *Journal of Historical Sociology,* **17**(4), December, pp. 428–63.

Hodgson, Geoffrey M. (2005) 'The Limits to Participatory Planning: A Reply to Adaman and Devine', *Economy and Society*, **31**(1), February, pp. 141–53.

Hodgson, Geoffrey M. (2006) 'What Are Institutions?', *Journal of Economic Issues*, **40**(1), March, pp. 1–25.

Hodgson, Geoffrey M. (forthcoming) 'The Concept of a Routine', in Becker, Markus (ed.) *The Handbook of Organizational Routines* (forthcoming).

Hodgson, Geoffrey M. and Knudsen, Thorbjørn (2004a) 'The Complex Evolution of a Simple Traffic Convention: The Functions and Implications of Habit', *Journal of Economic Behavior and Organization,* **54**(1), pp. 19–47.

Hodgson, Geoffrey M. and Knudsen, Thorbjørn (2004b) 'The Firm as an Interactor: Firms as Vehicles for Habits and Routines', *Journal of Evolutionary Economics*, **14**(3), July, pp. 281–307.

Hodgson, Geoffrey M. and Knudsen, Thorbjørn (2006) 'Why We Need a Generalized Darwinism: and Why a Generalized Darwinism is Not Enough', *Journal of Economic Behavior and Organization,* September (forthcoming).

Hodgson, Geoffrey M. and Knudsen, Thorbjørn (forthcoming) 'Dismantling Lamarckism: Why Descriptions of Socio-Economic Evolution as Lamarckian are Misleading', *Journal of Evolutionary Economics* (forthcoming).

Hofstadter, Richard (1941) 'William Graham Sumner, Social Darwinist', *New England Quarterly*, **14**, pp. 457–77.

Hofstadter, Richard (1944) *Social Darwinism in American Thought, 1860–1915* (Philadelphia: University of Pennsylvania Press).

Holmes, S. J. (1919) 'Social Amelioration and Eugenic Progress', *Scientific Monthly*, **8**(1), January, pp. 16–31.

Holmes, S. J. (1932) 'The Changing Effects of Race Competition', *Science,* **75**, 19 February, pp. 201–8.

Howitt, Peter and Clower, Robert W. (2000) 'The Emergence of Economic Organization', *Journal of Economic Behavior and Organization*, **41**(1), January, pp. 55–84.

Hull, Clark L. (1943) *Principles of Behavior: An Introduction to Behavior Theory* (New York: Appleton-Century).

Hull, David L. (1988) *Science as a Process: An Evolutionary Account of the Social and Conceptual Development of Science* (Chicago: University of Chicago Press).

Humphreys, Paul (1997) 'How Properties Emerge', *Philosophy of Science,* **64**(1), March, pp. 1–17.

Huxley, Thomas Henry (1894) *Collected Essays*, 9 vols (London: Macmillan).

Ingham, Geoffrey (1984) *Capitalism Divided? The City and Industry in British Social Development* (London: Macmillan).

James, William (1890) *The Principles of Psychology* (New York: Holt).

James, William (1892) *Psychology: Briefer Course* (New York and London: Holt and Macmillan).

Joas, Hans (1993) *Pragmatism and Social Theory* (Chicago: University of Chicago Press).

Joas, Hans (1996) *The Creativity of Action* (Chicago: University of Chicago Press).

Johnson, Gary R. (1998) Review of *Social Darwinism in European and American Thought, 1860–1945: Nature as Model and Nature as Threat* by Mike Hawkins, *American Political Science Review*, **92**(4), December, pp. 930–932.

Jones, Greta (1980) *Social Darwinism and English Thought* (Brighton, UK and Atlantic Highlands, NJ: Harvester and Humanities Press).

Jones, Lamar B. (1989) 'Schumpeter versus Darwin: In re Malthus', *Southern Economic Journal*, **56**(2), October, pp. 410–422.

Jones, Robert A. (1976) 'The Origin and Development of Media of Exchange', *Journal of Political Economy*, **84**(4), August, pp. 757–75.

Jones, Stephen R. G. (1984) *The Economics of Conformism* (Oxford: Basil Blackwell).

Jossa, Bruno (2005) 'Marx, Marxism and the Cooperative Movement', *Cambridge Journal of Economics*, **29**(1), January, pp. 3–18.

Jupille, Joseph and Caporaso, James A. (1999) 'Institutionalism and the European Union: Beyond International Relations and Comparative Politics', *Annual Review of Political Science*, **2**, pp. 429–44.

Kaldor, Nicholas (1950) 'The Economic Effects of Advertising', *Review of Economic Studies*, **18**(1), pp. 1–27.

Kaldor, Nicholas (1966) *Causes of the Slow Rate of Economic Growth in the United Kingdom: An Inaugural Lecture* (Cambridge: Cambridge University Press).

Kaldor, Nicholas (1985) *Economics Without Equilibrium* (Cardiff: University College Cardiff Press).

Keller, Albert Galloway (1915) *Societal Evolution: A Study of the Evolutionary Basis of the Science of Society* (New York: Macmillan).

Keller, Albert Galloway (1923) 'Societal Evolution', in Baitsell, George Alfred (ed.) (1923) *The Evolution of Man* (New Haven: Yale University Press), pp. 126–51.

Keller, Albert Galloway (1945) Review of *Social Darwinism in American Thought, 1860–1915* by Richard Hofstadter, *Scientific Monthly,* **60**(5), May, pp. 398–9.

Kelly, Alfred (1981) *The Descent of Darwin: The Popularization of Darwinism in Germany, 1860–1914* (Chapel Hill, NC: University of North Carolina Press).

Kelman, Herbert C. (1958) 'Compliance, Identification, and Internalization: Three Processes of Attitude Change', *Journal of Conflict Resolution*, **2**, pp. 51–60.

Kelman, Herbert C. (1961) 'Processes of Opinion Change', *Public Opinion Quarterly*, **25**, pp. 57–78.

Kelman, Herbert C. and Hamilton, V. Lee (1989) *Crimes of Obedience: Toward a Social Psychology of Authority and Responsibility* (New Haven: Yale University Press).

Keynes, John Maynard (1972) *The Collected Writings of John Maynard Keynes, Vol. X, Essays in Biography* (London: Macmillan).

Kilpatrick, Andrew and Lawson, Tony (1980) 'On the Nature of the Industrial Decline in the UK', *Cambridge Journal of Economics*, **4**(1), March, pp. 85–102.

Kilpinen, Erkki (2000) *The Enormous Fly-Wheel of Society: Pragmatism's Habitual Conception of Action and Social Theory* (Helsinki: University of Helsinki).

Kim, Jaegwon (1993) *Supervenience and Mind* (Cambridge and New York: Cambridge University Press).

Kirman, Alan P. (1989) 'The Intrinsic Limits of Modern Economic Theory: The Emperor Has No Clothes', *Economic Journal (Conference Papers)*, **99**, pp. 126–39.

Kitcher, Philip (1987) 'Why Not the Best?', in Dupré, John A. (ed.) *The Latest on the Best: Essays on Evolution and Optimality* (Cambridge, MA: MIT Press), pp. 77–102.

Kiyotaki, Nobuhiro and Wright, Randall (1989) 'On Money as a Medium of Exchange', *Journal of Political Economy*, **97**, pp. 927–54.

Klaes, Matthias (2001) '*Begriffsgeschichte:* Between the Scylla of Conceptual and the Charybdis of Institutional History of Economics', *Journal of the History of Economic Thought*, **23**(2), pp. 153–79.

Klamer, Arjo and Colander, David (1990) *The Making of an Economist* (Boulder: Westview Press).

Klein, Lawrence R. (1947) 'Theories of Effective Demand and Employment', *Journal of Political Economy*, **55**(2), April, pp. 138–77.

Kley, Roland (1994) *Hayek's Social and Political Thought* (Oxford: Clarendon Press).

Knight, Jack (1992) *Institutions and Social Conflict* (Cambridge: Cambridge University Press).

Knudsen, Thorbjørn (2002) 'The Significance of Tacit Knowledge in the Evolution of Human Language', *Selection*, **3**(1), pp. 93–112.

Knudsen, Thorbjørn (forthcoming) 'Organizational Routines in Evolutionary Theory', in Becker, Markus (ed.) *The Handbook of Organizational Routines* (forthcoming).

Kontopoulos, Kyriakos M. (1993) *The Logics of Social Structure* (Cambridge: Cambridge University Press).

Kropotkin, Petr A. (1902) *Mutual Aid: A Factor of Evolution* (London: Heinemann).

Krueger, Anne O. *et al.* (1991) 'Report on the Commission on Graduate Education in Economics', *Journal of Economic Literature*, **29**(3), September, pp. 1035–53.

Lacey, Hugh (1997) 'Neutrality in the Social Sciences: On Bhaskar's Argument for an Essential Emancipatory Impulse in Social Science', *Journal for the Theory of Social Behaviour,* **27**(2–3), pp. 213–41. Reprinted in Archer *et al.* (1998).

Landauer, Carl A. (1959) *European Socialism: A History of Ideas and Movements from the Industrial Revolution to Hitler's Seizure of Power,* 2 vols (Berkeley: University of California Press).

Landes, David S. (1969) *The Unbound Prometheus* (Cambridge: Cambridge University Press).

Lane, David A. (1993) 'Artificial Worlds and Economics', parts I and II, *Journal of Evolutionary Economics*, **3**(2), May, pp. 89–107 and **3**(3), August, pp. 177–97.

Lane, David, Malerba, Franco, Maxfield, Robert and Orsenigo, Luigi (1996) 'Choice and Action', *Journal of Evolutionary Economics*, **6**(1), pp. 43–76.

Latzer, Michael and Schmitz, Stefan (eds) (2002) *Carl Menger and the Evolution of Payments Systems* (Cheltenham, UK and Northampton, MA: Edward Elgar).

Laurent, John (2000) 'Alfred Marshall's Annotations on Herbert Spencer's *Principles of Biology*', *Marshall Studies Bulletin*, **7**, pp. 1–6.

Lavoie, Donald (1985) *Rivalry and Central Planning: The Socialist Calculation Debate Reconsidered* (Cambridge: Cambridge University Press).

Lawson, Tony (1987) 'The Relative/Absolute Nature of Knowledge and Economic Analysis', *Economic Journal*, **97**(4), December, pp. 951–70.

Lawson, Tony (1994) 'Hayek and Realism: A Case of Continuous Transformation', in Colonna, Marina, Hagemann, Harald and Hamouda, Omar F. (eds) (1994) *Capitalism, Socialism and Knowledge: The Economics of F. A. Hayek, Volume 2* (Aldershot: Edward Elgar), pp. 131–59.

Lawson, Tony (1997) *Economics and Reality* (London and New York: Routledge).

Lawson, Tony (1999) 'Connections and Distinctions: Post Keynesianism and Critical Realism', *Journal of Post Keynesian Economics*, **22**(1), Fall, pp. 3–14.

Lawson, Tony (2002) 'Mathematical Formalism in Economics: What Really is the Problem?', in Arestis, Philip, Desai, Meghnad and Dow, Sheila (eds) (2002) *Methodology, Microeconomics and Keynes: Essays in Honour of Victoria Chick, Volume Two* (London and New York: Routledge), pp. 73–83.

Lawson, Tony (2003a) 'Institutionalism: On the Need to Firm up Notions of Social Structure and the Human Subject', *Journal of Economic Issues,* **37**(1), March, pp. 175–207.

Lawson, Tony (2003b) *Reorienting Economics* (London and New York: Routledge).

Lawson, Tony (2004) 'On Heterodox Economics, Themata and the Use of Mathematics in Economics', *Journal of Economic Methodology*, **11**(3), September, pp. 329–40.

Lazaric, Nathalie (2000) 'The Role of Routines, Rules and Habits in Collective Learning: Some Epistemological and Ontological Considerations', *European Journal of Economic and Social Systems*, **14**(2), pp. 157–71.

Lazaric, Nathalie and Denis, Blandine (2001) 'How and Why Routines Change: Some Lessons from the Articulation of Knowledge with ISO 9002 Implementation in the Food Industry', *Économies et sociétés*, Série *Dynamique technoloqique et organisation,* **6**(4), pp. 585–611.

Le Conte, Joseph (1892) *The Race Problem in the South* (New York: Appleton).

Leibenstein, Harvey (1982) 'The Prisoners's Dilemma in the Invisible Hand: An Analysis of Intrafirm Productivity', *American Economic Review (Papers and Proceedings),* **72**(2), May, pp. 92–7.

Levitt, Barbara and March, James G. (1988) 'Organizational Learning', *Annual Review of Sociology*, **14**, pp. 319–40.

Lewis, Paul A. (1996) 'Metaphor and Critical Realism', *Review of Social Economy,* **54**(4), Winter, pp. 487–506.

Lewis, Paul A. (ed.) (2004) *Transforming Economics: Perspectives on the Critical Realist Project* (London and New York: Routledge).

Libet, Benjamin (1985) 'Unconscious Cerebral Initiative and the Role of Conscious Will in Voluntary Action', *Behavioral and Brain Sciences*, **8**, pp. 529–66.

Libet, Benjamin (2004) *Mind Time: The Temporal Factor in Consciousness* (Cambridge, MA: Harvard University Press).

Lindgren, Kristian (1992) 'Evolutionary Phenomena in Simple Dynamics', in Langton, Christopher G., Taylor, Charles, Farmer, J. Doyne and Rasmussen, Steen (eds) (1992) *Artificial Life II* (Redwood City, CA: Addison-Wesley), pp. 295–312.

Lluch, C. (1974) 'Expenditures, Savings and Habit Formation', *International Economic Review*, **15**, pp. 786–97.

Lopreato, Joseph and Crippen, Timothy (1999) *Crisis in Sociology: The Need for Darwin* (New Brunswick, NJ: Transaction).

Loria, Achille (1895) *Problemi Sociali Contemporanei* (Milano: Kantorowicz).

Loye, David (1998) *Darwin's Lost Theory of Love - A Healing Vision for the New Century* (Lincoln, NE: iUniverse).

Luhmann, Niklas (1982) *The Differentiation of Society* (New York: Columbia University Press).

Luxemburg, Rosa (1971) *Selected Political Writings of Rosa Luxemburg*, edited by Dick Howard (New York, Monthly Review Press).

Mäki, Uskali (1992) 'On the Method of Isolation in Economics', *Poznan Studies in the Philosophy of the Sciences and the Humanities*, **26**, pp. 319–54.

Mäki, Uskali (1994) 'Isolation, Idealization and Truth in Economics', *Poznan Studies in the Philosophy of the Sciences and the Humanities*, **38**, pp. 147–68.

Mäki, Uskali (1997) 'The One World and Many Theories', in Salanti, Andrea and Screpanti, Ernesto (eds) (1997) *Pluralism in Economics: New Perspectives in History and Methodology* (Aldershot: Edward Elgar), pp. 37–47.

Mäki, Uskali (2000) 'Kinds of Assumptions and Their Truth: Shaking an Untwisted F-Twist', *Kyklos*, **53**(3), pp. 317–36.

Malthus, Thomas Robert (1798) *An Essay on the Principle of Population, as it Affects the Future Improvement of Society, with Remarks on the Speculations of Mr. Godwin, M. Condorcet, and other Writers* (London: Johnson).

Mani, G. S. (1991) 'Is There a General Theory of Biological Evolution?' in Saviotti and Metcalfe (1991, pp. 31–57).

Mantel, Rolf R. (1974) 'On the Characterization of Aggregate Excess Demand', *Journal of Economic Theory*, **12**(2), pp. 348–53.

Mantzavinos, Chris (2001) *Individuals, Institutions and Markets* (Cambridge and New York: Cambridge University Press).

March, James G. and Simon, Herbert A. (1958) *Organizations* (New York: Wiley).

Margolis, Howard (1987) *Patterns, Thinking and Cognition: A Theory of Judgment* (Chicago: University of Chicago Press).

Marimon, Ramon E., McGrattan, Ellen and Sargent, Thomas J. (1990) 'Money as a Medium of Exchange in an Economy With Artificially Intelligent Agents', *Journal of Economic Dynamics and Control*, **14**, pp. 329–73.

Marshall, Alfred (1890) *Principles of Economics: An Introductory Volume*, 1st edn (London: Macmillan).

Marshall, Alfred (1949) *The Principles of Economics*, 8th (reset) edn (London: Macmillan).

Marx, Karl (1973a) *The Revolutions of 1848: Political Writings – Volume 1*, edited and introduced by David Fernbach (Harmondsworth: Penguin).

Marx, Karl (1973b) *Surveys From Exile: Political Writings – Volume 2*, edited and introduced by David Fernbach (Harmondsworth: Penguin).

Marx, Karl (1974) *The First International and After: Political Writings – Volume 3*, edited and introduced by David Fernbach (Harmondsworth: Penguin).

Marx, Karl (1976a) *Capital*, vol. 1, translated by Ben Fowkes from the fourth German edition of 1890 (Harmondsworth: Pelican).

Marx, Karl (1976b) 'Marginal Notes on Wagner', in Dragstedt, Albert (ed.) (1976) *Value: Studies by Marx* (London: New Park), pp. 195–229.

Marx, Karl (1978) *Capital*, vol. 2, translated by David Fernbach from the German edition of 1893 (Harmondsworth: Pelican).

Marx, Karl (1981) *Capital*, vol. 3, translated by David Fernbach from the German edition of 1894 (Harmondsworth: Pelican).

Marx, Karl and Engels, Frederick (1975) *Karl Marx and Frederick Engels, Collected Works, Vol. 3, Marx and Engels: 1843–1844* (London: Lawrence and Wishart).

Marx, Karl and Engels, Frederick (1976) *Karl Marx and Frederick Engels, Collected Works, Vol. 5, Marx and Engels: 1845–1847* (London: Lawrence and Wishart).

Marx, Karl and Engels, Frederick (1977) *Karl Marx and Frederick Engels, Collected Works, Vol. 8, Marx and Engels: 1848–1849* (London: Lawrence and Wishart).

Marx, Karl and Engels, Frederick (1983) *Karl Marx and Frederick Engels, Collected Works, Vol. 40, Letters 1856–1859* (London: Lawrence and Wishart).

Marx, Karl and Engels, Frederick (1985) *Karl Marx and Frederick Engels, Collected Works, Vol. 41, Letters 1860–1864* (London: Lawrence and Wishart).

Marx, Karl and Engels, Frederick (1987) *Karl Marx and Frederick Engels, Collected Works, Vol. 42, Letters 1864–1868* (London: Lawrence and Wishart).

Marx, Karl and Engels, Frederick (1989) *Karl Marx and Frederick Engels, Collected Works, Vol. 24, Marx and Engels: 1874–1883* (London: Lawrence and Wishart).

Marx, Karl and Engels, Frederick (1991) *Karl Marx and Frederick Engels, Collected Works, Vol. 45, Letters 1874–1879* (London: Lawrence and Wishart).

Marx, Karl and Engels, Frederick (1992) *Karl Marx and Frederick Engels, Collected Works, Vol. 46, Letters 1880–83* (London: Lawrence and Wishart).

Mayr, Ernst (1964) 'Introduction', in facsimile of the first edition of Darwin, Charles R. (1859) *On the Origin of Species by Means of Natural Selection, or the Preservation of Favoured Races in the Struggle for Life* (London: Murray), pp. vii–xxvii.

Mayr, Ernst (1982) *The Growth of Biological Thought: Diversity, Evolution, and Inheritance* (Cambridge, MA: Harvard University Press).

Mayr, Ernst (1985) 'How Biology Differs from the Physical Sciences', in Depew, David J. and Weber, Bruce H. (eds) (1985) *Evolution at a Crossroads: The New Biology and the New Philosophy of Science* (Cambridge, MA: MIT Press), pp. 43–63.

Mayr, Ernst (1988) *Toward a New Philosophy of Biology: Observations of an Evolutionist* (Cambridge, MA and London: Harvard University Press).

Mayr, Ernst (1991) *One Long Argument: Charles Darwin and the Genesis of Modern Evolutionary Thought* (Cambridge, MA and London: Harvard University Press and Allen Lane).

Mayr, Ernst (1992) 'The Idea of Teleology', *Journal of the History of Ideas*, **53**, pp. 117–35.

McDougall, William (1908) *An Introduction to Social Psychology* (London: Methuen).

McDougall, William (1924) 'Can Sociology and Social Psychology Dispense With Instincts?', *American Journal of Sociology*, **29**(6), May, pp. 657–73.

McGovern, William M. (1941) *From Luther to Hitler: The History of Fascist-Nazi Political Philosophy* (Boston: Houghton Mifflin).

McKelvey, William (1982) *Organizational Systematics: Taxonomy, Evolution, Classification* (Berkeley, CA: University of California Press).

Menger, Carl (1871) *Grundsätze der Volkwirtschaftslehre* (Tübingen: J. C. B. Mohr). Published in English in 1981 as *Principles of Economics*, edited by J. Dingwall and translated by B. F. Hoselitz from the German edition of 1871 (New York: New York University Press).

Milgram, Stanley (1974) *Obedience to Authority: An Experimental View* (New York and London: Harper and Row, and Tavistock).

Mirowski, Philip (1989) *More Heat Than Light: Economics as Social Physics, Physics as Nature's Economics* (Cambridge: Cambridge University Press).

Mirowski, Philip (1991) 'Postmodernism and the Social Theory of Value', *Journal of Post Keynesian Economics*, 13(4), Summer, pp. 565–82.

Mirowski, Philip (2002) *Machine Dreams: Economics Becomes a Cyborg Science* (Cambridge and New York: Cambridge University Press).

Mirowski, Philip and Somefun, Koye (1998) 'Markets as Evolving Computational Entities', *Journal of Evolutionary Economics* **8**(4), pp. 329–56.

Mitchell, Wesley C. (ed.) (1936) *What Veblen Taught* (New York: Viking).

Mitchell, Wesley C. (1937) *The Backward Art of Spending Money and Other Essays* (New York: McGraw-Hill).

Moore, A. W. (1922) 'Some Logical Aspects of Critical Realism', *Journal of Philosophy*, **19**, October, pp. 589–96.

Moore, Stanley (1980) *Marx on the Choice Between Socialism and Communism* (Cambridge, MA: Harvard University Press).

Moore, Stanley (1993) *Marx Versus Markets* (Philadelphia: University of Pennsylvania Press).

Morgan, Conwy Lloyd (1896) *Habit and Instinct* (London and New York: Edward Arnold).

Morison, Elting E. (1966) *Men, Machines and Modern Times* (Cambridge, MA: MIT Press).
Morris, Henry (1974) *The Troubled Waters of Evolution* (San Diego, CA: Creation-Life Publishers).
Mouzelis, Nicos (1995) *Sociological Theory: What Went Wrong? Diagnosis and Remedies* (London and New York: Routledge).
Mumford, Lewis (1944) *The Condition of Man* (New York: Harcourt, Brace).
Murphy, James Bernard (1994) 'The Kinds of Order in Society', in Mirowski, Philip (ed.) (1994) *Natural Images in Economic Thought: Markets Read in Tooth and Claw* (Cambridge and New York: Cambridge University Press), pp. 536–82.
Murray, J. D. (1989) *Mathematical Biology* (Berlin: Springer).
Musgrave, Alan (1981) '"Unreal Assumptions" in Economic Theory: The F-Twist Untwisted', *Kylklos*, **34**, Fasc. 3, pp. 377–87.
Myrdal, Gunnar (1939) *Monetary Equilibrium,* translated from the Swedish edition of 1931 and the German edition of 1933 (London: Hodge).
Myrdal, Gunnar (1957) *Economic Theory and Underdeveloped Regions* (London: Duckworth).
Nash, Stephen J. (2004) 'On Closure in Economics', *Journal of Economic Methodology*, **11**(1), March, pp. 75–89.
Nasmyth, George (1916) *Social Progress and Darwinian Theory: A Study of Force as a Factor in Human Relations* (New York and London: Putnam).
Nelson, Richard R. (1991) 'Why Do Firms Differ, and How Does it Matter?', *Strategic Management Journal*, **12**, Special Issue, Winter, pp. 61–74.
Nelson, Richard R. and Sampat, Bhaven N. (2001) 'Making Sense of Institutions as a Factor Shaping Economic Performance', *Journal of Economic Behavior and Organization*, **44**(1), pp. 31–54.
Nelson, Richard R. and Winter, Sidney G. (1982) *An Evolutionary Theory of Economic Change* (Cambridge, MA: Harvard University Press).
Nelson, Richard R. and Winter, Sidney G. (2002) 'Evolutionary Theorizing in Economics', *Journal of Economic Perspectives*, **16**(2), Spring, pp. 23–46.
Nicita, Antonio and Pagano, Ugo (eds) (2001) *The Evolution of Economic Diversity* (London and New York: Routledge).
Nielsen, Peter (2002) 'Reflections on Critical Realism in Political Economy', *Cambridge Journal of Economics*, **26**(6), November, pp. 727–38.
North, Douglass C. (1990) *Institutions, Institutional Change and Economic Performance* (Cambridge: Cambridge University Press).
North, Douglass C. (1991) 'Institutions', *Journal of Economic Perspectives,* **5**(1), Winter, pp. 97–112.
North, Douglass C. (1994) 'Economic Performance Through Time', *American Economic Review*, **84**(3), June, pp. 359–67.

North, Douglass C. (1995) 'Five Propositions about Institutional Change', in Knight, Jack and Sened, Itai (eds) (1995) *Explaining Social Institutions* (Ann Arbor, MI: University of Michigan Press), pp. 15–26.

North, Douglass C. (1997) 'Prologue' in Drobak, John N. and Nye, John V. C. (eds) (1997) *The Frontiers of the New Institutional Economics* (San Diego and London: Academic Press), pp. 3–28.

North, Douglass C. (2002a) Letter to G. M. Hodgson dated 10 September 2002.

North, Douglass C. (2002b) Letter to G. M. Hodgson dated 7 October 2002.

Nove, Alexander (1983) *The Economics of Feasible Socialism* (London: George Allen and Unwin).

Novicow, Jacques (1910) *La critique du darwinisme social* (Paris: Alcan).

O'Hara, Phillip Anthony (2000) *Marx, Veblen, and Contemporary Institutional Political Economy: Principles and Unstable Dynamics of Capitalism* (Cheltenham: Edward Elgar).

Oh, Songhwan (1989) 'A Theory of a Generally Acceptable Medium of Exchange and Barter', *Journal of Monetary Economics*, **23**, pp. 101–19,

Okishio, Nobuo (1961) 'Technical Change and the Profit Rate', *Kobe University Economic Review*, **7**, pp. 86–99.

Orléan, André (ed.) (1994) *Analyse économique des conventions* (Paris: Presses Universitaires de France).

Ostrom, Elinor (1986) 'An Agenda for the Study of Institutions', *Public Choice*, **48**, pp. 3–25.

Ouellette, Judith A. and Wood, Wendy (1998) 'Habit and Intention in Everyday Life: The Multiple Processes by which Past Behavior Predicts Future Behavior', *Psychological Bulletin*, **124**, pp. 54–74.

Packard, Vance (1957) *The Hidden Persuaders* (London: Longmans, Green).

Parra, Carlos M. (2005) 'Rules and Knowledge', *Evolutionary and Institutional Economics Review*, **2**(1), October, pp. 81–111.

Parsons, Talcott (1932) 'Economics and Sociology: Marshall in Relation to the Thought of his Time', *Quarterly Journal of Economics*, **46**(2), February, pp. 316–47.

Parsons, Talcott (1934) 'Some Reflections on "The Nature and Significance of Economics"', *Quarterly Journal of Economics*, **48**(3), May, pp. 511–45.

Parsons, Talcott (1935) 'Sociological Elements in Economic Thought, Parts I & II', *Quarterly Journal of Economics*, **49**, pp. 414–53, 646–67.

Parsons, Talcott (1937) *The Structure of Social Action*, 2 vols (New York: McGraw-Hill).

Parsons, Talcott (1966) *Societies: Evolutionary and Comparative Perspectives* (Engelewood Cliffs, NJ: Prentice-Hall).

Parsons, Talcott (1977) *The Evolution of Societies* (Engelewood Cliffs, NJ: Prentice-Hall).

Paul, Diane (1984) 'Eugenics and the Left', *Journal of the History of Ideas*, **45**(4), October–December, pp. 567–590

Pearl, Judea (2000) *Causality: Models, Reasoning, and Inference* (Cambridge and New York: Cambridge University Press).

Peirce, Charles Sanders (1878) 'How to Make Our Ideas Clear', *Popular Science Monthly*, **12**, January, pp. 286–302. Reprinted in Buchler, J. (ed.) (1955) *Philosophical Writings of Peirce* (New York: Dover Publications).

Peirce, Charles Sanders (1934) *Collected Papers of Charles Sanders Peirce, Volume V, Pragmatism and Pragmaticism*, edited by Hartshorne, C. and Weiss, P. (Cambridge, MA: Harvard University Press).

Pelikan, Pavel (1988) 'Can the Innovation System of Capitalism be Outperformed?', in Dosi, Giovanni, Freeman, Christopher, Nelson, Richard, Silverberg, Gerald and Soete, Luc L. G. (eds), *Technical Change and Economic Theory* (London: Pinter), pp. 370–398.

Pelikan, Pavel (1992) 'The Dynamics of Economic Systems, Or How to Transform a Failed Socialist Economy', *Journal of Evolutionary Economics*, **2**(1), March, pp. 39–63.

Perry, Ralph Barton (1918) *The Present Conflict of Ideals: A Study of the Philosophical Background of the World War* (New York: Longmans Green).

Petty, Richard E. and Cacioppo, John T. (1986) *Communication and Persuasion: Central and Peripheral Routes to Attitude and Change* (New York: Spinger-Verlag).

Phlips, Louis and Spinnewyn, F. (1984) 'True Indexes and Rational Habit Formation', *European Economic Review*, **24**, pp. 209–23.

Pittenger, Mark (1993) *American Socialists and Evolutionary Thought, 1870–1920* (Madison, WS: University of Wisconsin Press).

Plotkin, Henry C. (1994) *Darwin Machines and the Nature of Knowledge: Concerning Adaptations, Instinct and the Evolution of Intelligence* (Harmondsworth: Penguin).

Pohl, J. Otto (1999) *Ethnic Cleansing in the USSR, 1937–1949* (Westport, CT: Greenwood Press).

Polanyi, Michael (1967) *The Tacit Dimension* (London: Routledge and Kegan Paul).

Poldrack, Russell A., Clark, J., Pare-Blagoev, J., Shohamy, D., Creso Moyano, J., Myers, C. and Gluck, M. A. (2001) 'Interactive Memory Systems in the Human Brain', *Nature*, 29 November, **414**, pp. 546–550.

Pollak, Robert A. (1970) 'Habit Formation and Dynamic Demand Functions', *Journal of Political Economy*, **78**, July–August, pp. 745–63.

Popper, Karl R. (1990) *A World of Propensities* (Bristol: Thoemmes).

Popper, Karl R. and Eccles, John C. (1977) *The Self and Its Brain* (Berlin: Springer International).

Potts, Jason (2000) *The New Evolutionary Microeconomics: Complexity, Competence and Adaptive Behaviour* (Cheltenham: Edward Elgar).

Proudhon, Pierre Joseph (1969) *Selected Works,* translated and edited by S. Edwards (New York: Doubleday).

Purdy, David L. (1976) 'British Capitalism Since the War', Parts I and II, *Marxism Today*, September and October.

Quine, Willard van Orman (1951) 'Two Dogmas of Empiricism', *Philosophical Review*, **60**(1), January, pp. 20–43. Reprinted in Quine (1953).

Quine, Willard van Orman (1953) *From a Logical Point of View* (Cambridge, MA: Harvard University Press).

Quine, Willard van Orman (1960) *Word and Object* (Cambridge, MA: Harvard University Press).

Rabin, Matthew (1998) 'Psychology and Economics', *Journal of Economic Literature*, **36**(1), March, pp. 11–46.

Radner, Roy (1970) 'New Ideas in Pure Theory: Problems in the Theory of Markets Under Uncertainty', *American Economic Review (Papers and Proceedings)*, **60**(2), May, pp. 454–60.

Ramstad, Yngve (1994) 'On the Nature of Economic Evolution: John R. Commons and the Metaphor of Artificial Selection', in Magnusson, Lars (ed.) (1994) *Evolutionary and Neo-Schumpeterian Approaches to Economics* (Boston: Kluwer), pp. 65–121.

Reber, Arthur S. (1993) *Implicit Learning and Tacit Knowledge: An Essay on the Cognitive Unconscious* (Oxford and New York: Oxford University Press).

Reibel, R. (1975) 'The Workingman's Production Association, or the Republic in the Workshop', in Vanek, Jaroslav (ed.) (1975) *Self-Management: The Economic Liberation of Man* (Harmondsworth: Penguin), pp. 39–46.

Reynauld, Bénédicte (2000) 'The Properties of Routines: Tools of Decision Making and Modes of Coordination', in Saviotti, Pier Paolo and Nooteboom, Bart (eds) (2005) *Technology and Knowledge: From the Firm to Innovation Systems* (Cheltenham, UK and Northampton, MA: Edward Elgar), pp. 249–62.

Richards, Robert J. (1987) *Darwin and the Emergence of Evolutionary Theories of Mind and Behavior* (Chicago: University of Chicago Press).

Richerson, Peter J. and Boyd, Robert (2001) 'Built For Speed, Not for Comfort: Darwinian Theory and Human Culture', *History and Philosophy of the Life Sciences*, **23**, pp. 423–63.

Richerson, Peter J. and Boyd, Robert (2004) *Not by Genes Alone: How Culture Transformed Human Evolution* (Chicago: University of Chicago Press).

Richerson, Peter J., Boyd, Robert and Bettinger, Robert L. (2001) 'Was Agriculture Impossible During the Pleistocene But Mandatory During the Holocene? A Climate Change Hypothesis', *American Antiquity*, **66**, pp. 387–411.

Ritchie, David G. (1889) *Darwinism and Politics* (London: Swan Sonnenschein).

Ritchie, David G. (1896) 'Social Evolution', *International Journal of Ethics*, **6**(2), pp. 165–81.

Rizvi, S. Abu Turab (1994) 'The Microfoundations Project in General Equilibrium Theory', *Cambridge Journal of Economics*, **18**(4), August, pp. 357–77.

Robbins, Lionel (1932) *An Essay on the Nature and Significance of Economic Science* (London: Macmillan).

Robinson, Joan (1953) 'The Production Function and the Theory of Capital', *Review of Economic Studies*, **21**(1), pp. 81–106.

Robson, Arthur J. (2001a) 'The Biological Basis of Human Behavior', *Journal of Economic Literature*, **39**(1), March, pp. 11–33.

Robson, Arthur J. (2001b) 'Why Would Nature Give Individuals Utility Functions?', *Journal of Political Economy*, **109**(4), August, pp. 900–914.

Robson, Arthur J. (2002) 'Evolution and Human Nature', *Journal of Economic Perspectives*, **16**(2), Spring, pp. 89–106.

Rogers, Everett M. (1995) *Diffusion of Innovations*, 3rd edn (New York: Free Press).

Rogin, Leo (1937) Review of *Bourgeois Population Theory: A Marxist-Leninist Critique, American Economic Review*, **27**(2), June, pp. 412–14.

Rose, Steven, Kamin, Leon J. and Lewontin, Richard C. (1984) *Not in Our Genes: Biology, Ideology and Human Nature* (Harmondsworth: Penguin).

Rosenberg, Alexander (1995) *The Philosophy of Social Science,* 2nd edn (Boulder, CO: Westview Press).

Rosenberg, Alexander (1998) 'Folk Psychology', in Davis, John B., Hands, D. Wade and Mäki, Uskali (eds) (1998) *Handbook of Economic Methodology* (Cheltenham: Edward Elgar), pp. 195–7.

Ross, Edward Alsworth (1901) *Social Control: A Survey of the Foundations of Order* (New York: Macmillan).

Ross, Edward Alsworth (1903) 'Recent Tendencies in Sociology III', *Quarterly Journal of Economics*, **17**(3), May, pp. 438–55.

Roth, Alvin E. and Erev, Ido (1995) 'Learning in Extensive-Form Games: Experimental Data and Simple Dynamic Models in the Intermediate Term', *Games and Economic Behavior, Special Issue: Nobel Symposium*, **8**(1), January, pp. 164–212.

Rowthorn, Robert E. (1999) 'Unemployment, Wage Bargaining and Capital-Labour Substitution', *Cambridge Journal of Economics,* **23**(4), July, pp. 413–25.

Runciman, Walter G. (1972) *Relative Deprivation and Social Justice* (Harmondsworth: Pengion).

Runde, Jochen H. (1998) 'Assessing Causal Economic Explanations', *Oxford Economic Papers,* **50**(1), pp. 151–72.

Russell, Bertrand (1938) *Power: A New Social Analysis* (London: George Allen and Unwin).

Ruth, Matthias (1996) 'Evolutionary Economics at the Crossroads of Biology and Physics', *Journal of Social and Evolutionary Systems*, **19**(2), pp. 125–44.

Sahlins, Marshall D. (1977) *The Use and Abuse of Biology: An Anthropological Critique of Sociobiology* (London: Tavistock).

Salmon, Wesley C. (1998) *Causality and Explanation* (Oxford: Oxford University Press).

Samuelson, Paul A. (1962) 'Economists and the History of Ideas', *American Economic Review*, **52**(1), March, pp. 1–18.

Samuelson, Paul A. (1967) 'The Monopolistic Revolution', in Kuenne, R. (ed.) (1967) *Monopolistic Competition Theory* (New York: Wiley).

Sanderson, Stephen K. (2001) *The Evolution of Human Sociality: A Darwinian Conflict Perspective* (Lanham, MD: Rowman and Littlefield).

Saviotti, Pier Paolo and Metcalfe, J. Stanley (eds) (1991) *Evolutionary Theories of Economic and Technological Change: Present Status and Future Prospects* (Reading: Harwood).

Sayer, Andrew (1997) 'Critical Realism and the Limits to Critical Social Science', *Journal for the Theory of Social Behaviour*, **27**(4), pp. 473–488. Reprinted in Sayer, Andrew (2000) *Realism and Social Science* (Thousand Oaks, CA and London, UK: Sage).

Schelling, Thomas C. (1969) 'Models of Segregation', *American Economic Review,* **59**(2), June, pp. 488–93.

Schlicht, Ekkehart (1998) *On Custom in the Economy* (Oxford and New York: Clarendon Press).

Schmidt, Oskar (1879) 'Science and Socialism', *Popular Science*, **14**, pp. 557–91.

Schotter, Andrew R. (1981) *The Economic Theory of Social Institutions* (Cambridge: Cambridge University Press).

Schout, Adriaan (1991) 'Review of *Institutions, Institutional Change and Economic Performance* by Douglass C. North', *Economic Journal*, **101**(5), November, pp. 1587–9.

Schultz, Walter J. (2001) *The Moral Conditions of Economic Efficiency* (Cambridge and New York: Cambridge University Press).

Schumpeter, Joseph A. (1934) *The Theory of Economic Development: An Inquiry into Profits, Capital, Credit, Interest, and the Business Cycle*, translated by Redvers Opie from the second German edition of 1926; first edition 1911 (Cambridge, MA: Harvard University Press).

Schumpeter, Joseph A. (1942) *Capitalism, Socialism and Democracy* (London: George Allen and Unwin).

Schumpeter, Joseph A. (1954) *History of Economic Analysis* (New York: Oxford University Press).

Schweber, Silvan S. (1977) 'The Origin of the *Origin* Revisited', *Journal of the History of Biology*, **10**(2), Fall, pp. 229–316.

Searle, John R. (1995) *The Construction of Social Reality* (London: Allen Lane).

Searle, John R. (2005) 'What Is an Institution?', *Journal of Institutional Economics,* **1**(1), June, pp. 1–22.

Segerstråle, Ullica (2000) *Defenders of the Truth: The Sociobiology Debate* (Oxford: Oxford University Press).

Sellars, Roy Wood (1908) 'Critical Realism and the Time Problem', *Journal of Philosophy*, **5**(20, 22), September, pp. 542–48 and October, pp. 597–602.

Sellars, Roy Wood (1916) *Critical Realism: A Study of the Nature and Conditions of Knowledge* (Chicago: Rand-McNally).

Sened, Itai (1997) *The Political Institution of Private Property* (Cambridge: Cambridge University Press).

Shute, Daniel K. (1896) 'Racial Anatomical Peculiarities', *American Anthropologist*, **9**, April, pp. 123–7.

Simon, Herbert A. (1947) *Administrative Behavior: A Study of Decision-Making Processes in Administrative Organization* (New York: Free Press).

Simon, Herbert A. (1957) *Models of Man: Social and Rational. Mathematical Essays on Rational Human Behavior in a Social Setting* (New York: Wiley).

Simon, Herbert A. (1990) 'A Mechanism for Social Selection and Successful Altruism', *Science*, **250**, 21 December, pp. 1665–8.

Singer, Peter (1999) *A Darwinian Left: Politics, Evolution and Cooperation* (London UK, and New Haven CT: Wiedenfeld and Nicholson, and Yale University Press).

Sisson, K. and Marginson, P. (1996) 'Management Systems, Structures and Strategy', in Edwards, P. K. (ed.) (1996) *Industrial Relations* (Oxford: Basil Blackwell), pp. 89–122.

Smith, Norman E. (1979) 'William Graham Sumner as an Anti-Social Darwinist', *Pacific Sociological Review*, **22**, pp. 332–47.

Smith, Vernon L. (1982) 'Microeconomic Systems as an Experimental Science', *American Economic Review*, **72**(5), December, pp. 923–55.

Smolin, Lee (1997) *The Life of the Cosmos* (London: Weidenfeld and Nicholson).

Sober, Elliott and Wilson, David Sloan (1998) *Unto Others: The Evolution and Psychology of Unselfish Behavior* (Cambridge, MA: Harvard University Press).

Sosa, Ernest and Tooley, Michael (eds) (1993) *Causation* (Oxford: Oxford University Press).

Spencer, Herbert (1893) 'The Inadequacy of Natural Selection', *Contemporary Review*, **63**, pp. 153–66, 439–56.

Sperber, Dan (2000) 'An Objection to the Memetic Approach to Culture', in Aunger, Robert (ed.) *Darwinizing Culture: The Status of Memetics as a Science* (Oxford and New York: Oxford University Press), pp. 162–73.

Sperry, Roger W. (1964) *Problems Outstanding in the Evolution of Brain Function* (New York: American Museum of Natural History).

Sperry, Roger W. (1969) 'A Modified Concept of Consciousness', *Psychological Review*, **76**(6), pp. 532–6.

Sperry, Roger W. (1976) 'Mental Phenomena as Causal Determinants in Brain Function', in Globus, Gordon G., Maxwell, Grover and Savodnik, Irwin (eds) *Consciousness and the Brain: A Scientific and Philosophical Inquiry* (New York and London: Plenum), pp. 163–77.

Sperry, Roger W. (1991) 'In Defense of Mentalism and Emergent Interaction', *Journal of Mind and Behavior*, **12**(2), pp. 221–46.

Sraffa, Piero (1960) *Production of Commodities by Means of Commodities: Prelude to a Critique of Economic Theory* (Cambridge: Cambridge University Press).

Stafford, G. Bernard (1983) 'The Class Struggle, The Multiplier and the Alternative Economic Strategy' in Sawyer, Malcolm and Schott, Kerry (eds), *Socialist Economic Review 1983* (London: Merlin), pp. 1–21.

Stapleton, Laurence (1944) *Justice and World Society* (Chapel Hill: University of North Carolina Press).

Steedman, Ian (1977) *Marx After Sraffa* (London: NLB).

Steele, David Ramsay (1992) *From Marx to Mises: Post-Capitalist Society and the Challenge of Economic Calculation* (La Salle, Illinois: Open Court).

Sterelny, Kim, Smith, Kelly C. and Dickison, Michael (1996) 'The Extended Replicator', *Biology and Philosophy*, **11**, pp. 377–403.

Stern, Bernhard J. (1933) 'Sumner, William Graham', in Seligman, Edwin R. A. and Johnson, Alvin (eds) *Encyclopaedia of the Social Sciences* (New York: Macmillan), Vol. 9, p. 463.

Stich, Stephen P. (1983) *From Folk Psychology to Cognitive Science* (Cambridge, MA: MIT Press).

Stigler, George J. and Becker, Gary S. (1977) 'De Gustibus Non Est Disputandum', *American Economic Review,* **76**(1), March, pp. 76–90.

Stinchcombe, Arthur L. (1965) 'Social Structure and Organizations', in March, James G. (ed.) *Handbook of Organizations* (Chicago: Rand McNally), pp. 142–93.

Stinchcombe, Arthur L. (1990) *Information and Organizations* (Berkeley: University of California Press).

Sugden, Robert (1986) *The Economics of Rights, Co-operation and Welfare* (Oxford: Basil Blackwell).

Sugden, Robert (1991) 'Rational Choice: A Survey of Contributions from Economics and Philosophy', *Economic Journal*, **101**(4), July, pp. 751–85.

Sugden, Robert (2000a) 'Credible Worlds: The Status of Theoretical Models in Economics', *Journal of Economic Methodology*, **7**(1), March, pp. 1–31.

Sugden, Robert (2000b) 'Team Preferences', *Economics and Philosophy*, **16**(2), pp. 175–204.

Sumner, William Graham (1906) *Folkways: A Study of the Sociological Importance of Usages, Manners, Customs, Mores and Morals* (Boston: Ginn).

Sweezy, Paul M. (1942) *The Theory of Capitalist Development* (London: Dobson).

Szulanski, Gabriel (1996) 'Exploring Internal Stickiness: Impediments to the Transfer of Best Practice Within the Firm', *Strategic Management Journal*, **17**, Winter Special Issue, pp. 27–43.

Szulanski, Gabriel (2000) 'Appriopriability and the Challenge of Scope: Banc One Routinizes Replication', in Dosi, Giovanni, Nelson, Richard R. and Winter, Sidney G. (eds) *The Nature and Dynamics of Organizational Capabilities* (Oxford: Oxford University Press), pp. 69–98.

Tarde, Gabriel (1884) 'Darwinisme naturel et Darwinisme social', *Revue Philosophique,* **17**, p. 607.

Tarde, Gabriel (1890) *Les lois de l'imitation: étude sociologique* (Paris: Alcan).

Taussig, Frank W. (1895) Review of Achille Loria *Problemi Sociali Contemporani*, *Political Science Quarterly,* **10**(3), September, pp. 537–8.

Tedeschi, James T. (ed.) (1972) *The Social Influence Processes* (Chicago: Aldine-Atherton).

Tedeschi, James T. (ed.) (1974) *Perspectives on Social Power* (Chicago: Aldine-Atherton).

Thévenot, Laurent (1986) *Conventions economiques* (Paris: Presses Universitaires de France).

Thomas, Brinley (1991) 'Alfred Marshall on Economic Biology', *Review of Political Economy*, **3**(1), January, pp. 1–14.

Thomas, William and Znaniecki, Florian (1920) *The Polish Peasant in Europe and America*, vol. 2 (New York: Octagon).

Todd, Emmanuel (1985) *The Explanation of Ideology: Family Structures and Social Systems* (Oxford: Basil Blackwell).

Tomasello, Michael (2000) *The Cultural Origins of Human Cognition* (Cambridge, MA: Harvard University Press).

Trémaux, Pierre (1865) *Origine et transformation de l'homme et les autres êtres* (Paris: Hachette).

Trotsky, Leon D. (1937) *The Revolution Betrayed: What is the Soviet Union and Where is it Going?* (London: Faber and Faber)

Tulving, Endel and Schacter, Daniel L. (1990) 'Priming and Human Memory Systems', *Science*, **247**, no. 4940, 19 January, pp. 301–6.

Tuomela, Raimo (1995) *The Importance of Us: A Philosophical Study of Basic Social Notions* (Stanford, CA: Stanford University Press).

Usher, John M. and Evans, Martin G. (1996) 'Life and Death Along Gasoline Alley: Darwinian and Lamarckian Processes in a Differentiating Population, *Academy of Management Journal,* **39**(5), October, pp. 1428–66.

Van Parijs, Philippe (1980) 'The Falling-Rate-of-Profit Theory of Crisis: A Rational Reconstruction by Way of Obituary', *Review of Radical Political Economics*, **12**(1), Spring, pp. 1–16.

Vanberg, Viktor J. (1994) *Rules and Choice in Economics* (London and New York: Routledge).

Vanberg, Viktor J. (2000) 'Rational Choice and Rule-Based Behavior: Alternative Heuristics', in Metze, R., Mühler, K. and Opp, Karl-Dieter (eds) *Normen und Instituzionem: Entstehung und Virkungen* (Leipzig: Leipziger Universitätvarlag).

Vanberg, Viktor J. (2002) 'Rational Choice versus Program-Based Behavior: Alternative Theoretical Approaches and Their Relevance for the Study of Institutions', *Rationality and Society*, **14**(1), Summer, pp. 7–53.

Vanberg, Viktor J. (2004a) 'The Rationality Postulate in Economics: Its Ambiguity, Its Deficiency and Its Evolutionary Alternative', *Journal of Economic Methodology*, **11**(1), March, pp. 1–29.

Vanberg, Viktor J. (2004b) 'Austrian Economics, Evolutionary Psychology, and Methodological Dualism: Subjectivism Reconsidered', in Koppl, Roger (ed.) (2004) *Evolutionary Psychology and Economic Theory: Advances in Austrian Economics, Volume 7* (Amsterdam: Elsevier), pp. 155–99.

Veblen, Thorstein B. (1897) Review of *Die Marxistische Socialdemokratie* by Max Lorenz, in *Journal of Political Economy*, **6**(1), December, pp. 136–7.

Veblen, Thorstein B. (1899) *The Theory of the Leisure Class: An Economic Study in the Evolution of Institutions* (New York: Macmillan).

Veblen, Thorstein B. (1901a) 'Industrial and Pecuniary Employments', *Publications of the American Economic Association*, Series 3, pp. 190–235. Reprinted in Veblen (1919).

Veblen, Thorstein B. (1901b) 'Gustav Schmoller's Economics', *Quarterly Journal of Economics*, **16**(1), November, pp. 69–93. Reprinted in Veblen (1919).

Veblen, Thorstein B. (1906) 'The Socialist Economics of Karl Marx and His Followers I: The Theories of Karl Marx', *Quarterly Journal of Economics*, **20**(3), August, pp. 578–95. Reprinted in Veblen (1919).

Veblen, Thorstein B. (1907) 'The Socialist Economics of Karl Marx and His Followers II: The Later Marxism', *Quarterly Journal of Economics*, **21**(1), February, pp. 299–322. Reprinted in Veblen (1919).

Veblen, Thorstein B. (1909) 'The Limitations of Marginal Utility', *Journal of Political Economy*, **17**(9), November, pp. 620–636. Reprinted in Veblen (1919).

Veblen, Thorstein B. (1914) *The Instinct of Workmanship, and the State of the Industrial Arts* (New York: Macmillan).

Veblen, Thorstein B. (1919) The Place of Science in Modern Civilisation and Other Essays. New York, Huebsch.

Veblen, Thorstein B. (1923) *Absentee Ownership and Business Enterprise in Recent Times* (New York: Huebsch).

Veblen, Thorstein B. (1934) *Essays on Our Changing Order*, edited by Leon Ardzrooni (New York: The Viking Press).

Vickers, Douglas (1995) *The Tyranny of the Market: A Critique of Theoretical Foundations* (Ann Arbor: University of Michigan Press).

Vorzimmer, Peter J. (1969) 'Darwin, Malthus, and the Theory of Natural Selection', *Journal of the History of Ideas*, **30**, pp. 527–42.

Vromen, Jack J. (2003) 'Collective Intentionality, Social Reality and Evolutionary Biology', *Philosophical Explorations*, **6**(3), September, pp. 251–64.

Wainwright, Hilary (1994) *Arguments for a New Left: Answering the Free-Market Right* (Oxford: Basil Blackwell).

Wallace, Alfred Russel (1870) *Contributions to the Theory of Natural Selection: A Series of Essays* (London: Macmillan).

Walters, B. and Young, David (1999) 'Is Critical Realism the Appropriate Basis for Post Keynesianism?', *Journal of Post Keynesian Economics*, **22**(1), Fall, pp. 105–23.

Ward, Benjamin (1972) *What's Wrong With Economics?* (London: Macmillan).

Ward, Lester Frank (1903) *Pure Sociology: A Treatise On the Origin and Spontaneous Development of Society* (New York and London: Macmillan).

Ward, Lester Frank (1907a) 'Discussion' of Wells (1907), *American Journal of Sociology*, **12**(5), March, pp. 709–10.

Ward, Lester Frank (1907b) 'Social and Biological Struggles', *American Journal of Sociology,* **13**(3), November, pp. 289–99.

Ward, Lester Frank (1913) 'Eugenics, Euthenics, and Eudemics', *American Journal of Sociology*, **18**(6), May, pp. 737–54.

Wärneryd, Karl (1989) 'Legal Restrictions and the Evolution of Media of Exchange', *Journal of Institutional and Theoretical Economics*, **145**(4), December, pp. 613–26.

Wärneryd, Karl (1990a) 'Legal Restrictions and Monetary Evolution', *Journal of Economic Behavior and Organization*, **13**(1), March, pp. 117–24.

Wärneryd, Karl (1990b) *Economic Conventions: Essays in Institutional Economics* (Stockholm: Economic Research Institute).

Waters, C. Kenneth (1986) 'Natural Selection Without Survival of the Fittest', *Biology and Philosophy*, **1**(2), April, pp. 207–25.

Weber, Max (1978) *Max Weber: Selections in Translation,* edited and introduced by W. G. Runciman (Cambridge: Cambridge University Press).

Wegner, Daniel M. (2002) *The Illusion of Conscious Will* (Cambridge, MA: MIT Press).

Wegner, Daniel M. and Wheatley, T. (1999) 'Apparent Mental Causation: Sources of the Experience of the Will', *American Psychologist*, **54**, pp. 480–492.

Weikart, Richard (1993) 'The Origins of Social Darwinism in Germany, 1859–1895', *Journal of the History of Ideas*, **54**(3), July, pp. 469–88.

Weikart, Richard (2002) 'Darwinism and Death: Devaluing Human Life in Germany 1859–1920', *Journal of the History of Ideas*, **63**(2), July, pp. 323–44.

Weingart, Peter, Mitchell, Sandra D., Richerson, Peter J. and Maasen, Sabine (eds) (1997) *Human By Nature: Between Biology and the Social Sciences* (Mahwah, NJ: Lawrence Erlbaum Associates).

Weissman, David (2000) *A Social Ontology* (New Haven, CT: Yale University Press).

Wells, Alan (1970) *Social Institutions* (London: Heinemann).

Wells, D. Collin (1907) 'Social Darwinism', *American Journal of Sociology*, **12**(5), March, pp. 695–708.

Wiener, Martin J. (1981) *English Culture and the Decline of the Industrial Spirit 1850–1980* (Cambridge: Cambridge University Press).

Williamson, Oliver E. (1975) *Markets and Hierarchies: Analysis and Anti-Trust Implications: A Study in the Economics of Internal Organization* (New York: Free Press).

Wilson, Edward O. (1975) *Sociobiology: The New Synthesis* (Cambridge, MA: Harvard University Press).

Wilson, Edward O. (1978) *On Human Nature* (Cambridge, MA: Harvard University Press).

Wilson, John F. (1995) *British Business History, 1720–1994* (Manchester: Manchester University Press).

Wilson, Matthew (2005) 'Institutionalism, Critical Realism and the Critique of Mainstream Economics', *Journal of Institutional Economics*, **1**(2), December, pp. 217–31.

Wiltshire, David (1978) *The Social and Political Thought of Herbert Spencer* (Oxford: Oxford University Press).

Winston, G. C. (1980) 'Addiction and Backsliding: A Theory of Compulsive Consumption', *Journal of Economic Behavior and Organization*, **1**(3), September, pp. 295–324.

Winter, Sidney G., Jr (1990) 'Survival, Selection, and Inheritance in Evolutionary Theories of Organization', in Singh, Jitendra V. (ed.) (1990) *Organizational Evolution: New Directions* (London: Sage), pp. 269–97.

Winter, Sidney G. Jr (1995) 'Four Rs of Profitability: Rents, Resources, Routines, and Replication' in Montgomery, Cynthia A. (ed.) (1995) *Resource-Based and Evolutionary Theories of the Firm: Towards a Synthesis* (Boston: Kluwer), pp. 147–78.

Wittgenstein, Ludwig (1958) *Philosophical Investigations* (Oxford: Basil Blackwell).

Wood, Wendy, Quinn, Jeffrey M. and Kashy, D. (2002) 'Habits in Everyday Life: Thought, Emotion, and Action', *Journal of Personality and Social Psychology*, **83**, pp. 1281–97.

Woods, Erville B. (1920) 'Heredity and Opportunity', *American Journal of Sociology*, **26**(1), July, pp. 1–21.

Woodward, Jane (2003) *Making Things Happen: A Theory of Causal Explanation* (Oxford and New York: Oxford University Press).

Wright, Erik Olin (1994) *Interrogating Inequality: Essays on Class Analysis, Socialism and Marxism* (London: Verso).

Wuarin, Louis (1896) *Une vue d'ensemble de la question sociale: le problème, la méthode* (Paris: Larose).

Young, Allyn A. (1928) 'Increasing Returns and Economic Progress', *Economic Journal*, **38**(4), December, pp. 527–42.

Young, H. Peyton (1993) 'The Evolution of Conventions', *Econometrica*, **61**(1), January, pp. 57–84.

Young, H. Peyton (1996) 'The Economics of Convention', *Journal of Economic Perspectives*, **10**(2), Spring, pp. 105–22.

Young, Robert M. (1969) 'Malthus and the Evolutionists: The Common Context of Biological and Social Theory', *Past and Present*, No. 43, May, pp. 109–41.

Young, Robert M. (1985) *Darwin's Metaphor: Nature's Place in Victorian Culture* (Cambridge: Cambridge University Press).

Zilboorg, Gregory (1921) 'Reflections on a Century of Political Experience and Thought', *Political Science Quarterly*, **36**(3), September, pp. 391–408.

Zucker, Lynne G. (1987) 'Institutional Theories of Organization', *Annual Review of Sociology*, **13**, pp. 443–64.

Index